CW01044275

SUPPORTED BY

EDITED BY
ANNA FERRARI
BENJAMIN HINSON
WITH GHISLAINE WOOD

Visions of Ancient Egypt

First published in Great Britain by
Sainsbury Centre for Visual Arts
Norwich Research Park
University of East Anglia
Norwich, NR4 7TJ
sainsburycentre.ac.uk

ISBN 978-1-7397200-0-1

SAINSBURY
CENTRE

British Library Cataloguing-in-Publication Data. A catalogue record is available from the British Library.

Editors: Anna Ferrari and Benjamin Hinson with Ghislaine Wood
Book Design: Johnson Design
Copy editor: Mandy Greenfield
Index: Brenda Stones
Printed and bound in the UK by Pureprint Group, Sussex

SUPPORTED BY

Sotheby's EST. 1744

ILLUSTRATIONS

COVER: Awol Erizku, *Nefertiti (Black Power)*, 2018. Sainsbury Centre, purchased with support from the Art Fund.

PAGE 2: Fragment of a sunk relief: heads of female attendants, *c.*1370 BC. Sainsbury Centre.

CONTENTS

JAGO COOPER
Executive Director,
Sainsbury Centre
Professor of Art and Archaeology

DIRECTOR'S FOREWORD

The iconic imagery of ancient Egypt has captivated the imagination of enquiring minds for millennia. Its art, architecture and treasures are the first port of call for anyone seeking inspiration and a deeper cultural understanding of the great stories of humanity. The Nile Valley is synonymous with the origins of cultural innovation and human creativity and yet, all too often, an outsider's view of the region has been oversimplified and manipulated. It is home to one of the oldest and most diverse areas of continuous cultural development in the world, but all too often time is compressed in people's minds and the sheer scale of cultural diversity undervalued.

This book, and the accompanying exhibition, provides a comprehensive rethink of how visions of ancient Egypt have been created and shared over time. This provides a timely critique of the uncritical imposition of Western perspectives and the lurking dangers of a reinvention of Orientalism in scholarship more widely. The chapters collaboratively bring together a diverse range of expertise that includes more reflexive understandings of cultural representation and foreground African-led perspectives. The gleaming neon lights of Awol Erizku's *Nefertiti (Black Power)* shining out from the cover of this book embody this beautifully. It uses light to cut through time and transform ownership of a Nefertiti profile, so widely recognised and yet here reframed within a global political landscape. The use of the Chinese characters 黑色力量 to spell out the words 'Black Power' underlines an updated international framework far beyond the traditional Eurocentric roots of Western scholarship. Through the inclusion of cross-disciplinary perspectives, globally representative scholars and contemporary art perspectives, the true richness and diversity of Egypt are repositioned in this book. The changing ways in which *Visions of Ancient Egypt* are then presented and received are a revelation – both as a heartland of global cultural development and as a more personal one of self-reflection for the visitor, in how often assumed cultural reference points of Egyptian imagery and association can be broken down and reseen through a different lens.

'Visions' is a word that conjures up the need for imagination, and that is what the essays in this book and the accompanying exhibition do so emotively. The power of imagination is that unique and defining quality of human culture across the world. However, true imagination requires the creative space and inspiration for its inception. *Visions of Ancient Egypt* is that perfect place for the power of imagination to thrive. The playful interplay of iconic imagery and critical rethinking, guided by expert insight, helps to shape thought and challenge expectations as the mind journeys across the landscapes of the Nile Valley. Such a journey would not have been possible without the incredibly kind support of Viking and Sotheby's. It is only through committed collaboration between colleagues invested in over many years that such an ambitious project as this can be realised and brought to an international audience. ⊙

WENDY ATKIN-SMITH
Managing Director,
Viking UK

SPONSOR'S FOREWORD

We are delighted and proud to support the *Visions of Ancient Egypt* exhibition at the Sainsbury Centre. Egypt has inspired explorers for generations, and this major exhibition portrays the enduring appeal of this ancient land and its historical and cultural treasures as it displays some incredible works of art to the public for the first time.

To be able to explore one of the greatest civilisations through art, design, fashion and architecture is an exciting experience. It is also one that resonates with the Viking ethos to offer enriching journeys in which guests can immerse themselves in the culture of each destination they visit.

Just like the explorers before them, our guests are curious travellers, and they choose Egypt as a destination because of its unparalleled access to history and antiquities. This rings as true today as it did a century ago, and it is what we continue to hear from the guests who sail with us on the Nile. We are proud to be the only Western company to build, own and operate ships on the Nile – and we will always maintain our commitment to creating meaningful experiences that are focused on the destination.

Egypt, in particular, offers boundless meaningful experiences. On our *Pharaohs & Pyramids* itinerary, guests follow in the wake of pharaohs along the banks of the Nile between Luxor and Aswan, as Viking's expert Egyptologists provide insights into one of history's greatest civilisations. The itinerary includes the fascinating city of Cairo, where guests can visit iconic sites such as the Great Pyramids of Giza, the necropolis of Sakkara and the Mosque of Muhammad Ali. As well as exploring these famous sites, guests can look forward to Privileged Access® to the tomb of Nefertari in the Valley of the Queens and the tomb of Tutankhamun in the Valley of the Kings. Excursions to the Temple of Khnum in Esna, the Dendera Temple complex in Qena and the temples at Abu Simbel can also be explored through engaging experiences.

Opening in September 2022, the *Visions of Ancient Egypt* exhibition coincides with the anniversaries of several key events: the bicentenary of Jean-François Champollion's decipherment of hieroglyphs; the opening of the new Grand Egyptian Museum outside Cairo on the Giza Plateau; and the launch of *Viking Osiris*, a brand-new Viking ship built specifically for the Nile River. 2022 is also the 100th anniversary of the discovery of King Tutankhamun's tomb by Howard Carter and his benefactor, the 5th Earl of Carnarvon. Guests who sail on board *Viking Osiris* will experience Privileged Access® to memories from 1922 and the events surrounding the discovery of King Tutankhamun's tomb, building on Viking's long-standing relationship with the Carnarvon family.

With our destination focus and our commitment to provide culturally enriching journeys, Viking shares the Sainsbury Centre's passion for connecting different cultures and opening up the world, even when we're close to home. Egypt is a compelling destination that has ignited the imagination of travellers for hundreds of years, and we are proud to support this important exhibition, which promises to offer a fresh perspective on an ancient civilisation. ⊙

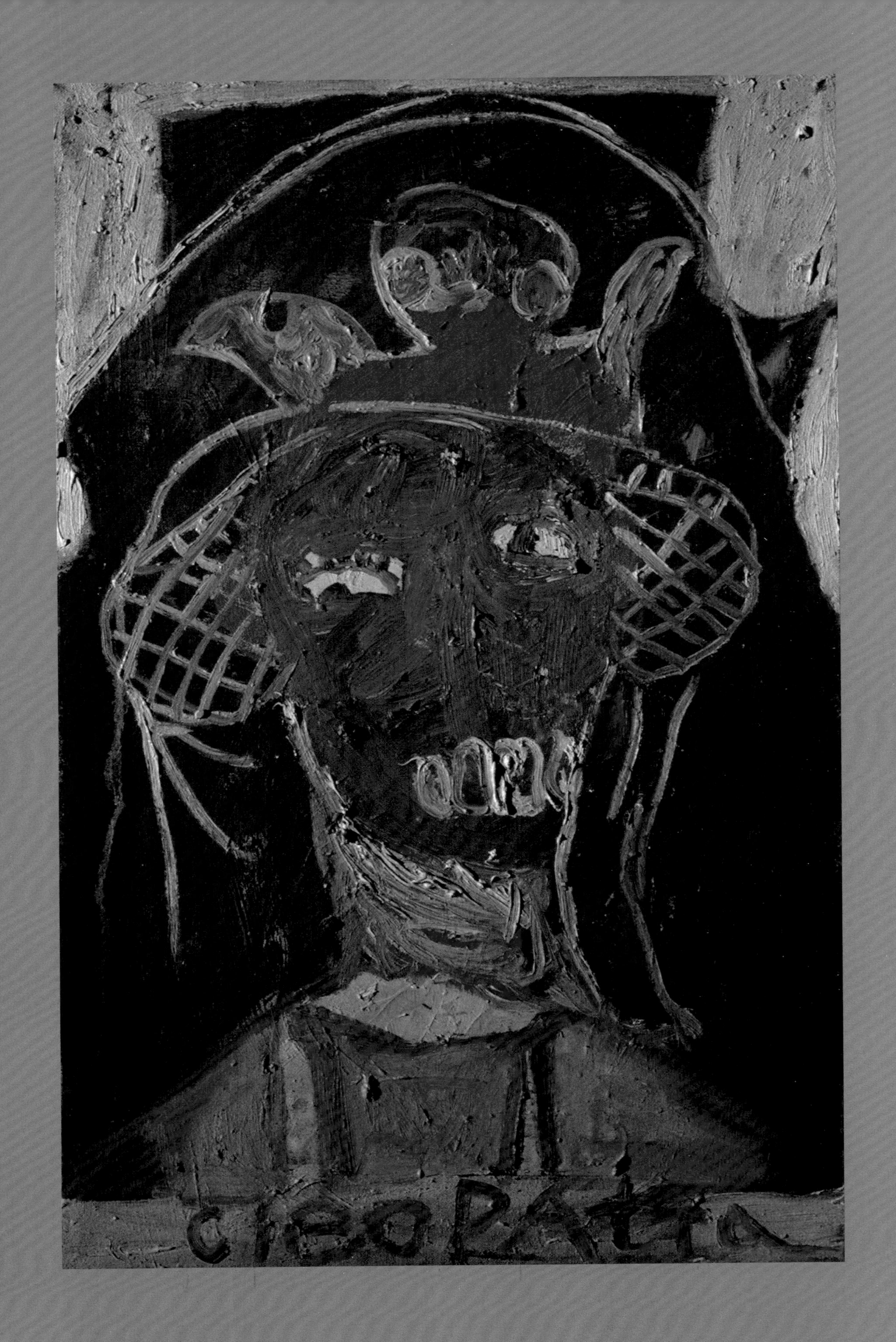

ANNA FERRARI &
BENJAMIN HINSON

INTRODUCTION

The year 2022 marks two milestones, perhaps the two most famous moments in the history of Western Egyptology: 200 years since Jean-François Champollion deciphered the hieroglyphic script, and 100 years since Howard Carter rediscovered the tomb of Tutankhamun. There is therefore no better moment to reflect on ancient Egypt's impact on art and design.

For many, this impact is synonymous with Tutankhamun and the 1920s. The spectacular discovery of the 'Boy King's' tomb captured the world's imagination and sparked a passion for ancient Egypt that saturated popular culture. However, the influence of ancient Egypt on art, design and performance reaches back through history, into Antiquity itself. The exhibition and the accompanying essays in this book explore its enduring appeal and the particular moments at which uses of Egyptian motifs and iconography flourished.

Nonetheless, the phenomenon is more than just an aesthetic. It is a visual reflection of how ancient Egypt's heritage has been contested, appropriated and reinterpreted by different audiences for different purposes over time. At each of the periods when artists have looked to ancient Egypt, the reuse of Egyptian imagery also tells us something about those reusing it. This remains true of the present day; in a modern world aware of potential problems with (mis)representing other cultures, should the continued appeal of ancient Egypt be seen as appreciation or appropriation? That this book comes on the centenary of Tutankhamun's rediscovery is also timely, as the excavation coincided with growing nationalism within Egypt and calls for independence. This exemplifies the context for this book – the influence of Egypt on art and design cannot be understood without highlighting the often political motivations underlying it.

Egypt's own voice in this narrative has historically been silent. The story is traditionally seen through a Western lens – a story of Europe, and particularly Western Europe, 'inspired' by Egypt. How Egypt engaged with its own past has been far less explored. A prevailing trope is that Egypt's double religious conversion to Christianity and then Islam formed a clear break between ancient and modern, severing Egyptian attachment to the pharaonic past.[1] In the nineteenth century this idea acted as justification for European control of Egypt. Egyptians were painted as indifferent to the past and – especially after 1835, when antiquities legislation threatened European access to monuments – as active threats to it. The aim of this was to portray continued European looting as 'preservation'. Even in subsequent accounts that took a more critical stance on past attitudes, Egyptians were painted as bystanders rather than active agents in their own history.[2] However, at many of the moments covered in this book, Egyptians continued to engage with their pharaonic past in complex and multifaceted ways. This crucial part of the story, traditionally ignored, is gradually being reassessed to give it the prominence it deserves.[3]

For the first time, this exhibition and book weave these threads together, inviting scholars and contemporary Egyptian artists to reflect, and to explore how Egypt itself has responded to its ancient past – and continues to do so – through art and design. Crucially, as part of the wider narrative, the exhibition brings together key works by modern and contemporary Egyptian artists, shedding light on a continued engagement with their pharaonic heritage.

◁ FIG. 0.1: Chris Ofili, *Cleopatra*, 1992. Royal College of Art Collection.

NOT 'EGYPTOMANIA'

Many have heard of the word 'Egyptomania'. Its origin is popularly attributed to John Soane, whose architectural lectures of 1806–9 derided the burgeoning 'Egyptian mania' of the day.[4] However, it can actually be traced back to 1797 – specifically 20 March, and a letter from Frederick Augustus Hervey, Bishop of Derry, to Wilhelmine Encke, Countess of Lichtenau.[5] Interestingly, Soane and Hervey were at one time close acquaintances, and until 1780 Hervey was his patron; it is possible that Soane did not independently invent the term.

However, in this book 'Egyptomania' is deliberately not used. That Soane saw 'Egyptian mania' as worthy of derision is important. The word 'mania' conjures up primarily negative connotations – faddish, irrational. Indeed, although Hervey was full of praise for it, from Soane onwards 'Egyptomania' was usually used pejoratively. An anonymous review of Encke's memoirs, referring to the very letter mentioned above, described 'that Egyptomania ... which threatened at one time to replunge our chairs and tables into barbarism'.[6] Nonetheless, this academic derision masks a more complex truth, because there was a growing contemporary popular market for objects and interiors inspired by Egypt. Indeed, Soane himself produced numerous Egyptian-inspired designs in his earlier career, although he later distinguished between the 'sublimity' of actual Egyptian art and what he saw as inappropriate commercial adaptations.

A shortcoming of 'Egyptomania' is that it is often used indiscriminately to describe all of the periods when artistic interest in Egypt resurged. This generalises the phenomenon and suggests an underlying similarity in reasoning. 'Mania' also suggests that the phenomenon swept all corners of society, but before the late nineteenth century the 'Egyptian style' was limited. The gradual popularisation is one of several underlying themes running across the story. A further problem is that 'Egyptomania' does not cover the entire material or thematic scope of the story. It is commonly used to refer only to material that, whilst using Egyptian iconography, adapts it either in style or function. However, this precludes much of the surrounding material that is necessary for understanding why such objects exist. For example, an Orientalist painting of Cairo is not 'Egyptomania', but reflects wider mid-nineteenth-century understandings of Egypt and thus the social and cultural background within which 'Egyptomania' developed at that time.

Scholarship now increasingly acknowledges how Egyptology primarily developed as a colonial, Western European endeavour.[7] As an extension of this, ancient Egypt's African context is beginning to be re-evaluated and acknowledged, and the same is also true of artists looking to ancient Egypt in their works.[8] By contrast, studies of 'Egyptomania' have been slower to explore this context. The visual manifestations of 'Egyptomania' have been well documented, but analysis of *why* Egypt rather less so.[9] Some exhibitions have explored the relationship between Orientalist and Egyptological visions of Egypt.[10] However, 'Egyptomania' is still commonly presented as an aesthetic divorced from the same underlying colonial contexts that influenced Egyptology. The artistic appeal of pharaonic Egypt cannot be separated from Orientalism, and indeed the pharaonic as the abiding image of Egypt in people's minds (ignoring the subsequent Greco-Roman, Coptic and Islamic histories) itself reflects romantic, Orientalist ideas of Egypt as an ancient but timeless land. Furthermore, as the essays in this book explore, it is no coincidence that the moments at which artistic interest in Egypt flourished correspond to moments when political interest in Egypt peaked. This exhibition is cognisant of the fact that both it and the museum space it occupies have their roots in such colonialism. It is therefore our challenge to present the material without celebrating or echoing Orientalist tropes, but to fully acknowledge that artistic reception of pharaonic Egypt is ultimately reflective, and the product, of them.

Another recurring problem is to treat the artistic appeal of Egypt as unique. Rather, it is only one manifestation of wider social trends of antiquarianism and historical revival. For example, we cannot understand why religious elites in the Renaissance employed Egyptian iconography without placing it in the wider contexts of both revived interest in Classical history and the contemporary reception of Egyptian art itself. From the Renaissance, the revival of Classical Antiquity became a prevailing theme. Ancient Egypt was rediscovered within the Classical Roman cultural landscape, where objects had been looted to in ancient times, and was read about through Greek and Roman writers. Similarly, the seventeenth-century excavations in Rome, which uncovered much Egyptian and Egyptianising material, were aiming more generally to uncover Classical artworks. Artists would go on to encounter this material through the Grand Tour, and in the eighteenth-century antiquarian trends in scholarship emerged, with Egyptianising material held in collections – most importantly in Italy – enfolded into these broader studies of antique art.[11]

At this time, Helleno-centric ideas of Western culture held sway and those who promoted the Egyptian style did so as a conscious foil. Piranesi's 'defence' of Egyptian and Etruscan architecture was a polemic against the prevailing taste for Greek art posited by figures like the archaeologist and art historian Johann Joachim Winckelmann, who was familiar with Egyptian art but held an essentially negative view of it. Winckelmann saw Egyptian art as invariant and unchanging – a view adopted from Plato's writings and thus revived Greek thinking.[12] Interestingly, Piranesi's use of Egypt as a foil to Classical models would be repeated centuries later, when modernist artists like Henry Moore looked to Egypt and other non-Western cultures as 'non-canonical' sources of inspiration. Classical prejudices remained well into the nineteenth century; only after 1822, when the decipherment of hieroglyphs and a growing study of Egypt led to a greater understanding of its history, was Egypt's place in the history of art reconsidered, to give it a central role as the origin of these Classical civilisations. At this point, the dynamic inverted and the Egyptian style became predominant – so much so that figures like Augustus Pugin, mirroring Piranesi's appeal above, reverted to criticising it.[13]

Scholars today use several alternative terms to describe the effect of Egypt on artists and designers: German tradition has the *Nachleben* ('afterlife') of Egypt; English literature has the 'Egyptian Revival'.[14] Perhaps these are conscious decisions to lend seriousness to what has historically been seen as irrational. Interestingly, 'Egyptomania' came back into fashion in the wake of the Tutankhamun exhibitions of the 1970s and the reignited popular craze for Egypt.[15] Some authors have deliberately leaned into the word's connotations.[16] These debates continue; in a recent body of essays, authors within the same volume both argue for and against 'Egyptomania'.[17]

It is difficult to know exactly how best to frame the phenomenon, and each term exposes its own shortcomings. 'Egyptian Revival' is rather art historical and tends towards describing a limited scope of material, mainly furniture and interiors. Furthermore, the term 'Revival' suggests something died out in the first place; rather, since at least the Renaissance, interest in Egyptian (or mock-Egyptian) culture has been alive for at least some sections of society. On the other hand, terms such as 'Inspiration' or 'Allure' are too neutral for something that relies on uneven power dynamics with Egypt.[18] Ultimately, what the various terms describe above all is perhaps an exercise in appropriation – or is it different when the culture is ancient?

For all these reasons, this exhibition and its accompanying book have been entitled *Visions of Ancient Egypt*. This word 'Visions' suggests what we hope to convey: that ancient Egypt as seen through art and design is a mediation, a constructed fantasy rather than something necessarily grounded in reality, but also a multiplicity rather than one cohesive image.

EGYPT AS EVER-CHANGING

One of the problems with defining the artistic appeal of ancient Egypt is that it re-emerges repeatedly across history, in multiple contexts and employed for multiple purposes. Its presence in art, design and fashion has persisted for centuries – sometimes jostling for position amongst other tastes, at other times pushing to the forefront of popular culture. Why has it been so popular?

▽ FIG. 0.2: Eugenio Lombardi, *The Death of Cleopatra*, *c.*1890–1900. Russell-Cotes Art Gallery & Museum.

Unlike many other ancient cultures, Egypt was never 'lost'. Echoes of it lingered through two main strands. The first is religious tradition; Egypt was the setting for many Old Testament events. The second strand is Classical tradition. Physical objects such as obelisks were brought to Rome, where they remained visible for centuries afterwards, and Classical authors wrote about Egypt. Because of these accounts, rediscovered in the Renaissance, Egypt was held as the precursor to Greek and Roman civilisation. The name Egypt (itself derived from the ancient Greek *Aigyptos*) and what it meant were therefore always present in the Western mind, even if it was a distorted vision.

Another reason for Egypt's popularity is its mutability. Whilst the monumental traces of Egyptian civilisation have survived well, for most of European history they were divorced from any cultural context. Most known objects had either been transported into European collections or were viewed in Rome, and hieroglyphs were unreadable until the mid-nineteenth century. This allowed new interpretations and narratives of the material to be crafted. The iconography and the very idea of Egypt could mean different things to different people, and could be exploited to suit various agendas. This is demonstrated clearly in architecture, where Egyptian elements have been used as a cipher for justice, wisdom and law (inspiring the design for courthouses and jails); for permanence and stability (and thus Victorian industrial works, such as Bristol's Clifton Suspension Bridge); for the arcane and esoteric (as typified by Freemasons halls across the world); or for the sublime and ideas of death (obelisks and pyramids are commonly used as grave-markers).

This introduces another recurring theme, that of the tension between the 'authentic' Egypt of archaeology and the 'constructed' Egypts of popular imagination. In art and design, these have sometimes merged closely and sometimes diverged widely. Indeed, 'Egyptomania' is often seen as distinct from Egyptology: one being an academic science, and the other characterised as irrational and popular. However, as this book explores, Egyptology is not a neutral science but is itself a reception of ancient Egypt.[19]

Perhaps no figure typifies the continual reinvention of ancient Egypt, and also the chasm between Western and native Egyptian engagements with it, better than Cleopatra, its last Ptolemaic queen. Her image and actions have been subject to constant manipulation in Western art.[20] Although descended from a line of non-Egyptian Macedonian rulers, Cleopatra apparently went to great lengths to integrate herself with Egyptian culture. She consciously constructed an image for an Egyptian audience; in 34 BC, at the 'Donations of Alexandria', she even appeared as the goddess Isis herself.

However, after her death Cleopatra's legacy was beyond her control. She appears in the works of

▽ FIG. 0.3: Agnes Pringle, *The Flight of Anthony and Cleopatra from the Battle of Actium*, c.1897. Laing Art Gallery.

multiple Roman authors, who painted a picture of Oriental excess and of a cruel and seductive ruler.[21] Yet these accounts are deeply biased, laced with Roman misogyny and xenophobia. Cleopatra represented the antithesis of Roman values: a strong, non-Roman, female leader. Furthermore, these accounts had specific reasons for tarnishing Cleopatra's character. She was not their main focus; they were primarily about the life of Mark Antony, who at that moment was engaged in a war with Octavian, nephew of Caesar and eventual Emperor Augustus, who would conquer Egypt in 30 BC. Roman propaganda therefore needed to demonise Mark Antony. However, criticism of him could not go too far or Octavian's triumph would not have been seen as one against a challenging enemy. Nor could the conflict be portrayed as a civil war between Romans. Cleopatra was therefore fair game – a foreign woman, the 'other', who was emasculating and barbarianising Mark Antony, contrasting Oriental excess with Octavian as a champion of traditional Roman values. These Roman sources, many of which focused on Cleopatra's physicality, in turn became the kernel for a Western tradition that associated her with beauty and seduction. They persevere even into the works of Shakespeare, whose *Antony and Cleopatra* drew heavily on Plutarch's accounts. However, here the play focused on a doomed love, with Cleopatra as a mother and lover.

From the eighteenth century, key artistic motifs based on Cleopatra's life began to crystallise, each of which reflected contemporary Western attitudes. One was the Death of Cleopatra, in reality an excuse to depict 'tasteful' nudes (Fig. 0.2). Another was Cleopatra fleeing the battle of Actium, a cowardly figure, or as a supplicant, lying frailly over Mark Antony's tomb, both reflecting male ideals of femininity and subservience (Fig. 0.3). Particularly popular legends were the meeting of Cleopatra and Mark Antony, depicted as Orientalised, exotic, excessive banqueting scenes, and Cleopatra as the femme fatale who seduced and then killed men – an outlet for Orientalised erotic fetishes. In the eighteenth and nineteenth centuries art increasingly also depicted Cleopatra as a pale, fleshy European, appealing to Western concepts of beauty. In Joshua Reynolds's celebrated *Kitty Fisher as Cleopatra* (1759), the famous courtesan is depicted as the ancient queen, dropping a pearl into a goblet, in reference to the legend wherein Cleopatra drank a priceless pearl in a cup of wine to demonstrate to Mark Antony her supreme wealth (Fig. 0.4).

△ **FIG. 0.4:** Joshua Reynolds, *Kitty Fisher as Cleopatra Dissolving the Pearl*, 1759. Kenwood House.

Cleopatra also remained popular onstage, but again adaptations reflected underlying Western attitudes. For example, George Bernard Shaw's 1898 play *Caesar and Cleopatra* portrays Cleopatra as much younger than she was in reality, and with a Roman governor; it is difficult not to see this as reflecting the 'stewardship' that Victorian colonial powers such as Britain saw themselves as imparting on Egypt. Into the twentieth century, Hollywood took Cleopatra in a slightly different direction, refashioning her as an icon of beauty and glamour. This vision was exemplified by Elizabeth Taylor, although her portrayal was the culmination of more than fifty years of silver-screen adaptations, beginning with Theda Bara in 1917, that solidified the characterisation (Fig. 0.6). Each of these portrayals, whilst tying into a broader Hollywood tradition of depicting the queen, makes important statements about those portraying her. For example, studios promoted a fictitious Egyptian identity around the American-born Bara, linking into ideas of the occult and mysticism, which are themselves so often entwined with ancient Egypt.

This image of Cleopatra, and especially her portrayal as a Western ideal of beauty, has, thankfully,

△ FIG. 0.5: Tamara Dobson in *Cleopatra Jones*, 1973. Kobal Collection.

begun to be challenged. Even in 1973, the Blaxpoitation 'classic' *Cleopatra Jones* deliberately chose Cleopatra as the titular character's name, speaking to broader issues of the queen's identity and race, and especially black reclamation of ancient Egypt as part of African heritage (Fig. 0.5). More recently, Esmeralda Kosmatopoulos's installation *I Want to Look Like Cleopatra* takes images of the queen's face from ancient coins – among the only surviving depictions of her actual appearance – and marks them up with a cosmetic surgeon's suggestions on how to make her look more like Elizabeth Taylor; who is the 'real' Cleopatra? (Fig. 0.7). Similarly, Nigerian-British artist Chris Ofili's 1992 painting *Cleopatra* boldly recasts the queen as a black African, wearing a crown and posed in a regal three-quarter-length portrait (Fig. 0.1).

Contrast Western tradition with Egyptian accounts. In the seventh century, the Coptic bishop John of Nikiou wrote that no ruler had ever surpassed her: 'She executed many noble works and important institutions. And this woman, the most illustrious and wise amongst women, died in the fourteenth year of the reign Caesar Augustus.'[22]

Even in ancient times, a competing myth of the powerful female ruler was alive – Zenobia, Queen of Palmyra, reportedly likened herself to Cleopatra. The Roman historian Ammianus Marcellinus, writing in the fourth century AD, also said the Egyptians still worshiped her memory.[23] John of Nikiou's account in particular became the basis for her study among Islamic writers, who, rather than focusing on her beauty, portrayed Cleopatra as a protective ruler, wise scholar, linguist and scientist; apocryphal tradition even had her as the builder of Alexandria's lighthouse and library. For example, in *Muruj al-Dhahab* ('Meadows of Gold'), the tenth-century Arab scholar al-Mas'udi recounts: 'She was a sage, a philosopher who elevated the ranks of scholars and enjoyed their company. She also wrote books on medicine, charms and cosmetics in addition to many other books ascribed to her which are known to those who practice medicine.'[24]

▷ FIG. 0.6: Elizabeth Taylor in *Cleopatra*, 1963. Kobal Collection.

▽ FIG. 0.7: Esmeralda Kosmatopoulos, *I Want to Look Like Cleopatra* (detail), 2020.

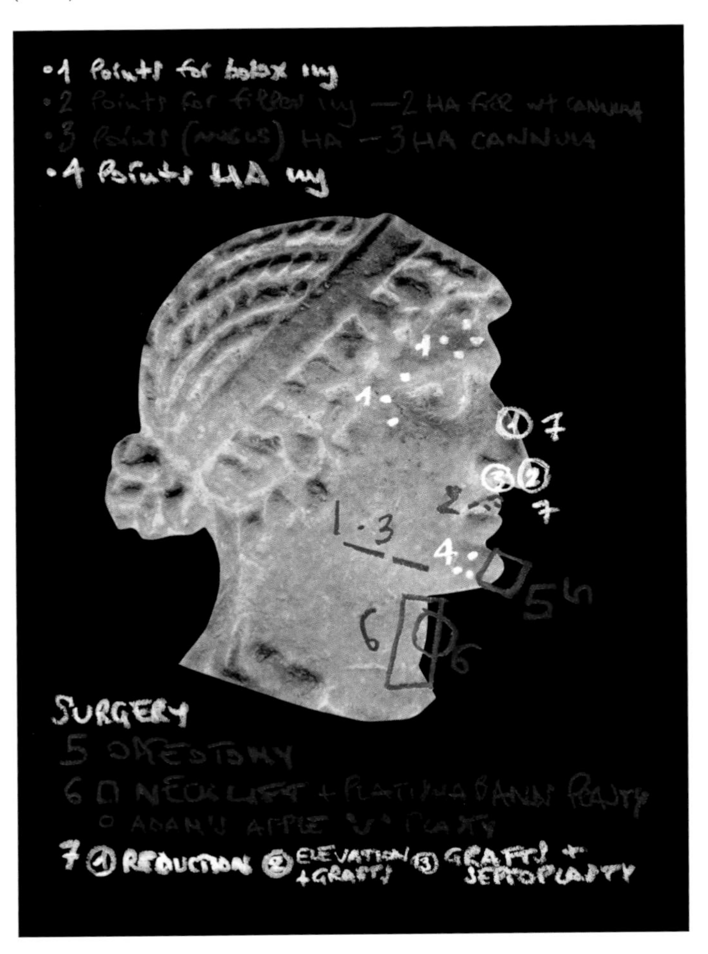

△ FIG 0.8: The Temple of Dendera in Dominique Vivant Denon, *Voyage dans la Basse et la Haute Égypte*, first published in 1802. New York Public Library.

Whilst the Classical and Islamic accounts paint two very different pictures, Roman accounts did not entirely ignore or discredit Cleopatra's intelligence; according to Plutarch, she spoke seven languages, and Cicero described her as 'scholarly'. Cleopatra was apparently also the only Ptolemaic ruler to learn the Egyptian language. However, this did not fit the narrative that Roman commentators wished to portray. Ancient propaganda crafted a character – one that has influenced opinion ever since.

THE FRENCH IN EGYPT

Perhaps a key example of how Egypt has been constantly reinvented and recast occurred at the turn of the nineteenth century when, in 1798, French general Napoleon Bonaparte invaded Egypt with 38,000 troops and a contingent of more than 150 scholars. Bonaparte's invasion of Egypt was motivated by the desire to thwart the British by cutting off access to their commercial interests in India, which was reached via the overland passage, while gaining a valuable French colony and inscribing France – and, by extension, himself – into the glorious lineage of Egyptian rulers. The military campaign proved a disaster that saw Bonaparte flee back to France in 1799, and the French eventually withdrew after a series of crushing defeats against the British. However, the scholarly publications that followed, including Vivant Denon's *Voyage dans la Basse et la Haute Égypte pendant les campagnes du Général Bonaparte* (Travels in Upper and Lower Egypt) (1802) and the *Description de l'Égypte, ou Recueil des observations et des recherches qui ont été faites en Égypte pendant l'expédition de l'armée française* (Description of Egypt. or, collection of observations and research conducted in Egypt during the expedition of the French army) (published between 1809 and 1828), spun it as a great scholarly achievement (Fig. 0.8).[25] In the nineteenth century Denon's *Voyage* was the most successful European publication about Egypt: it was promptly translated into English, Dutch and Italian, and by the turn of the twentieth century it had been reprinted more than forty times.[26] Denon, an artist and antiquarian who joined the scholars in Egypt, described Egyptian monuments from Alexandria to Aswan but, as Egyptian historian Laïla Enan underscores, Denon's text is a wartime account, in which he recorded with chilling detachment the brutal French repression of Egyptian people who were killed, exploited, robbed and raped.[27]

Terminology is crucial here. While in French history this period of 1798–1801 has euphemistically been referred to as 'Bonaparte's *campagne d'Égypte*' or the 'expedition', such expressions, which stem from

Napoleonic propaganda, elide the fact that it was a bloody invasion and occupation, and instead emphasise the sense of exploration and scientific discovery.

The monumental multi-volume *Description de l'Égypte* reimagined Egypt, highlighting its ancient grandeur and its links with great Classical figures at the expense of its more recent Islamic past. In the opening lines of the Preface, Jean-Baptiste Joseph Fourier claimed that, situated between Africa and Asia, Egypt 'presents only great memories', evoking it as a site that had drawn great Greek scholars such as Homer, Pythagoras and Plato as well as Roman leaders from Pompey to Caesar and Mark Antony.[28] In doing so, the *Description* claimed that the Egyptian past was linked to the West's, justifying France's imperial ambitions. As the new conqueror of Egypt, Bonaparte could imagine himself as a new Alexander the Great, who had conquered Egypt in 332 BC – a flattering comparison, which signalled the ambitions of the French general who had yet to become emperor. The frontispiece of the *Description*, which shows Bonaparte as a victorious Classical hero in a chariot, above an imagined scene conflating monuments from across Egypt (crucially excluding anything post-pharaonic), makes this explicit (Fig. 0.9).

In his pivotal book *Orientalism* (1978), Edward Said critically examined the *Description* as one of the Western literary works that participated in the West's construction of the Eastern 'other'. The literary creation of this 'other' served to impose and justify imperialism. Said argued that the scholarly enterprise was integral to Bonaparte's ambitions to control Egypt in order to 'render it completely open, to make it totally accessible to European scrutiny' and to transform it from 'a land of obscurity and part of the Orient hitherto known at second hand through the exploits of earlier travellers, scholars, and conquerors' into 'a department of French learning'.[29] The *Description* reframed Egyptian history in terms of Western moments of contact with Egypt that held particular importance from the Western perspective, supplanting Egypt's own history and disrupting its sense of coherence and continuity.[30] While Said exposed the construction of a binary opposition between East and West, scholar Elliott Colla has highlighted the complexity of colonial relations. Instead of opposing the terms 'Expedition' and 'Occupation', for example, he argues that both 'Expedition *and* Occupation' apply to the French in Egypt, allowing for ambiguities and ambivalent relations, without excluding colonial violence.[31]

Both the *Voyage* and the *Description* articulated one of the most enduring reinventions and appropriations of ancient Egypt. In fact it was so successful that two centuries after Bonaparte landed in Egypt there were still few remarks about the violence of the colonial encounter, despite Denon's widely accessible book.[32] In 1998, exhibitions and cultural events marked the bicentenary of the French expedition, provoking a debate in the Egyptian press about the appropriateness for Egyptians of commemorating this period of their history. Napoleonic propaganda, much like that of the Romans, has proven a powerful and long-lasting vision of ancient Egypt.

In 2022, how can we mark two important moments for Egyptology, both of which are enmeshed in Egypt's colonial history? This exhibition and book seek to highlight the complexities of colonial relations and the ways in which different accounts and myths have served different agendas. ⊙

▽ FIG 0.9: Frontispiece of the *Description de l'Égypte*, 1809, vol.1. New York Public Library.

ϹΦΙΝΓΙΑ
ΛΕΑΙΝΑ
ΛΥΝΞ
ΚΡΟΚΟΔΙΛ

1 A MILLENNIUM AND A HALF OF EGYPT: ARTISTIC ENGAGEMENTS FROM ROME TO THE RENAISSANCE

BENJAMIN HINSON

Artistic engagements with ancient Egypt are as old as Egypt itself. This essay outlines the earliest ways in which ideas of ancient Egypt were mediated through art, spanning the period from ancient Rome through to medieval and Renaissance Europe. This scope may seem surprising: how can there be any commonality across such breadth of time? However, when medieval and Renaissance artists first encountered ancient Egypt, it was as part of the rediscovery of Classical Antiquity; the material they encountered was that which had formed part of Rome's ancient cityscape and the Classical written accounts of Egypt. Ancient Egypt was therefore seen through a Classical lens, a filter that would persist until the nineteenth century. In order to understand how medieval and Renaissance artists repurposed ancient Egypt, therefore, we must first understand the ways in which it was repurposed by the Romans. Across this timespan there is a key consistency: at no point did 'Egypt' have one fixed meaning in peoples' minds. Egypt was a mutable concept, whose meanings and significance could be adapted in different contexts as required.

◁ FIG. 1.1: Nilotic mosaic (detail), second to first centuries BC. Archaeological Museum, Palestrina, Lazio, Italy.

EGYPT AND ITS NEIGHBOURS

Discussion of Egypt's artistic legacy typically begins with the Romans. However, before the Romans, the Greeks established trading posts in Egyptian cities, served as mercenaries for pharaohs, wrote about Egypt, absorbed Egyptian ideas and eventually, under Alexander the Great, conquered it. It could be suggested that Alexander had Egyptophile tendencies; Diodorus Siculus reported that he had planned a monumental pyramid for his father's tomb.[1] Many of the Egyptian monuments that have proven most inspirational to artists, such as the temples of Philae and Edfu, were actually built under Ptolemaic (Macedonian Greek) rule.

Nonetheless the Romans enmeshed themselves with Egypt on an unprecedented scale. In 30 BC they conquered Egypt; Emperor Augustus had coins minted bearing a crocodile and the legend *aegypto capta* ('Egypt having been conquered').[2] Subsequently he had a pair of obelisks looted from Heliopolis and redisplayed in Rome. One was placed in the Circus

Maximus; the other formed the centrepoint of his solar meridian in the Campus Martius.[3] This was a political statement, symbolising Egypt's subjugation to Rome. Subsequent emperors continued to loot monuments; both Domitian and Hadrian even had new obelisks commissioned, complete with accurate hieroglyphic texts praising them in terms drawn from Egyptian religio-royal convention.[4]

However, Rome's engagement with Egypt was multifaceted. Centuries before Augustus, the cult of the Egyptian goddess Isis had spread across the Mediterranean (Fig. 1.2). Several Greek islands had sanctuaries by at least the fourth century BC. By the second century BC Isis had reached the Italian mainland, and by the reign of Sulla (88–78 BC) she had entered Rome. From there she spread across the provinces of the expanding Empire, along river trade routes and following troop movements, even reaching Britain.[5] By Roman times, Isis had absorbed elements of many other Egyptian goddesses, and she became further syncretised with Classical goddesses such as Aphrodite, Ceres, Fortuna and Venus, transitioning into a 'universal' goddess. It is often stated (controversially) that her personality and iconography influenced later Christian theology, with the very imagery of Mary and the infant Jesus claimed to derive from the *Isis lactans* motif of Isis nursing her son Horus. Other Egyptian deities also became popular in the Roman Empire. Serapis, a composite deity deriving from the joint worship of Osiris and Apis and originally promoted by the Ptolemies, was worshipped as both a sun god (as Zeus Serapis) and, through association with both Osiris and Dionysus, as a god of fertility and resurrection (Fig. 1.3). He became Isis' consort, and was worshipped alongside her at Rome's main Isis sanctuary, the Iseum Campense. Harpocrates (Horus-the-child), often linked with Eros and Hercules, remained Isis' son and was worshipped as part of a triad. Anubis was also worshipped, and was associated with both Hades and Hermes (as the composite god Hermanubis) and linked with Isis, as either son or consort.

◁ FIG. 1.2: Statuette of Isis, second century AD. Liverpool World Museums.

▽ FIG. 1.3: Bust of Serapis, Roman copy after a Ptolemaic original. Museo Pio-Clementino, Vatican City.

Gods of Egyptian origin were therefore firmly embedded within Roman religion.[6] Despite this, Classical authors portrayed a polarised view of Egyptian gods. Although they praised the wisdom of Egypt's priests, they considered the worship of animals disdainful.[7] Surprisingly, therefore, in the Roman world Anubis remained animal-headed. On the other hand, some poets such as Tibullus were openly influenced by the Isis cult.[8] Religious ambivalence reflected Classical writings on Egypt more generally, which despite occasional alienation showed a fascination with and admiration for Egypt. Among the authors who wrote accounts of Egypt were Herodotus (*Histories*, Book 2); Manetho (*History of Egypt*); Diodorus Siculus (*Bibliotheca Historica*, Book 1); Strabo (*Geography*, Book 17); and Plutarch (*De Iside et Osiride*).

The Isis cult employed a mixture of Egyptian and Egyptianising material. Isis sanctuaries often incorporated Egyptian sculptures; the Iseum Campense was bedecked with monuments taken from Egypt, including an XVIIIth-dynasty sphinx and a Roman-made partner.[9] Traditionally Egyptian religious objects were used in her rituals, such as the sistrum, a form of rattle and sacred instrument in pharaonic Egypt (see Fig. 1.2). However, another key object used in Isis worship, so-called Osiris-Hydreios or Canopus jars, were a Roman innovation, developed in the first century AD and materialising an association of Osiris with the Nile (Fig. 1.4).[10] Despite their appearance and name, they bear no relation to the canopic jars used in mummification. This misassociation was the product of early archaeologists, who understood the Roman jars as proof that Osiris was worshipped at the Egyptian city of Canopus; subsequently the term 'canopic' was erroneously also given to the mummification jars of similar shape.

Political attitudes towards Egypt varied between emperors. Some, such as Agrippa and Tiberius, made staunch efforts to stamp out Isis worship. By comparison, Caligula officially reinstated Isis within the pantheon after Tiberius' repressions, and rebuilt the Iseum Campense. The Flavian dynasty consciously associated themselves with Isis and Serapis; Vespasian visited Serapis' temple whilst in Alexandria and, after victory in the Judaean War, slept in the Iseum Campense. Under the Flavians, Apis and Serapis were adopted on imperial coinage. After Augustus, however, the pharaoh most associated with this story is Hadrian. On a visit to Egypt in AD 130 his lover Antinous sacrificed himself in the Nile. In response, Hadrian founded the site of Antinoöpolis, and the image of Antinous as Osiris became a popular motif for sculptors for centuries afterwards (Fig. 1.5). Hadrian's villa at Tivoli was outfitted with numerous Egyptian and Egyptianising sculptures; Hadrian himself has often been considered a fully-fledged Egyptophile.[11]

△ **FIG. 1.4:** Osiris-Hydreios jar, second century AD. Koninklijke Verzamelingen, Den Haag.

Within Egypt, the picture was different. No emperor was formally crowned pharaoh. However, on Egyptian stelae they are still depicted as such, performing traditionally Egyptian rites. On one stela, Diocletian is shown offering to the Buchis bull (Fig. 1.6). Pragmatically, the emperor being presented visually as a traditional Egyptian ruler, respecting the worship of Egyptian gods, helped to maintain order. However, even though Diocletian's titles remain within a cartouche, the words Caesar and *Autokrator* are used, not 'pharaoh'. This stela demonstrates not imperial support of Egyptian religion, but a statement of imperial authority. However, it also shows Egyptian methods of rationalising this new situation. The cartouches next to Diocletian's figure

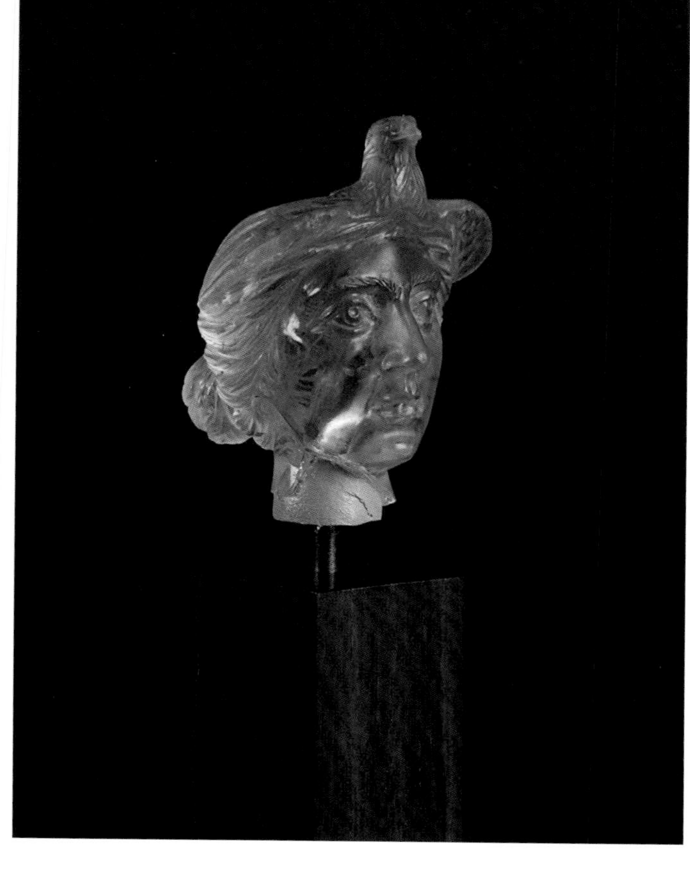

◁ FIG. 1.5: Statue of Osiris-Antinous, *c.*1800. This sculpture, made for the Grand Tour, is an exact replica of the monumental statue of Osiris-Antinous in the Vatican. Gallery Desmet.

△ FIG. 1.6: Stela of Diocletian offering to the Buchis Bull, AD 288. British Museum.

▷ FIG. 1.7: Amethyst head of Faustina the younger as Isis-Aphrodite-Nekhbet, second century AD. Wyvern Collection.

are blank, allowing the image to act as an idealised abstract of the concept of 'pharaoh' rather than as reference to a specific figure.

Other figures consciously portrayed themselves with an Egyptian audience in mind. A delicately carved amethyst head depicts Isis-Aphrodite, a syncretic goddess of beauty, love and rebirth, with the falcon attribute of Nekhbet, the Egyptian goddess who was the pharaoh's divine protector (Fig. 1.7). Ptolemaic queen mothers had frequently associated themselves with Nekhbet; this head possibly represents Faustina the younger, queen to emperor Marcus Aurelius, who revived the practice for propagandistic means. As Isis-Aphrodite, she was the ideal woman, mother and queen; and as Nekhbet, who had been so closely associated with the Ptolemaic queen mothers, she was making a statement designed to appeal to Egyptians: that she was the royal matriarch carrying the heirs to the Ptolemies. It was not only emperors who could manipulate Egyptian imagery to make political messages.

Considering the above themes, the traditional interpretation has been that Egyptian presence was associated directly with imperial propaganda, or with cultic contexts.[12] However, Egyptian elements also occurred in public and domestic decoration, primarily wall paintings and mosaics, with no cultic purpose. Rather they were a statement of elite identity. In 'Nilotic' scenes, visual identifiers were employed to evoke Egypt – boats, papyrus, hippopotamuses, crocodiles and, perhaps surprisingly, pygmies.[13] These were often accompanied by imported objects and locally made sculptures. As with the emergence of the Isis cult, Nilotic imagery predated the Empire, being attested since at least the mid-first century BC and possibly the second century. The most famous example is the Palestrina Mosaic, which depicts the entire Nile course from origin to delta (Fig. 1.1).[14] Within houses, Nilotic scenes occurred primarily in reception rooms

◁FIG. 1.8: Silver-gilt *skyphos*, first century BC to first century AD. Wyvern Collection.

and gardens, areas for receiving guests or entertaining. They were intended to evoke domestic luxury, wealth, cosmopolitanism and cultural aspiration.[15] Such images took the viewer on a journey away from the home and to an exotic land, but at the same time tamed it.[16]

However, 'Nilotic' scenes were not just straightforward representations of Egypt. They held often polyvalent meanings. For example, on a silver *skyphos* (drinking cup) from Alexandria, Nilotic imagery encodes a hidden story, enabling the object to provoke discussion and for the viewer to showcase their erudition by 'decoding' its message (Fig. 1.8). On one side, a naked figure with pointed headdress reminiscent of the pharaonic white crown crouches with his hand in a hippopotamus' mouth; on the other, a second figure with similar headdress, holding a basket and forked stick, steps on a crocodile's back. It is believed that these figures represent the kings Menes (possibly the early dynastic pharaoh Narmer) and Achthoes (Meryibre Khety, first pharaoh of the IXth dynasty), who were held in Classical times as embodiments of good and evil rulership respectively. In particular, the scenes illustrate a Classical literary reference to how both kings met their deaths.[17]

Egypt was not only encountered by elites, however. Huge numbers of smaller and more affordable Egyptian objects circulated along trade routes, embedding them into the everyday life of the Roman Empire. These objects were key in spreading ideas of Egypt to the population away from urban centres, and were the primary means of encounter with Egypt for most people. Inevitably, however, it is harder to quantify such objects, because those that survive are often without archaeological provenance.

In the above contexts, the implicit assumption is of Egypt as 'other' and 'un-Roman'. Scholarship has historically drawn a distinction between 'Egyptian/Oriental' and 'Roman' cults, and has separated authentic Egyptian objects brought to Rome from 'aegyptiaca' – Egyptianising objects made in the Roman world. However, these dichotomies are problematic. There is much evidence to suggest that boundaries were more fluid in the Roman mind. 'Roman' and 'Egyptian' were mutable, overlapping ideas; Egypt was at once both other *and* part of Rome, and various concepts of Egypt could be employed at various times to craft various messages.[18] An object's context, not its appearance, was key.

A good example is the first-century pyramidal tomb of Gaius Cestius. Still standing today, it was much steeper than a 'traditional' Egyptian pyramid, but its distinctive shape became the prototypical example for artists centuries later (Fig. 1.9).[19] Its shape has historically led to assumptions that its design was consciously 'un-Roman'. However, despite its exterior, the interior was decorated in a traditionally Roman style, and the monument can equally be read as a political statement celebrating Roman triumph in North Africa. The pyramid shape was, furthermore,

△ FIG. 1.9: View of the Pyramid of Caius Cestius, Rome, *c.*1806–19. Sir John Soane's Museum.

mediated through Classical associations that linked the pyramids not just with Egypt generally, but more specifically with their purpose as funereal monuments, associated with lavish consumption and great age, and with their status as Wonders of the World. Therefore, whilst its shape might bring to mind ideas of Egypt, it was these above connotations that mattered – a highly visible monument, a modern-day wonder, marking its owner's wealth and power.[20]

To return to the beginning, even Augustus' propaganda was multivocal. Looting obelisks claimed Egypt as conquered and therefore 'othered' it, but at the same time also enfolded Egypt into the Empire's story, and proclaimed Rome as inheriting Egypt's legacy. The inclusion of an Egyptian solar obelisk as the centrepoint of the meridian was also symbolic; Augustus linked himself with the sun god Apollo, and a new inscription dedicated this obelisk to the sun god. This built on the object's original meaning, in a new setting, and made a statement about Augustus' divine leadership. Furthermore, his public political opposition to Egypt seems to have related more to his war with Cleopatra than to any cultural bias. His residence, and the Domus Flavia on the Palatine Hill, incorporated Egyptian decorations.[21] Furthermore, Egyptian cults were allowed to continue, but outside the *pomerium* (Rome's religious boundary) – a statement of Rome as inclusive to others, but marking 'Roman' from 'non-Roman'.[22]

In short, Egypt influenced Roman artistic and material culture in a range of ways. The Romans did not ascribe one meaning to Egypt; multiple 'concepts' of Egypt could be employed by different groups in different contexts.

EGYPT'S LEGACY IN EUROPE

After the fall of Rome, the first Europeans to re-engage physically with Egypt were religious pilgrims retracing the biblical stories. The earliest recorded visit is that of Lady Egeria (travelled AD 381–84), in her *Itinerarium*

Egeriae. In the Middle Ages the practice intensified. The first travellers tried to make sense of Egypt's monuments by rationalising them according to what they knew of Egypt through the Bible. For the pyramids, this was to identify them as the Granaries of Joseph, from Genesis. Most famously, the pyramids appear in the thirteenth-century 'Joseph Cycle' in San Marco Basilica, Venice.

Engagements with ancient Egypt peaked in the Renaissance. Ancient Rome's Egyptian and Egyptianising monuments were rediscovered as part of the turn towards recovering Classical civilisation, and were unearthed during urban expansions and renovations. A key object rediscovered at this time was the *Mensa Isiaca*. This bronze tablet inlaid with silver, depicting various deities and ritual scenes, was rediscovered in the sixteenth century and became perhaps the object that was most responsible for renewed Renaissance interest in ancient Egypt. It is now understood as first-century Roman, probably from an Isis sanctuary, but until the nineteenth century it was believed to be genuinely Egyptian. Other objects had remained known throughout the centuries, but gained renewed interest. In the thirteenth century the Cosmati family of sculptors was able to turn to a limited number of still-visible Egyptian monuments, most importantly sphinxes, as inspiration. 'Cosmatesque' sphinxes were sculpted for the basilica of San Giovanni in Laterano at Rome (unusually, a male and female pair) and for Viterbo, and lions were sculpted for several Roman churches, such as Santi Apostoli and San Lorenzo in Lucina.[23] Whilst Egyptian in inspiration, Cosmatesque sculptures were stylistically far removed. Similarly, the Palestrina Mosaic discussed above was still visible into the sixteenth century.[24] It was moved in the 1620s and was subsequently much restored, making its appearance today a palimpsest of Roman and seventeenth-century ideas of Egyptian landscapes.

These re-encounters, alongside the concurrent rediscovery of the testimonies of Greek and Roman authors on Egypt, were fundamental to Renaissance understandings of, and interest in, ancient Egypt. However, the Classical context of these finds meant that Egypt was understood through the lens of Classical Antiquity, and was seen as part of a Classical history. Nonetheless, within this framework, Egypt also became an area of serious interest and enquiry on its own terms. Objects like the Colonna Missal, which collate together many of the Egyptian and Egyptianising monuments known in sixteenth-century Italy, show an understanding of Egyptian art as a discrete category with distinct visual features (Fig. 1.10).

As material was rediscovered, Egyptian iconography became repurposed to suit new agendas. Because hieroglyphs remained unreadable and objects were found within a Roman milieu, without their original historical context, it became possible for different meanings to be overlaid, and for Egyptian iconography to be appropriated differently to service various groups.[25] Elites were quick to exploit ancient Egypt. Classical writings had fostered an idea of Egypt as the birthplace of law and order; linking oneself to Egypt was therefore a way to enhance legitimacy. One of the most overt ways in which this emerged was through papal re-appropriation of obelisks. Similar to the ancient Romans, obelisks were given new political meaning in an Italian context, but as symbols of papal rather than imperial authority. Many obelisks were reused and altered in this way, perhaps most famously the obelisk in Piazza Navona, which Gian Lorenzo Bernini reused as part of his *Fountain of the Four Rivers*.

◁ FIG. 1.10: Colonna Missal, *c*.1530–38. Fol. 79r. John Rylands Library.

△ FIG. 1.11: The Myth of Osiris and Apis, Sala dei Danti, Borgia apartments, 1492–94. The Vatican.

Each of the four great rivers of the known world crouch in awe of the obelisk, a cipher for papal might. The sculpture's commissioner, Pope Innocent X, was a Pamphili; not only was the sculpture placed in front of the Pamphili Palace, but the obelisk itself was adorned with his family crest. Re-appropriated obelisks were particularly important in Pope Sixtus V's urban programme. Under his architect Domenico Fontana, the obelisk now in St Peter's Square was placed there in 1586; in 1587 one of the obelisks from Augustus' mausoleum was moved to the Esquiline Hill (plans to excavate this obelisk had been in motion since 1519); also in 1587, two obelisks were re-excavated at the Circus Maximus, one erected in 1588 near the Lateran Palace, the other a year later in Piazza del Popolo. These obelisks were 'Christianised' by being surmounted by the papal *monti*. A medal was even issued in Sixtus' final year, showing the obelisks he re-erected.

Popes engaged with other aspects of Egypt also. Rodrigo di Borgia, who became Pope Alexander VI, went as far as to craft an imaginary family lineage reaching directly back to Egypt itself, providing semi-mythical enforcement for his rule. The Borgia apartments (Sala dei Santi) in the Vatican, painted by Pinturicchio to depict the lives of Alexander's patron saints, included overt references to the myths of Osiris, Isis and Apis (Fig. 1.11).[26] This was intended to demonstrate Alexander's genealogy from Osiris, and therefore his legitimacy to rule through descent from Egyptian ancestors; the initials AL.VI even appear on the pediment of Osiris' throne, and the Apis bull was linked with the heraldic Borgia bull. Nonetheless, although Egyptian-inspired in theme, very little about the apartments' decoration is 'accurately' Egyptian. For example, the depiction of Osiris' pyramid tomb drew from Filarete's depiction of the *Meta Romuli* on the bronze doors of St Peter's Basilica (ironically, this pyramid was demolished under Alexander VI), and the sphinxes on his throne resemble medieval Cosmatesque sphinxes more than Egyptian originals. The iconography thus simultaneously drew on Egyptian, Christian and Roman associations, enabling the Borgias to claim links to all three.

Through the rediscovered Classical texts, which portrayed Egypt as a land of philosophy and great sagacity, Egypt was also associated with lost mysticism and wisdom to Renaissance humanist scholars. Classical authors frequently described hieroglyphs as an allegorical system developed by Egyptian priests to preserve, but also conceal, their knowledge. These accounts cultivated a Renaissance idea of ancient Egypt as the ultimate origin of sacred and true wisdom pre-dating the Classical philosophers, *sapientia veterum*. Some took the understanding even further – if Egypt was the source of wisdom, then it followed that it was also the source of *prisca theologia*, the single, true theology underpinning all religions. In other words, Christianity in fact had its roots in ancient Egypt. Hieroglyphic inscriptions became not a potential window into deciphering the historical past, but pictorial representations of secrets and knowledge, transcending language itself to reveal the very essence of existence.

Tying into this were two key works. The first, *Corpus Hermeticum*, was written by 'Hermes Trismegistus'. It was initially translated into Latin in the fifteenth century, by the humanist scholar Marsilio Ficino. Hermes Trismegistus was believed to be an Egyptian priest, and the originator of Egyptian law and religious doctrine that was passed on to Plato, granting him an unsurpassed level of wisdom and knowledge. The second work is *Hieroglyphica*, purportedly written by the Egyptian priest Horapollo, which was rediscovered in 1419. It claimed to explain the meanings of 189 hieroglyphic symbols, with each sign being a rebus encoding an entire concept, idea or natural phenomenon. Neither work was authentically pharaonic – the *Corpus Hermeticum* was a compendium of second- or third-century writings by numerous authors, and *Hieroglyphica* dated to the fifth century – but both were almost universally believed to be authentic ancient treatises on Egyptian wisdom.[27]

These works had a profound influence not only on humanist philosophy – Ficino's translation of *Corpus Hermeticum* had at least twenty-two editions between 1471 and 1641 – but on art. Filarete's *Libro Architettonico* (1460–66) understood Egyptian architecture as the origin of all others, a *prisca architettura* paralleling Egypt's place as *prisca theologia*.[28] Around 1450, Ciriaco d'Ancona produced several architectural sketches; he was unusual in having actually visited Egypt, and apparently took a copy of Horapollo with him to assist in the translation of inscriptions.[29] Humanist ideas around hieroglyphs also led to the development of a system of 'neo-hieroglyphs', attempts at new

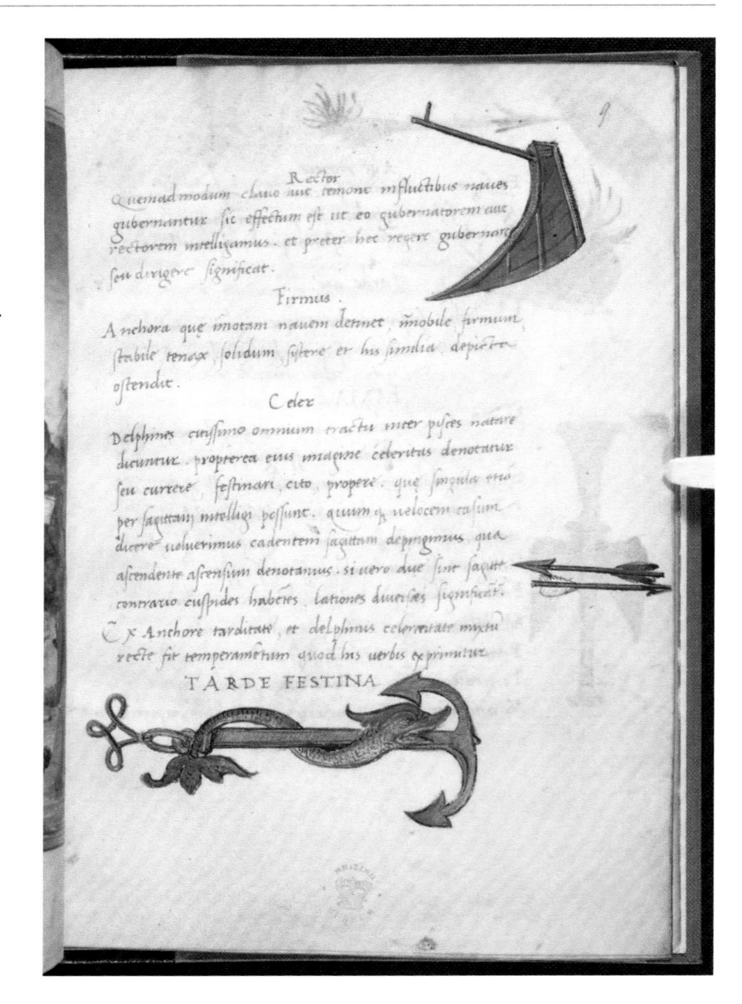

△ FIG. 1.12: Filippo Alberici's *Hieroglyphica*, *c.*1507. Fol. 9r. The British Library.

compositions expressing philosophical ideas through symbols, based on understandings of the ancient script through Horapollo. In 1499 Francesco Colonna wrote *Hypnerotomachia Poliphili*, a story taking place in a fantastical landscape with pyramids, statues and obelisks, heavily inspired by Classical accounts. Images from the book included neo-hieroglyphic inscriptions; and in particular one of the book's images, of an obelisk on an elephant, inspired Bernini's *Elephant and Obelisk* in Piazza della Minerva. Numerous neo-hieroglyphic 'dictionaries' were written to aid compositions, such as Filippo Alberici's *Hieroglyphica* (*c.*1507), Hewarth von Hohenburg's *Thesaurus Hieroglyphicorum* (1610) and, most influentially, Piero Valeriano's *Hieroglyphica* (1556).

Humanist interest rapidly expanded beyond Italy. Albrecht Dürer was fascinated by hieroglyphs, providing the images for Willibald Pirckheimer's 1512–13 translation of Horapollo. For his monumental 1517–18 woodcut *Arch of Honour*, made in honour of

Emperor Maximilian I, Dürer took a Latin eulogy of the emperor made by Pirckheimer and then translated this into 'hieroglyphs' using *Hieroglyphica* as a dictionary; this text forms the centrepiece of the arch.[30] French artists were also receptive to neo-hieroglyphics, as were those in the Low Countries; Lambert Lombard, who was keenly interested in Egypt, particularly helped to disseminate neo-hieroglyphs through his works.[31] Across the Channel, Filippo Alberici's *Hieroglyphica* was actually intended as a gift for King Henry VII, representing the earliest-known penetration of the 'Egyptian renaissance' into England.[32] Many of its entries can be linked directly to neo-hieroglyphs from the *Hypnerotomachia Poliphili* (Fig. 1.12). The page shown here contains pseudo-hieroglyphs for 'ruler/guide' (a ship's prow) and 'fast' (two crossed arrows). The third image, of a dolphin around an anchor, came from the *Hypnerotomachia* through Roman coins, where this symbol was understood as a hieroglyphic expression of Augustus' motto, *festina lente* ('make haste slowly'). By the end of the Renaissance, therefore, artists were looking to ancient Egypt – or at least humanist interpretations of it – across Europe.

EGYPT'S LEGACY IN THE ARABIC WORLD

Whilst Europeans were only just rediscovering Egypt, Arabic scholars, scientists and geographers had engaged with it for centuries. At an everyday level, the pharaoh was as prominent in Islam as in Judaism and Christianity, personifying a pre-Islamic period of ignorance and polytheism.[33] The Qur'an posited links between Islam and Egypt through Hajar, the Egyptian wife of Abraham, and several of the hadiths (the collected sayings of the Prophet) praised Egypt.[34] These all played a role in forming general Islamic views of Egypt. However, alongside these general concepts was a rich tradition of detailed writing about Egypt's monuments. The study of ancient nations was a prominent part of Arabic historiographies, exploring the idea of humanity's common origin, and many geographers chronicled Egypt (Fig. 1.13). Particularly extensive surveys were written by 'Abd al-Laṭīf ibn Yūsuf al-Baghdādī (d.1231); Abu Jafar al-Idrisi (d.1251); Taqī al-Dīn al-Maqrīzī (d.1442); and Jalal al-Din al-Suyuti (d.1505).[35] Egypt's monuments told conflicting stories: their pagan origin and ruined state evoked the vanity of human attempts to transcend mortality, but at the same time their age pointed to a time beyond the human scale, towards the eternal and divine itself. They were both a warning, and something to marvel at.[36]

Like Christian travellers, medieval Islamic authors also attempted to incorporate ancient Egypt into a 'known' historical framework, although this time Islamic history. The pyramids gained particular attention; al-Baghdādī wrote that they had been preserved because companions of the prophets had visited and left pious graffiti on them (possibly a way of explaining the actual ancient travellers' graffiti found on the pyramids); and one sheikh, Naṣir al-Din, chose for himself a pyramid-shaped tomb, within sight of the originals.[37] Al-Idrisi's account of the pyramids included a description of the route from Bab Zuwayla in Cairo to the monuments themselves.[38] These engagements show that the pyramids were not treated as something alien, but as part of an Islamic landscape, connected to

▽ FIG. 1.13: The Nile Delta, from *Ashkal al-'ālam* (Forms of the World), based on Abu Ishaq al-Istakhri's *Kitab al-masālik w'al-mamālik* (Book of Routes and Kingdoms), thirteenth century (original manuscript); this copy made in Baghdad, 1835. Fol. 63a. The British Library.

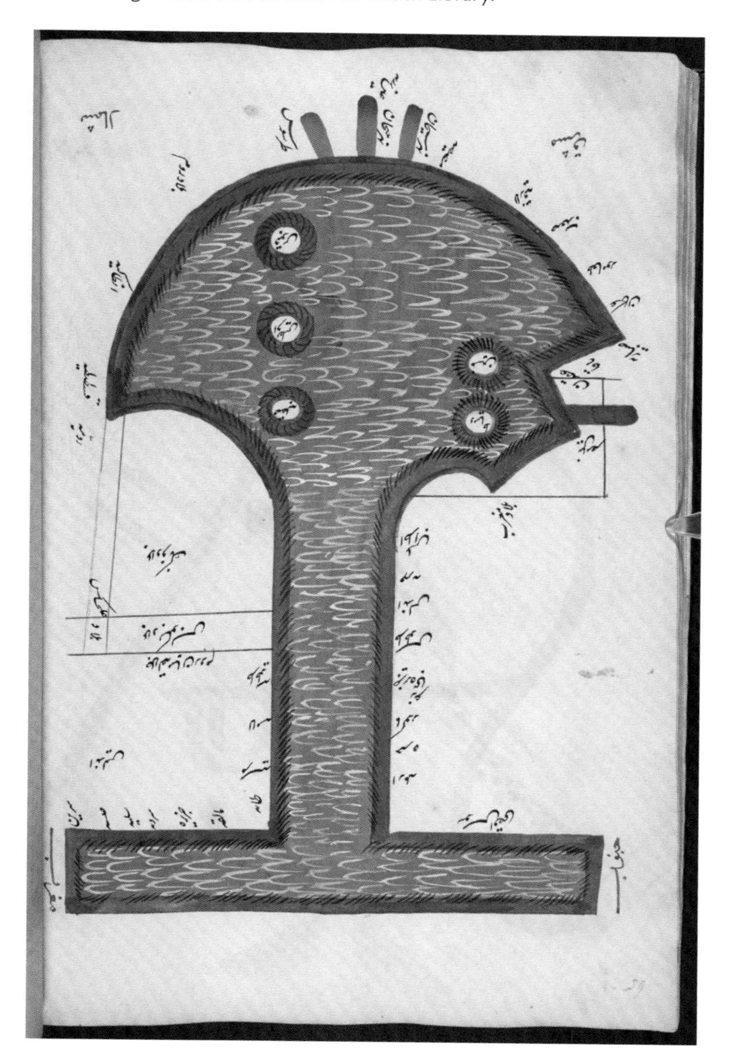

Cairo's sacred sites. However, Islam also felt a tension in relation to the pyramids. Rulers did not want their accomplishments to be judged inferior to those of the ancient past, and so linking the pyramids to ancient Islamic history helped to enfold them into Islam's accomplishments, and also to assuage broader cultural anxieties comparing the standing of Islam with the past.[39] Popular stories included the construction of the pyramids by a legendary antediluvian King Surid; as a repository of Hermes Trismegistus' wisdom and knowledge; or by the legendary people of 'Ād, famed for their building skill.[40] These stories tied the monuments into an Islamic ancestral past.

The literary tradition was rich. Many writers repeated the accounts of their predecessors verbatim, suggesting a continuous engagement with the material; in their studies of the pyramids, al-Maqrīzī and al-Idrisi were able to cite thirty-four different works on the topic.[41] However, although rich, the tradition was not universally relevant or acknowledged. Indeed, in the twelfth century the pyramids' outer casings were used in the construction of Cairo, and other monuments were also periodically demolished or reused for masonry.[42] More generally, the written philosophical wonder of monuments contrasted with an ongoing practice of the inhabitation of sites, and with popular religious beliefs that associated pharaonic remains with fertility and magic. In the thirteenth century Al-Nabulsi described a popular tradition at Biahmu in the Faiyum, where people visited the Middle Kingdom royal statues, using the water beneath them as cures. The obelisks of Alexandria were also believed to have healing powers, gaining the moniker *'Amuda al-I'iya'* (pillars of illness).[43] These themes reflected the more usual engagement with pharaonic Egypt for most of the population.

Alchemy was another key engagement with ancient Egypt – and in particular hieroglyphs. Informed by the same Classical sources as later Renaissance humanists, hieroglyphs were perceived as encoding scientific wisdom. It was believed that Hermes Trismegistus had taught the ancient Egyptians the arcane sciences, and this information was recorded on temple walls; to read hieroglyphs was therefore to unlock these secrets.[44] Many alchemists and scholars attempted to decipher the script, perhaps the most well known being the tenth-century writer Ibn-Wahshiyah, whose work was used by later European scholars attempting their own translations.[45] Alchemists engaged directly with sites and artefacts; indeed, alchemy was known as *'ilm* or *san'at al-barabi*, 'the science or craft of the Egyptian temples' (Fig. 1.14).[46] Ibn Umail, a tenth-century alchemist, wrote of visiting a chapel at Abusir known colloquially as *Sijn Yusuf*, the 'Prison of Joseph', another attempt to link ancient sites to Islamic scriptural tradition.[47] This site has been identified as a cult chapel to the (later deified) high priest Imhotep, another key figure in Hermeticism.

Linked to these beliefs was treasure-hunting.[48] Reinforced by Qur'anic descriptions of the pharaoh's wealth, Egyptian monuments were perceived as great sources of affluence, protected by magic. Some of these ideas of magical protection may be based on observation; one common idea was that demons wielding knives would decapitate intruders, possibly based on actual New Kingdom tomb seals showing the jackal of Anubis atop bound and decapitated human figures.[49] These ideas led to the establishment of a medieval treasure-hunting industry, which became so prolific that the state came to rely on the financial yields of treasure, and from the reign of Ibn Tulun (r. AD 868–84/254–270 AH) it was state-controlled. This practice, of course, only caused further ruin to the monuments. Treasure-hunting was treated as an occult science and was taken seriously by scholars such as al-Kindi, writing in the ninth century.[50] It overlapped heavily with alchemy; alchemists supported treasure-hunting as a means of finding scientific works, and also wrote treasure-hunting manuals because spells needed 'neutralising' before one could enter and find the riches. These manuals often included pseudo-hieroglyphs, designed to increase their credibility. Importantly, the descriptions and depictions of monuments in these manuals sometimes provide the only surviving information on now-lost sites and objects. For example, al-Iraqi's thirteenth-century *Kitāb al-aqālīm al-ṣab'ah* contains an illustrated copy of an actual (now-lost) stela of King Amenemhat II.[51]

In summary, by the end of the fifteenth century ancient Egypt was a source of serious study for both European and Arabic scholars and artists. The European tradition re-emerged after a hiatus, whereas Arabic engagements with ancient Egypt redeveloped much faster. However, both traditions were ultimately indebted to the same source: the Classical world. ⊙

▷ FIG. 1.14: Abū al-Qāsim al-'Irāqī, Study of a 'Hidden Book' by Hermes Trismegistus. The 'hidden book' analysed here was actually a hieroglyphic stela of Amenemhat II. *Kitāb al-aqālim al-sab'ah* (Book of the Seven Climes), thirteenth century (original manuscript); this copy is nineteenth-century. Fol. 15a. The British Library.

هذا ما رمزه الحكيم هرمس المثلث بالحكمة المتوج بالنعمة في المصحف المكنون
المتسوين في جميع الطبايع في العمل الاول بالتدبير الروحاني
العقاب الثاني
منقاره ذهب
عقاب على شجر
طير مقصص الاجنحه
غراب حالك السواد
عقاب ثابت

2 AMBIGUOUS EXCHANGES: TRANSCULTURAL DIALOGUES BETWEEN ANCIENT EGYPT AND THE WEST

DANA ARNOLD

On 12 May 1825 the alabaster sarcophagus of pharaoh Seti I of the XIXth-Dynasty (*c.*1294–79 BC) arrived at the home of the architect John Soane. Soane's house, situated in Lincoln's Inn Fields in London, was also a museum housing his vast collection of antiquities, books and artworks.[1] From the outside, Soane's house/museum appeared to be a Georgian town house, but on entering the visitor was confronted by an unexpected range of spatial experiences and spectacular illumination, both of which served to enhance the exhibits on display.[2] The purchase of the sarcophagus was Soane's greatest and most expensive acquisition. It became the centrepiece of Soane's collection and was situated on the lowest floor of the house in an area known as the crypt, which soared through the full height of the building. The crypt was topped by a glass lantern that created dramatic lighting effects down into the whole space (Fig. 2.2). Soane's acquisition of the sarcophagus attracted international attention, if not envy, and was widely reported in the press. The sale of the sarcophagus had been agreed a month earlier, prompting *The Morning Post* to remark, 'We believe that there is no country in Europe which would not be proud of possessing such a rarity ... if it were possible to purchase it from the liberal and patriotic individual [Soane] who is now its proprietor.'[3]

The sarcophagus had been discovered by the archaeologist Giovanni Battista Belzoni whilst working for Henry Salt, the Consul General of Egypt. Belzoni had indelibly inscribed his name on the sarcophagus and it is sometimes referred to as 'The Belzoni sarcophagus'.[4] In 1820 Belzoni promoted his discovery through the publication of *Narrative of the Operations and Recent Discoveries within the Pyramids, Temples, Tombs, and Excavations in Egypt and Nubia* and a year later the accompanying *Plates Illustrative of the Researches and Operations of G. Belzoni in Egypt and Nubia*, both of which were purchased by Soane.[5] In anticipation that the Trustees would purchase the sarcophagus, Salt arranged the shipment of it to the British Museum, where it arrived in September 1821. But after lengthy negotiations, the asking price of £2,000 remained too high and in 1824 the Trustees finally declined the

◁FIG. 2.1: Soane office, RA Lecture Drawing to illustrate an Egyptian temple: Perspective of the First Court of the Temple at Edfu, after Denon, c.1806–19 (detail). Sir John Soane's Museum.

◁ FIG. 2.2: Volume titled *Sketches and Drawings of the House and Museum of J. Soane Esq RA, 1825–1836*. Sir John Soane's Museum.

offer. Soane, who had been interested in acquiring the sarcophagus since its arrival in London, stepped in.

In March of the following year, to celebrate his purchase and the forthcoming arrival of the sarcophagus at his home, Soane held receptions on three consecutive evenings. It was also an opportunity to show off his substantial collection of antiquities, sculpture including casts, and other artefacts that were carefully displayed in his house. The guests, numbering almost 900, were invited to view 'The Belzoni Sarcophagus and other antiquities ... by lamplight'. The events on all three evenings were widely reported in newspapers, with attendees from royal and political circles.[6] The dazzling array of guests was eclipsed by Soane's strategy for the display of the sarcophagus, together with the rest of his impressive collection. He personally supervised the lighting of his house to manipulate the space by exploiting the contrast between light and dark. In this way he created a romantic atmosphere in which his guests could fully appreciate the sarcophagus – perhaps giving a sense of the experience of its initial discovery in 1817.[7] But Soane was not the first to attempt a re-creation of this archaeological find.

Belzoni was no stranger to self-promotion and the staging of spectacles, having enjoyed a career as a strongman before becoming an Egyptologist. Indeed, as we have seen, to ensure his place in posterity he had inscribed his name on the sarcophagus. To publicise his discovery, stimulate public interest and, hopefully, raise the price the British Museum was prepared to pay, Belzoni hired the appropriately themed Egyptian Hall on Piccadilly (Fig. 2.3).[8] The Hall, completed in 1812, was one of the first examples of an Egyptian Revival building in England.[9] It had been commissioned by William Bullock as a museum to house his collection, which had little to do with Egypt, largely comprising curiosities brought back from the South Seas by Captain Cook. This collection was sold in 1819, and the Hall proved to be a very successful space in which to stage spectacles or large exhibitions. Belzoni's show of the tomb of Seti I, *Facsimile of the Tomb of Psammuthis, King of Thebes*, comprised a full-size model of the principal chambers and contents of the tomb, constructed from drawings and wax-impressions of the original.[10] To accompany the show, Belzoni published *Description of the Egyptian tomb, discovered by G. Belzoni, a pamphlet issued on the occasion of Belzoni's exhibition at the Egyptian Hall in Piccadilly. Includes 'Mrs Belzoni's Trifling Account of The Women of Egypt, Nubia, And Syria'*. It was far more sensationalist than his earlier publications. Here he emphasised the experience of discovering the tomb – notably the lack of air, the dust and numerous decaying mummies.[11] For the visitor to the Egyptian Hall, the tomb and ancient Egypt itself were just spectacles; the venue was coincidental. Indeed, in an ominous nod to the 'living exhibitions' that became an appalling feature of world's fairs later in the century,[12] the Egyptian exhibit was followed in 1822 by that of a family of Laplanders, who were displayed in front of a painted backdrop alongside their

▷ FIG. 2.3: Thomas H. Shepherd, *Bullock's Museum* (Egyptian Hall or London Museum), Piccadilly, 1815. Wellcome Collection.

◁ FIG. 2.4: James Gillray, *Extirpation of the Plagues of Egypt; – Destruction of Revolutionary Crocodiles-or-The British Hero cleansing ye Mouth of ye Nile*, 1798. National Maritime Museum.

reindeer, which had been imported to provide short sleigh-rides to visitors.[13]

The story of Seti is indexical of the *goût d'Égypte*, or taste for Egyptian style, that gripped Europe in the eighteenth and early nineteenth centuries. Most obviously, the nature of the discovery, removal and ultimately the sale of the sarcophagus tells of the wide-scale appropriation and commodification of Egyptian visual culture by an occupying force. This domination by the coloniser of the colonised has been ably discussed elsewhere and is not the focus of this essay.[14] I would like to investigate how encounters with ancient Egypt during this period interacted with Western thinking, artistic practices and patterns of popular consumption. First, I examine the *goût d'Égypte* as a fashion or aesthetic against the background of changing cultural dialogues between Egypt and its European consumers. I will then explore how Egypt disrupted canonical Western thinking about the origins of its own culture. Much of the chronology of these two strands of enquiry runs in parallel. The common thread between them is the notion of modernity.

APPROPRIATING ANCIENT EGYPT

Napoleon Bonaparte initially marched into Egypt in 1798 as part of his empire-building agenda across North Africa and the Middle East.[15] As symbols of Bonaparte's military success, Egyptian motifs were absorbed into the French Empire style that proved very fashionable in all manner of design across Europe. This act of colonisation has its own complexities as the French were replaced by the British a few years later. The defeats of the French by the British at the battles of the Nile (1798), followed by Trafalgar (1805) and finally Waterloo (1815) seeped into popular culture through the spectacles and large exhibitions similar to that staged by Belzoni. The political background to the *goût d'Égypte* may explain some of the fashion for the style in early nineteenth-century Britain, which was short-lived, running in parallel with the Napoleonic Wars.[16] The Egyptian style was distinct from the taste for Classical design that it eclipsed; it had novelty, signalled the expansion of the British Empire and the defeat of Britain's longtime enemy, the French (Fig. 2.4).

The Egyptian style was not, however, completely new to Britain. The use of Egyptian motifs can be found in the work of architects and designers such as William Chambers and Robert Adam during the latter part of the eighteenth century. Similarly, Josiah Wedgwood's catalogue of 1773 presented sphinxes and other Egyptian motifs. Travel to Egypt was rare at this time, so knowledge of Egyptian sources was superficial, gleaned mostly from publications of varying accuracy, including, for example, Benoît de Maillet's *Description de l'Égypte* (1735), Richard Pococke's *A Description of the East and Some Other Countries* (1743), and Frederic Louis Norden's *Voyage d'Égypte et de Nubie* (1755). In addition,

◁ FIG. 2.5: Josiah Wedgwood & Sons, Teapot, c.1800–10. Private Collection.

▽ FIG. 2.6: Josiah Wedgwood & Sons, Canopic jar, 1790. V&A Wedgwood Collection.

Bernard de Montfaucon's ten-volume *L'Antiquité expliquée et representée en figures* (Antiquity explained and depicted in figures) (1719–24) illustrated ancient artefacts and monuments from a broad sweep of time, including ancient Egypt.

Interest in Egyptian-style designs grew and, by the turn of the eighteenth century, Wedgwood was producing modern manufactures including a teapot and stand using Egyptian motifs, hieroglyphics and novelty elements such as a crocodile lid (Fig. 2.5). Alongside the generic Egyptian-style decorative motifs, Wedgwood pieces such as the Canopic Jar were derived directly from the pages of Montfaucon (Fig. 2.6). Adam, Chambers and Wedgwood, amongst others, offered the elite modern design and manufactures that responded to fashionable taste. Despite the commodification of its aesthetic, ancient Egypt remained at a distinct distance in terms of both time and space.

The remark 'The past is a foreign country' is not a new observation.[17] But the past was experienced at first hand by the many eighteenth-century European travellers. Men and women followed the established itineraries of the Grand Tour, with the sights and sites of Italy, especially Rome, as the primary destination. In the latter part of the century, alongside Naples, Pompeii and Herculaneum, excursions to Greece expanded both the geographical spread of the Grand Tour and tourists' engagement with the past. Travellers also ventured beyond these boundaries to visit the

△ FIG. 2.7: Dominique Vivant Denon, *Voyage dans la Basse et la Haute Égypte*, 1829. Sphinx close to the pyramids. Plate 20. Rare Book Division, The New York Public Library.

Ottoman Empire, India and Egypt. Direct experience of Egypt led to fresh understandings and interpretations of its ancient culture. Moreover, archaeological excavations unearthed a past that was previously unknown. Knowledge of this new past, specifically its art and architecture, was disseminated to a broad range of publics through prints and lithographs complemented by scholarly tomes and surveys. Alongside these rich visual resources, the discovery of the Rosetta Stone in 1799 meant that Egypt's verbal past could now be unlocked.

The first systematic study of Egyptian antiquities was undertaken by the French archaeologist Dominique Vivant Denon. He was a loyal supporter of Napoleon Bonaparte, at whose invitation he travelled to Egypt with other scholars as part of his military and scientific expedition of 1798–99. Denon's findings were published in his *Voyage dans la Basse et la Haute Égypte pendant les campagnes du Général Bonaparte*, published as two volumes in 1802. *Voyage* was a highly detailed survey that confirmed Denon's reputation as an archaeologist.[18] Equally important was the subsequent use of *Voyage* as a source and inspiration for architects and designers. Its popularity was immediate – two editions in English were published in the same year, two in German in 1803, with an Italian edition following in 1808.[19]

In his Preface, Denon reminded the reader that he had been engaged in travelling through a country 'which was known to Europe by name only; it therefore became important to describe everything ... I have made drawings of objects of every description.'[20] *Voyage* offered a reconstruction of the archaeology of Egypt using a scientific system of standardisation. This system drew on the visual language of recording architecture established by the Italian Renaissance architect Andrea Palladio in his studies of ancient Rome. This mode of viewing Egypt refracted this previously unknown culture through a European lens. In this way, Denon's visual 'descriptions' reconstructed Egypt's archaeology using language that was recognisable to both his audiences across Europe.[21] This kind of reconstruction helped to present Egypt as part of the Classical European tradition. We can see evidence of this process of Occidentalising the views of Egypt if we look at Denon's engraving of the Sphinx (Fig. 2.7). The figures, trees and animals, and the construction of the landscape of the image, illustrated the artist's stated aim to emphasise the 'picturesque' qualities of the scene. Denon was also at pains to link this image of Egypt to the classicising aims of architects, designers and artists of the West. 'I had only time to view the sphinx ... if the head wants what is called "style", that is to say, the straight and bold lines which give expression to the figures under which the Greeks have designated their deities, yet sufficient justice has been rendered to the fine simplicity and character of nature which is displayed in this figure.'[22] To the present-day reader it is remarkable that Denon ignores the Africanness[23] of the Sphinx, and does not fully acknowledge the location of Egypt in North Africa and not Europe.[24] Indeed, ancient Egypt continued to disrupt European epistemologies, including systems of history, and the history of art, to which I will return.[25]

Denon's visual description of Egyptian architecture offers a synthesis of the picturesque views and measured drawings that had been the hallmark of earlier publications, notably Stuart and Revett's *Antiquities of Athens*.[26] For example, in the description of the Temple of Hermopolis (plate 33), we are presented with a narrative contemporary scene of the Temple with figures in the foreground (Fig. 2.8). Denon also provides a groundplan and a scale, which give some sense of size and layout. In his verbal description of the effect of the Temple of Hermopolis upon the viewer, Denon compares it to the achievements of the Greeks: 'Is it the Egyptians who have invented and brought to perfection such a beautiful art? This is a question that I am unable to answer; but even on first glimpse of this edifice we may pronounce, that the Greeks have never devised nor executed anything in a grander style.'[27] But we must remember that ancient Egypt was a civilisation that was older than the Greco-Roman world.

Denon's well-illustrated archaeological investigations drove design in several ways, including quotations of the images as decoration or the adaptation of architectural form for the design of varying kinds of modern manufactures. Perhaps the most notable example of the reuse of Denon's images of his archaeological finds

▷ FIG. 2.8: Dominique Vivant Denon, *Voyage dans la Basse et la Haute Égypte*, 1829. Ruins of the Temple of Hermopolis (El-Ashmunein); Egyptian tombs of Lycopolis (Asyut); Plan of the Tombs, Plate 33. Rare Book Division, The New York Public Library.

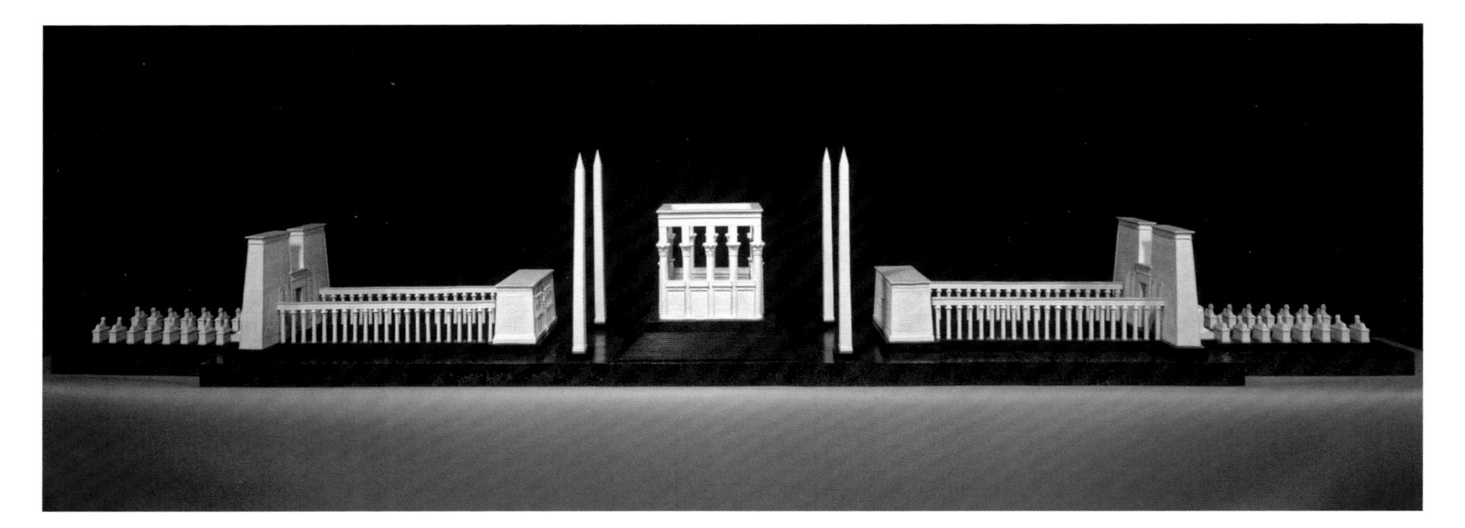

is the Sèvres Egyptian Service. There were two made: the first service was a gift from Napoleon to Alexander I of Russia in 1808;[28] the second service, dating from 1810–12, comprises a stunning architectural centrepiece and seventy-two plates commissioned by the Empress Josephine, just before her divorce from Napoleon in 1809.[29] The centrepiece is a remarkable model combining several ancient Egyptian edifices from different places and periods, arranged in a symmetrical layout (Fig. 2.9).[30] The Temple of Philae stands in the middle, flanked on either side by two obelisks, after which we see the Temple of Dendera, with colonnades leading to the Temple of Edfu, and finally at either end of the centrepiece we have two figures of Memnon and rams. Denon's careful recording of these buildings and sculptures made it possible to re-create them in fine detail. By contrast, the hieroglyphics on the architectural models were fictitious. Perhaps as they were still undecipherable, they did not attract Denon's attention, and were instead reduced to decorative motifs. Memnon appears again on one of the plates entitled 'Statues dites de Memnon', which has a central scene of the colossi of Amenhotep III at Luxor, taken from plate 44 of Denon's *Voyage* (Fig. 2.10).[31] Motifs from Denon's visual descriptions of ancient Egypt also influenced designers. We see this, for example, in the Medal Cabinet by Charles Percier and Martin-Guillaume Biennais (Fig. 2.11). The pylon form of the cabinet, the decoration of the front and back panels with scarab, and two *uraei* (cobras) on lotus stalks are archaeologically informed motifs. But of particular note is the upper part of this cabinet, which bears very close resemblance to plate 80 of Denon's *Voyage* showing the pylon at Apollonopolis Parva (now Qus) in Upper Egypt.[32]

△ FIG. 2.9: Sèvres porcelain factory, Egyptian Service, architectural centrepiece, 1810–12. Victoria and Albert Museum.

▷ FIG. 2.10: Sèvres porcelain factory, Egyptian Service, plate shows the statues of Amenhotep III at Luxor, 1810–12. Victoria and Albert Museum.

▽ FIG. 2.11: Martin Guillaume Biennais, after a design by Charles Percier, Medal Cabinet in the Egyptian taste, *c.*1810. Victoria and Albert Museum.

◁FIG. 2.12: Thomas Hope, *Household Furniture and Interior Decoration*, 1807. The Egyptian Room. Plate 8. Victoria and Albert Museum.

Denon's experience of Egypt was perhaps more extensive and intense than that of other travellers at this time. Nevertheless, Egypt made a considerable impression on them – not least on the collector and designer Thomas Hope, who travelled extensively in Europe and beyond. In 1787 he embarked on a series of journeys, during which he visited Turkey, Egypt, Syria, Greece, Sicily, Spain, Hungary, Palestine, Portugal, France and Germany. He settled in London around 1796, and by 1799 had bought a house in Duchess Street, London, designed by Robert Adam.[33] Hope remodelled the interior with a series of themed rooms to display his ever-growing collection of objects purchased during and after his travels, including antique sculpture, vases and artefacts, alongside modern paintings and sculpture. In 1802 he hosted a grand opening of his house/museum for the social elite, with invitees including the Prince of Wales. The divide between private residence and public gallery blurred further when, only two years later, Hope decided to issue admission tickets to members of the Royal Academy. Subsequently there were numerous other visitors to the house, including leaders of society, artists, scholars and designers.

Visitors to the Duchess Street mansion experienced a range of styles, including Egyptian, Greek, Roman, Indian and French Empire. The themed rooms included the Vase Room containing his extensive collection of Greek vases; the Aurora Room – a mirrored space built around a statue of Aurora, the goddess of dawn; a Statue Gallery; and the Egyptian Room. Alongside his own travels in Egypt, Hope's approach to the *goût d'Égypte* was influenced by the plates from Denon's *Voyage*, as well as earlier studies by designers including Piranesi. And we see in his designs a far more serious archaeological engagement with ancient Egypt than had previously been in evidence in the work of Adam, Chambers and Wedgwood. The Egyptian Room was located on the first floor and was intended to be accessible to the visiting public. Hope's design of this room included the display of original Egyptian sculpture placed alongside furniture designed by Hope in an Egyptian manner, and was intended to demonstrate the importance of the ancient Egyptians to the origins of Western culture (Fig. 2.12).[34] The furnishings included a pair of armchairs and a couch in the Egyptian Revival style (Fig. 2.13). The arrangement of the Egyptian Room, including the placement of this suite of furniture, is recorded in a meticulous line drawing in Hope's very influential publication *Household Furniture and Interior Decoration* (1807).[35]

Denon's *Voyage* was not the only publication to come out of Napoleon's Egyptian campaign of 1798–1801. The *Description de l'Égypte* was a highly ambitious collaborative work of more than 150 scholars and scientists who, like Denon, had been part of Bonaparte's expedition. The survey, with the full title *Description de l'Égypte, ou Recueil des observations et des recherches qui ont été faites en Égypte pendant l'expédition de l'armée française*, ran to many volumes published between 1809 and 1829. *Description* comprised text, plates and a cartographic section, *Carte de l'Égypte*, with fifty plates of maps, including the first accurate maps of Egypt, Syria and Palestine. The survey aimed to record and catalogue all known aspects of ancient and modern Egypt, as well as its natural history, and can be seen as the 'great collective appropriation of one country by another'.[36] This kind of appropriation is a form of colonialism, where cultural elements are copied from a minority culture by members of a dominant culture. They are then used outside their original cultural context. Both Denon's *Voyage* and the multi-volume *Description* typify the standardisation and Occidentalisation that were germane to the mapping processes of cultural appropriation. Egypt was subsumed into established systems of knowledge and visual representation to endorse contemporary empire-building agendas. Returning to Chambers, Adam, Wedgwood and Hope, we must not forget that their designs were seen as modern by contemporaries. And this leads me to the think about how, through this cultural mapping and reconfiguring, Egypt was pressed into the service of European notions of modernity.

▽ FIG. 2.13: Thomas Hope, Regency Egyptian Revival style armchairs, c.1802. Powerhouse Museum Collection, MAAS Collection.

EGYPT BEFORE THE DISCOVERY OF EGYPT

My second, parallel line of enquiry focuses on the transcultural dialogues between Europe and ancient Egypt. This tells a different story of a perhaps more ambiguous set of cultural exchanges between Europe and ancient Egypt. European interest in the architecture of ancient Egypt pre-dated the Enlightenment and can be traced back to 30 BC, when Egypt became part of the Roman Empire (see Chapter 1). Alongside the use of Egyptian architectural motifs, there was a growing interest in portable objects such as obelisks, which meant that Egyptian remains were accessible in cities such as Rome. Thirteenth-century Rome underwent yet another period of lively interest in Egypt 'where Sphinxes turned up in stylistically remarkably correct adaptations ... and, for the first time, pyramids were incorporated in Christian tomb monuments'.[37] Reference to these architectural elements was revived during the Renaissance (see Chapter 1). And this had relevance for the eighteenth- and early nineteenth-century dialogues with ancient Egypt. Indeed, ancient Egypt had been absorbed into the debates of the Greco-Roman controversy, about whether Greece or Rome was superior, by the mid-eighteenth century.

My interest here is in how the 'discovery' of ancient Egypt disrupted European ideas about its history, civilisation and culture. Here again, the notion of modernity comes to the fore. The Renaissance revival and identification with the Classical world to further the predominant humanistic cultural agenda of the fifteenth and sixteenth centuries can be seen as the advent of modernity. This identification with the Classical world went hand-in-hand with the rejection of the immediate medieval past and set new parameters for the notions of cultural supremacy. Knowledge of this remote paradigm of Western civilisation was developed and spread through the printing press. Words and images of the past circulated in an ever-increasing pan-European currency of knowledge of the ancients. The self-conscious adaptation of the Greco-Roman past became itself a focus of debate in *La querelle des Anciens et des Modernes*, or 'Battle of the Books', that dominated seventeenth- and eighteenth-century intellectual debate. Fuelled by the development of the printing press, which made knowledge of both artefacts and ideas from across time more accessible, the debate focused on whether the ancients or the moderns were superior. It was the importance of either the past or the present for the future that was at stake here. And it was only towards the end of the eighteenth century that the past began to be differentiated from the present in European thought. In this way, the past became a means to meet the demands of the present and was devised accordingly. But Egypt offered a new past – a different 'foreign country' to be explored, both metaphorically and physically.

Johann Joachim Winckelmann was the first art historian to make the distinction between Greek, Greco-Roman and Roman art, leading to controversial debates about which was the superior society. His 1755 major work *Gedanken über die Nachahmung der griechischen Werke in der Malerei und Bildhauerkunst* (*Reflections on the Painting and Sculpture of the Greeks*) emphasised the supremacy of ancient Greek art and established a chronology of the development of art beginning with Greece.[38] Winckelmann's writings sparked the Greco-Roman controversy in the 1760s, a debate as to the relative superiority of Greek and Roman architecture and ornament. The Romans found a champion in Giovanni Battista Piranesi, whose vast oeuvre of engravings of ancient Roman sites demonstrated his perception of Roman practicality as an improvement over Greek experiment. The *Della Magnificenza e d'Architettura de' Romani* (*On the Grandeur and the Architecture of the Romans*) of 1761 involved a sequence of illustrations depicting Roman invention, backed up with intelligent text. His view was that Roman technology was superior to Greek. His main thesis was based on the idea that the Romans had learned about design not from the Greeks, as British and French scholars argued, but from the earlier inhabitants of Italy, the Etruscans. Piranesi contested that Etruscan design was in turn derived from the Egyptians. In making this argument, he was asserting that Europe's visual culture was rooted in a civilisation that lay outside its geographical borders. The non-European basis of architecture and design did not find favour, and Winckelmann's position that the beginnings lay in ancient Greece has remained largely unchallenged.

Piranesi's advocacy of Egyptian design as a superior source for contemporary design found strongest voice in his 1769 *Diverse maniere d'adornare i cammini ed ogni altra parte degli edifizi desunte dall'architettura Egizia, Etrusca, e Greca con un Ragionamento Apologetico in defesa dell'Architettura Egizia, e Toscana* (*Diverse Ways of ornamenting chimneypieces and all other parts of houses taken from Egyptian, Etruscan, and Grecian architecture with an Apologia in defence of the Egyptian, Tuscan architecture*).[39] His focus was on the use of Etruscan, Greek and especially Egyptian elements in the design of chimneypieces. Compared to his earlier archaeological investigations, *Diverse maniere* was a text of two distinct halves. There was a thirty-five-page Preface of highly theorised polemical text, advocating the supremacy of Roman design and its Etruscan and Egyptian roots, published in Italian, English and French. Piranesi's Preface counters the anticipated criticism of the inappropriateness of Egyptian and Etruscan art as sources for design. He was one of the first to advocate non-Greek styles in architecture and the decorative arts. He contested that although these styles were not customary and might not be found to be 'agreeable' and 'delicate', but rather 'bold, hard, and stiff',[40] he objected to the dismissal of Egyptian art as too bulky and crude, and thus the artists employing it as too unsophisticated to recognise and employ standards of perfection established by the Greeks. Moreover, Piranesi argued that the Egyptians were not culturally deficient, unadvanced technically and aesthetically in their abilities to copy nature in its most perfect form. Rather, the Egyptians deliberately chose their monumental, blocky style, and that choice was a matter of artistic intention, to preserve long-held and revered traditions. All that said, Piranesi did underscore the importance of the designer's imagination in the adoption and adaptation of forms from the past.[41]

The second part of the book was a pattern book comprising sixty-six plates, of which fifty-three were of chimneypieces.[42] In his discussion of the use of antiquity, Piranesi advocated not only creating in the manner of the Egyptians or the Romans, but also combining the various styles, 'uniting [them] in an artful and masterly manner'.[43] For example, Egyptian figures are juxtaposed with Roman trophies or Pompeian motifs of winged Victories, a string of masks entwined by a snake (a motif that Piranesi considered

▽ FIG. 2.14: Giovanni Battista Piranesi, *Diverse Maniere d'adornare i cammini* (Diverse Ways of ornamenting chimneypieces), Spaccato della bottega ad uso di caffè detta degl'Inglesi situata in piazza di Spagna ... (A section of the English Coffee House in the Piazza di Spagna ...), 1769. Smithsonian. Gift of Mr and Mrs Gustave Gilbert.

Etruscan), and Egyptian figures flank pilasters engraved with hieroglyphics. In *Diverse maniere* Piranesi also included two plates illustrating his painted scheme for the Caffè degli Inglesi in Piazza di Spagna, Rome, of *c.*1760 (Fig. 2.14). We have some idea of the reaction of contemporaries, which was not always favourable. On visiting the Caffè, the Welsh painter Thomas Jones remarked in 1776, '[the Caffè was] a filthy vaulted room the walls of which were painted with sphinxes, obelisks and pyramids from capricious designs of Piranesi, and fitter to adorn the inside of an Egyptian sepulchre, than a room of social conversation.'[44]

Piranesi's view of the supremacy of Rome over Greece chimed with the debates about the meaning of architecture that had been a principal concern of *La querelle des Anciens et des Modernes*, which dominated French thought in the seventeenth and eighteenth centuries. And this brings us back to Soane, who was greatly influenced by these debates. He was especially inspired by Enlightenment thinkers such as the Abbé Laugier, who was in favour of the *Modernes*. And, like Laugier, Soane came down firmly on the side of the superiority of contemporary architecture over the achievements of the ancients. In his *Essai sur l'architecture* of 1753, Laugier outlined the fundamentals of architectural language and sought to distil the essentials from architectural style. In the second edition of his *Essai* in 1755, Laugier included his seminal image of the primitive hut as the basis of architecture. The belief in modernity and in the essence of architecture informed Soane's approach to architectural theory and practice. From 1806 Soane was Professor of Architecture at the Royal Academy and was responsible for delivering six public lectures annually, through which he was able to influence future generations of architects, as well as his contemporaries. The notes and images for these lectures remain.[45]

Soane's first Royal Academy lecture was in 1809 and he sought to outline the origin of civil, military and naval architecture, with an emphasis on first principles. His wish was to 'trace architecture from its most early periods'.[46] Here we can see his view of ancient Egyptian architecture and how it fitted into the broader history of architectural theory and practice. Soane did not visit Egypt, and his knowledge of ancient Egyptian architecture was derived primarily from his copies of Piranesi's *Diverse maniere* and especially from Denon's *Voyage*, from which he made several pages of notes and translated material for inclusion in Lecture 1.[47] Soane presents parallel views of Egyptian design. He is most influenced by Denon's description and images when he speaks of its effect as being sublime. His lecture included a passage from Denon: 'The Egyptians, not having borrowed anything from others, have not added any foreign ornament, no superfluity to that which necessity dictates. Ordonnance and simplicity were their principles, and they have raised these principles to sublimity.'[48]

Soane also noted that 'At Luxor is a temple [of Amenhotep III] ... it is a wonderful proof of the perseverance and industry of the Egyptians, and also of the sublimity of their ideas.'[49] Like Denon, Soane also found the Temple of Hermopolis to be a form of *architecture parlante*, or speaking architecture: '... show this work to a peasant. At once without having any idea of architecture, he would say, "this is The House of a God" ... the Greeks have neither invented or done anything of greater character.'[50] Moreover the illustrations to the lectures quote directly from the plates in Denon. We see this, for example, in the *Lecture Drawing to illustrate an Egyptian temple, Plan & perspective of the Temple of Hermopolis, after Denon* (Fig. 2.15).[51] This is based on plate 33 in *Voyage, Temple of Hermopolis (El-Ashmunein); Egyptian tombs of Lycopolis (Asyut); plan of the tombs*. Similarly, the *Lecture Drawing to illustrate an Egyptian temple: Perspective of the First Court of the Temple at Edfu, after Denon*, is also almost identical to the corresponding plate in Denon.[52] The obvious difference between the lecture drawings and Denon's plates is that the former are in colour and, as such, perhaps give greater emphasis to the sublime grandeur of their subjects (Fig. 2.1). That said, for Soane, Denon's careful mapping of the architecture of ancient Egypt disrupted both the accepted chronology of European architecture and its roots in Greco-Roman tradition. Instead, through Denon and to some extent Piranesi's exploration of Egyptian design, Soane found a link between the fundamentals of architecture and modernity. There was then, for Soane, something in ancient Egyptian design that was both the essence of architecture and protomodern. He saw it as never straying from the first principles that Laugier had articulated and illustrated in his *Essai*, ' ... even in their subsequent and most splendid works they never lost sight of their primitive model'.[53]

In tandem with his praise and admiration for ancient Egypt, Soane also commented on Egyptian Revival fashion. By contrast, he was highly critical of this style, as it ignored the first principles that, for him, were a hallmark of Egyptian design:

△ FIG. 2.15: Soane office, RA Lecture Drawing to illustrate an Egyptian temple: Plan and perspective of the Temple of Hermopolis, after Denon, c.1806–19. Sir John Soane's Museum.

> If I have been correct in describing the characteristics and essential features of Egyptian architecture, what can be more puerile and unsuccessful than paltry attempts to imitate the character and form of their works in small confined spaces? And yet, such is the prevalence of that monster fashion, and such the rage for novelty, that we frequently see attempts of this kind by way of decoration. Particularly to many of the shop fronts of the metropolis. Nor does this evil of applying without recurrence to first principles end here. The Egyptian mania has spread further: even our furniture is decorated with the symbolic forms of the religions and other customs of Egypt.[54]

This brings us back to Seti. At first glance, Soane's acquisition of the sarcophagus and the celebrations that followed can be seen as indexical of the growing interest in Egypt, combined with the collecting and thoughtful display of objects. This is evident in the burgeoning number of private collections in Britain and Europe, as well as the ever-expanding holdings of national museums.[55] As the horizons of travel and exploration expanded across Africa and Asia, so did the amassing of objects. In contrast to the familiar remnants of the European Greco-Roman past, these were outside the established, canonical systems of classifying knowledge. There is no doubt of the colonising agenda of the surveys of Egypt in the early nineteenth century. We can see this in the way the archaeological remains were recorded and visually described using techniques that were developed within the Western/European canon of architectural drawing. And it is clear that ancient Egypt was seen as exotic, and its visual culture fetishised. But knowledge about ancient Egypt also disrupted European ideas about its history, civilisation and culture, and had agency in the debates about the notion of modernity. ⊙

N° 7. Abou-Simbel. Gd Temple. Le dieu-Soleil Ra & Rhamses II.
P. Sébah

3 EGYPT THROUGH NINETEENTH-CENTURY PHOTOGRAPHY

OMNIYA ABDEL BARR & ELLA RAVILIOUS

In January 1839 astronomer François Arago, director of the Paris Observatory, gave a speech to announce Louis-Jacques-Mandé Daguerre's invention, the daguerreotype, a unique one-off photographic image formed on a silvered copper plate. In his speech Arago noted how useful the invention would have been for the survey of Egypt a few decades previously, when the scientists and scholars accompanying Napoleon Bonaparte's military expedition were preparing the twenty-two-volume *Description de l'Égypte*. He stated that, with this invention, one man alone could copy 'millions of hieroglyphs'. Photography and Egyptology were tied together from that moment on. In November that same year the first photographers set sail to Egypt. Photography amplified the fascination for ancient Egypt in popular culture and revolutionised the study of ancient Egypt in Europe and North America. It is testament to the pre-existing keen levels of interest in ancient Egypt during the birth of photography that so many early photographs depict Egypt or its artefacts. Photography became embedded within the similarly expanding discipline of Egyptology. Both William Henry Fox Talbot and Louis-Jacques-Mandé Daguerre's new photographic inventions were swiftly put to work to disseminate ideas about ancient Egypt in Europe.

The daguerreotype was used to create the aquatint illustrations for the publication *Excursions Daguerriennes: Vues et monuments les plus remarquables du globe*, published in 1840–42 and commissioned by the optician and daguerreotypist Noël Paymal Lerebours. The book project gathered daguerreotypes from multiple photographers, which were traced and engraved to create the printed illustrations. The project swung into action only weeks after the announcement of Daguerre's process in 1839. The volume therefore featured illustrations based on daguerreotypes of Egypt's architectural monuments taken by the pioneering photographers described below.

The French painter Horace Vernet travelled to Egypt in November 1839 with his student Frédéric Goupil-Fesquet. In Alexandria they met Pierre-Gustave Joly de Lotbinière, a Swiss-Canadian landowner who had been in Paris en route to Egypt when Daguerre's invention was announced. The three were received in Ras al-Tin Palace by the Ottoman viceroy Muhammad

◁ FIG. 3.1: Pascal Sébah, The Abu Simbel temple (the Sun Temple of Ramses II), *c.*1875. Victoria and Albert Museum.

Ali Pasha (r.1805–48), who was keen to champion technology and therefore asked Vernet to demonstrate the daguerreotype process for him, and allowed the painter to take his photograph. The daguerreotypes this trio took for *Excursions Daguerriennes* were the earliest photographs taken in Egypt and Africa, and the resulting volume they sit within is a fascinating boundary object in both material and conceptual terms. Materially, it sits between the established art forms of painting and printmaking and the infant art of photography; and conceptually, one can see *Excursions Daguerriennes* within the framework of the Grand Tour and the tradition of the seminal publication *Description de l'Égypte*, identified by Edward Said as 'that great collective appropriation of one country by another'.[1]

Excursions Daguerriennes also created the conditions for later photographic survey projects published in book form, such as *Égypte, Nubie, Syrie: Paysages et Monuments* of 1849–50 by Maxime Du Camp, and set the scene for tourist and survey photography of Egypt. The daguerreotypes made for the project no longer exist. Following closely behind Vernet, Goupil-Fesquet and Lotbinière, however, was Joseph-Philibert Girault de Prangey, a French artist, photographer and draughtsman whose daguerreotypes of Egypt made in 1844 are the earliest surviving photographic records of the country and its ancient monuments (Fig. 3.2).

William Henry Fox Talbot, who had interests in etymology as well as photography, took Arago's plea to photographically reproduce hieroglyphs to the letter and rendered his latest invention, a new paper-based photographic process called the Talbotype or calotype, for use in recording them. The esoteric publication that

▽ FIG. 3.2: Joseph-Philibert Girault de Prangey, Ramesseum, Thebes, 1844. The Metropolitan Museum of Art.

resulted marked a path for photography in archaeology that was to become deeply entangled in Egyptian antiquities and in beliefs about ancient Egypt. Indeed, one can see a lineage from Talbot's photographs of hieroglyphs to current research by Christina Riggs into the photography of Howard Carter's excavation of Tutankhamun's tomb in the 1920s, in the way photographs shaped opinion on Egypt's ancient past.[2]

Talbot was to work concertedly on deciphering the ancient cuneiform script from Mesopotamia (Iraq), but his foray into Egyptology resulted in his 1846 pamphlet *The Talbotype Applied to Hieroglyphics* (Fig. 3.3). Talbot was embedded in British scientific circles and produced the booklet with Egyptologist and antiquary Samuel Birch, artist, curator and Egyptologist Joseph Bonomi the Younger, skull-collector and Egyptologist George Robins Gliddon and antiquary, merchant and collector Anthony Charles Harris. Gliddon was a major figure in scientific racism, who, through his study of skulls and hieroglyphs, concluded that the ancient Egyptians were white. As Riggs outlines, 'His books *Crania Americana* (1839) and *Crania Aegyptiaca* (1844) laid the groundwork for scientific racism in America ... Using ancient art, chimpanzees and, of course, the mummies' skulls, it argued that the Ancient Egyptians were light-skinned Caucasians and black Africans their slaves.'[3]

The booklet that Talbot and his colleagues produced concerned the hieroglyphs found by Harris inscribed on a tablet at Ibrîm, now at the site of Lake Nasser, and included a translation of the hieroglyphs done by Birch. The calotypes showing the hieroglyphs were not made in Egypt and do not show the actual tablet, but instead reproduce Bonomi's illustrations of the hieroglyphs, which were in turn based on drawings Harris made of the tablet *in situ*. In 1966 the Argentine Egyptologist Ricardo A. Caminos published an essay on the booklet in which he noted that, unbeknownst to Harris, this tablet had been previously 'discovered' by William John Bankes in around 1815–19, and again by Robert Hay between 1824 and 1827, and was duly 'discovered' a fourth time after Harris and Talbot's publication in the 1840s by Archibald Henry Sayce in 1893–94, who was clearly unaware of their previous work.[4] This tale illustrates how Egypt was seen to be a *tabula rasa* ready for re-inscription by Western knowledge actors – in fact to own his discovery and claim it as his find, Harris carved his own name on the tablet in 1845.[5] Such renaming/graffiti regularly took place in the region during the nineteenth century and was at times captured in the photographic record, as we shall see.

Towards the late 1840s and early 1850s the calotype process reached Egypt. Less well-known

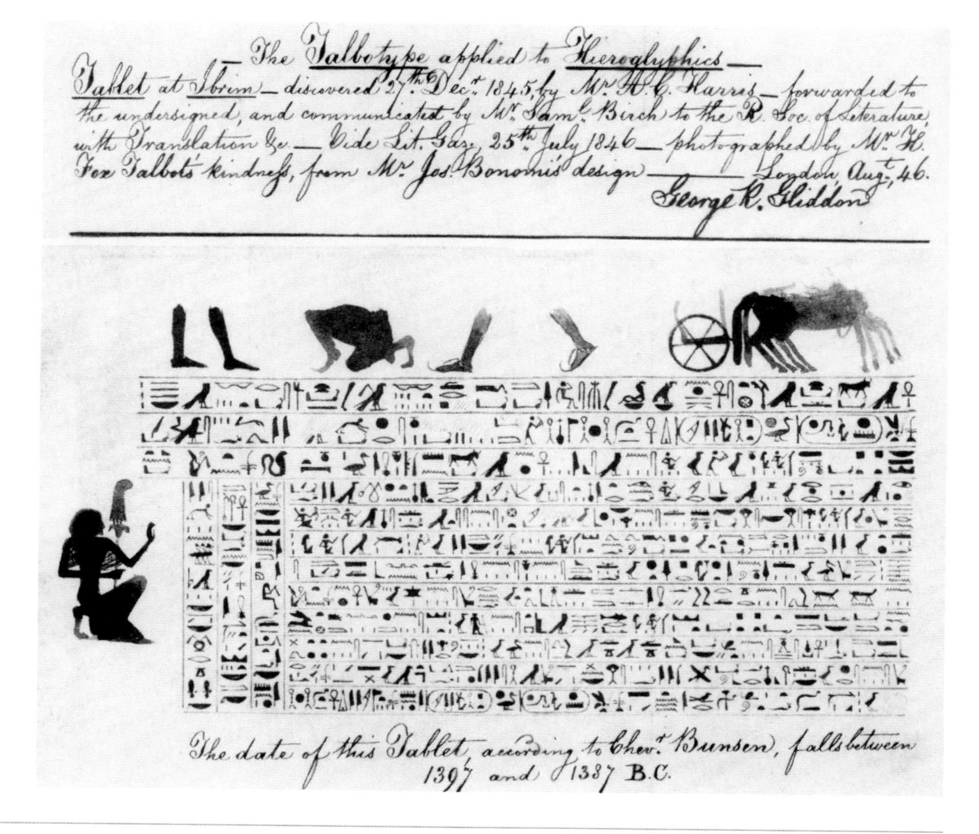

▷ FIG. 3.3: William Henry Fox Talbot, copy of a translation of a hieroglyphic tablet, c.1845. The Science and Society Picture Library.

early photographers of Egypt included Claudius Galen Wheelhouse, a ship's surgeon who was in the region accompanying Lord Lincoln, the British minister for war, on a yachting trip in 1850–51. An album of his photographs exists in the collection of the Royal Photographic Society at the Victoria and Albert Museum and documents both medieval and ancient Egyptian architecture in soft, vignetted views. Reverend George Wilson Bridges, who had learned calotypy from Talbot, also found himself in Egypt and took images of ancient sites, which can be seen as early embodiments of the separate ways in which local people and Western visitors were portrayed in photography. In one image we see Bridges standing in the centre holding his gun and gazing off into the distance, with Egyptians sitting behind him on the ground in front of a dark opening, probably the entrance of a tomb, while the Pyramid of Khafre at Giza looms behind them . The challenges of photography during this period were considerable, as the process involved extensive heavy and fragile equipment, chemicals that did not work as expected in the heat, light-sensitive materials and, after the calotype process gave way to the collodion process, the transport of fragile glass-plate negatives.

Better known is Maxime Du Camp's series, based on his 1849–50 journey across the region with the writer Gustave Flaubert. These magnificently soft but crisp photographs set in place the tropes for photography of ancient Egypt, portraying a curiously empty monumental landscape (Fig. 3.4). The quiet emptiness of some of the most famous photographs from this set gives them an archetypal pull, prompting thoughts of Shelley's poem 'Ozymandias' – but their stillness is a construct. Although the photographic technology of the time did not have the capacity to capture figures in motion, it is wrong to assume it was the technology that

▽ FIG. 3.4: Maxime Du Camp and Louis Désiré Blanquart-Evrard, *Égypte Moyenne: Le Sphinx* (Middle Egypt: The Sphinx), 1849–50. Victoria and Albert Museum.

de-peopled these photographs – it was possible to have chosen to include people, as other images in Du Camp's volume feature his companion Flaubert or his employed Nubian sailor Hadji-Ishmael in shot. As Elizabeth Anne McCauley notes, 'the photographs produced during the trip appear as silent, almost unfeeling studies analogous to the text that accompanies them in the Gide and Baudry publication':[6]

> Looking at the prints, one would have no idea that these two Frenchmen spent their evenings in the arms of dancing girls, were plagued by fleas and venereal disease, and amused themselves by shooting birds, crocodiles, and even dogs. Although the slowness of the medium made genre scenes or lively portraits impossible, the presence of various figures to give a sense of scale proves that it was possible to obtain clear images of individuals who are instructed not to move.[7]

Julia Ballerini's analysis of the role of Hadji-Ishmael in Du Camp's photographs includes the palpable disdain in which Du Camp held his servant, describing the photographer 'ordering Ishmael to scramble here and there, continually looking at him through the camera lens and ordering his immobility by telling him that the camera is a cannon that will kill him if he makes the slightest move'.[8]

This disdain for the contemporary people of Egypt is a marked trope in nineteenth-century photography of the country. The astronomer Sir Charles Piazzi Smyth travelled to Egypt in 1865 and photographed inside the pyramids for the first time, using magnesium flash to illuminate the interiors sufficiently to obtain the image – practically the first instance of the technology being used in this way.[9] Ali Behdad has discussed how, in an 1897 reading for a Magic Lantern show of his images of the great pyramid of Giza, Smyth – explaining his obsessive fixation on the pyramids – expressed the view that 'the ghost-like figures of the Arabs might as well have been omitted, for with their black, unphotographicable [*sic*] faces they make very bad ghosts; and besides the modern Arabs of Egypt are such ephemeral occupiers of the soil, that they have no right to any place among the more ancient monuments of Egypt'.[10] Views such as these were not uncommon.

▽ FIG. 3.5: Philip Henry Delamotte, The Egyptian Court at the Crystal Palace, 1854. Victoria and Albert Museum.

What such stories illustrate is the passion for ancient Egypt in Europe in the mid-nineteenth century, its place in overlapping academic, artistic, scientific and photographic circles, and the commitment to a discourse of 'discovery' that erased contemporary Egyptians. This was formulated on the re-inscription, translation and ownership of Egypt's ancient heritage for European audiences, creating new fuel for the popular obsession with ancient Egypt.

These acts of re-inscription and translation for a popular British audience can be seen in the 'Egyptian Court' at the Crystal Palace in Sydenham, designed in 1854 by Owen Jones and sculpted by Joseph Bonomi, the artist whom we met previously in Talbot's Egyptology circle. This flagship project in a popular public attraction brought Egypt to the masses in England and was photographed extensively by many photographers; particularly notable were Philip Henry Delamotte's albumen prints and Negretti & Zambra's stereo views.

This grand court contained reduced-size replicas of an array of ancient Egyptian sites, from the temples of Abu Simbel, Karnak and Dendera to the tombs of Beni Hasan and the portico at Philae, all arranged metres from each other and brightly coloured, to represent a concept of the monuments as they were originally built. The effect must have been dazzling, though Jones received considerable criticism for his approach, as he was 'thought by some to have created gaudy and flawed interpretations of the ancient monuments'.[11]

The Egyptian Court was one of the most heavily photographed areas of the reopened Crystal Palace (Fig. 3.5). Photographic images could be bought as souvenirs and appeared in a wide variety of

◁ FIG. 3.6: Louis Haghe after David Roberts, Statues outside the temple of Abu Simbel, Egypt, coloured lithograph, 1849. Wellcome Collection.

photographic formats, including lantern slides and stereo views – the former being used performatively to tour images and representations around the country. Jones' version of ancient Egypt, and its wide dissemination through various media, spread visions of ancient Egypt in colour – the Egypt-themed cinema frontages, fairground rides and bingo halls of twentieth-century England arguably have roots in Jones' Egyptian Court.

Behdad rightly states that 'the relation between orientalist painting and photography is not that of a linear influence but that of a circular reciprocity'.[12] Each discipline was deeply enmeshed with the other. Linda Nochlin explains how 'naturalist' painters like Jean-Léon Gérôme painted in a realist style and included authentic details, such as the damaged Iznik tiles behind the watchers in his painting *The Snake Charmer*, to convince viewers that they were seeing an objective vision of 'the Orient', though in fact such details served to promote a message that Egyptian people had let their own cultural treasures sink into decay. This decay was sought-after by Western artists to comply with what Nochlin outlines when she states, 'the very notion of the picturesque in its 19th century manifestations is premised on the fact of destruction. Only on the brink of destruction, [were] customs, costumes and religious rituals of the dominated finally seen as picturesque.'[13] Photography was an ideal way to seek out, create and promote such picturesque visions of decaying cultural treasures, and

▽ FIG. 3.7: Francis Frith, Abu Simbel, 1856–60. Victoria and Albert Museum.

it contributed to Orientalist discourses suggesting that Egyptians were not capable of caring for their heritage.

As Behdad asserts:

> painters such as Jean Léon Gérôme (1824–1904), Ludwig Deutsch (1855–1935), and William Holman Hunt (1827–1910) became increasingly dependent on the works of amateur and professional photographers of the Orient with well-established photographic studios in Egypt, such as in Luxor Antonio Beato (est. 1862), and others in Cairo such as Henri and Emile Béchard (est. 1868), Beniamino Facchinelli (est. 1870s), Pascal Sébah (est. 1973), the Abdullah frères (est. 1886) and Gabriel

Lékégian (est. 1887) to create what was considered documentary realism.[14]

After the opening of the Suez Canal in 1869, French, German, English, Armenian and Italian photographers all operated in Egypt to service this booming trade.

This symbiosis between artists and photographers is evident in the output of Francis Frith, who explicitly set out to follow in the footsteps of the artist David Roberts (Figs. 5.6–7). Roberts' popular set of lithographs based on his drawings of the region, *The Holy Land, Syria, Idumea, Arabia, Egypt, and Nubia* were published in London serially between 1842 and 1849. Maria Golia describes how Frith aimed to 'correct' Roberts' work a decade later through the medium of photography, thereby drawing on Roberts' popularity but utilising the promise of photography to present something purporting to be even closer to reality.[15]

A trope that photography swiftly borrowed from painting and used extensively in photographs of the Arab world was staffage. In painting, staffage refers to anonymous human or animal figures added as subordinate elements to landscape painting as decoration or to show scale. We see this manifest increasingly in nineteenth-century photographs of ancient Egyptian monuments, where hired guides, servants or passing locals were, like Hadji-Ishmael, asked to pose in photographs of monuments to demonstrate their size and add picturesque detail.

What is noticeable about such photographs is the way people are posed so as to portray a disjuncture between them and the monuments they are standing next to. Whether seated in a group in front of the monument as if they are passing nomads, sitting on top of a chunk of carving or standing minutely next to some giant arch, Egyptians are portrayed as stiff, obedient ciphers, distracted servants puzzled by the

▽ FIG. 3.8: Francis Bedford, The Prince of Wales and party among the ruins in the Hypostyle Hall, Temple of Amun, Karnak, March 1862. Royal Collection Trust.

photographer's interest or direction, or as romantic versions of Bedouin. They are seldom shown as understanding, or interacting with, the monuments they are placed alongside. This contrasts with images of Westerners at the same sites, who appear in more relaxed and interested poses, celebrating their 'conquest of the pyramids' (Fig. 3.8).

Contradicting the pervasive Orientalist narrative that Egyptians were blind to their own heritage and, unlike Western powers, unable to respect it or care for it properly was the widespread nineteenth-century tourist practice of graffitiing the ancient monuments of Egypt. This had a longer history dating back into Antiquity itself, but was embraced enthusiastically by nineteenth-century Western travellers, as we saw with Harris' inscription on the tablet at Ibrîm. It is clearly visible in the photographic record, as an image by Pascal Sébah demonstrates (Fig. 3.1). In this photograph Ramses II's torso and arm are plastered with visitors' names, initials and comments carved into the sculpture. Here the re-inscription of Egyptian heritage is bold and literal.

What begins to be visible from the 1860s, as noted above, is the formation of photographers basing themselves in Egypt, opening studios catering to tourists and the art-reference market. An interesting figure in this new economy was Gustave le Gray, who achieved fame in his native France in the 1850s for his magnificent seascapes, shot using combination printing (printing different negatives of the same scene onto the same sheet of paper) to achieve definition in both sea and sky, and for his views of the forest at Fontainebleau. He trained other photographers, from Henri Le Secq to Maxime Du Camp, and, in 1864, moved to Cairo. His work there had been overlooked until scholars Sylvie Aubenas and Mercedes Volait revisited this era of his life – but le Gray continued to photograph in Egypt, in addition to teaching drawing (Fig. 3.9).[16]

After the opening of the Suez Canal in 1869 and the expansion of tourism in Egypt, as typified by Thomas Cook's organised tours, many foreign photographers came to work in Egypt, some settling there, such as the European, Armenian and Ottoman photographers mentioned above. The German photographer Wilhelm Hammerschmidt settled in Cairo in 1860 to work as a photographer, also opening a shop that supplied Cairo's photographers with their chemicals and paper, showing the expansion of the trade (Fig. 3.10).

As the century drew to a close, signs of new photographic cultures were emerging in Egypt. Whilst Egyptian servants and assistants took part in the processes of many of the Western photographers, their efforts were mostly unrecorded. However, from around 1896 an eight-year-old boy from Luxor, Attaya

▷ FIG. 3.9: Gustave le Gray, The Hypostyle Hall of the Temple of Amon, Karnak, 1867. The J. Paul Getty Museum.

▷ FIG. 3.10: Wilhelm Hammerschmidt, The Theban west bank, the Memnon Colossi, 1857–59. Griffith Institute, University of Oxford.

Gaddis, took work as an assistant in Antonio Beato's studio in Luxor. Gaddis took over the business in 1907, a year after Beato's death, and became one of Egypt's first-known native photographers. He established his studio in Luxor in 1912, which remains active in the same location at the front of the Winter Palace Hotel (est. 1886). Today the family-run studio is preserving the founder's legacy and currently sells prints and postcards from their collection of 4,000 negatives.[17]

Nineteenth-century Egypt is considered the birthplace of world travel photography (Fig. 3.11). Early photographers ventured out in the desert heat, with heavy and fragile equipment and sometimes encountering dangers, to capture Egypt's ancient heritage. The result is a remarkable achievement preserved in national and international collections. In Egypt today, photography groups are becoming extremely popular gatherings for people to meet and explore sites and monuments. In this digital world we often forget how difficult and challenging it was in the past to travel to far-away sites and succeed in returning from these missions with unbroken negatives. This wealth of material has survived, thanks to both private and institutional efforts. The past two decades particularly have seen exhaustive digitisation efforts undertaken in many institutions that hold such photographs, enabling large audiences to explore, research and use these images. Such efforts have taken place in Europe, America and more locally in Egypt but, as Lucie Ryzova has analysed, such activity within the region has not been without its problems.[18]

As Egypt was so widely photographed in the nineteenth century, the material available online is extremely rich and diverse. These views portray sites and local scenes from some of the most popular tourist destinations, showing the elegant ruins of the ancient past, with occasional glimpses of daily life. They enable us to investigate the past and trace how the country has developed and changed. Yet one can argue that they were also idealising a certain image of Egypt.

CONTEMPORARY USE OF NINETEENTH-CENTURY PHOTOGRAPHS IN EGYPT

Ever since Egyptians occupied Tahrir Square in 2011 a growing interest in the country's past has emerged. This was reflected in the ways in which the younger generation started expressing their commitment to their nation. Large murals and graffiti filled the square with ambitious and exciting paintings, projecting hope but also fear. Some were using imagery influenced by Egypt's past. These visual expressions introduced the younger generations to their ancient heritage, and that connection has grown in contemporary Egyptian culture. This same process took place after the 1919

Sphinx de Ghizeh N° 10

revolution and with the discovery of the tomb of Tutankhamun in 1922, when Egyptians looked for a national identity to connect with, especially while struggling to gain independence from the British occupation (see Chapter 9).

In this past decade in Egypt, forms from the pharaonic past were re-adopted in various mediums. The effect of this artistic movement in the streets, showing visual expressions influenced from the past, had real impact on the creative industries. Many businesses, large and small, were encouraged to emphasise Egypt's 'glorious past' and to research and rediscover ancient heritage in connection with their projects, supported by the wide range of images accessible online. This style of representation remains popular and has been welcomed in Egyptian media and advertising campaigns, as well as in interior and product designs.

David Roberts' lithographs are perhaps among the most widely used in contemporary interior design in Egypt, yet we also see copies from Lekegian's and Sébah's prints adorning the walls of hotels, local restaurants and cafés. For those who can afford more, some of these original photographs are bought online from auction sites, reframed and used in lavish interior spaces. In a recent discussion with an Egyptian architect designing a *dahabiyya* (Nile boat) for one of Egypt's most prominent businessmen, he mentioned including two albumen prints bought online, taken by Lekegian and featuring the statue of Ramses II in the Temple of Luxor and the columns in Medinet Habu.[19]

Another Egyptian product designer, Dina Hafez, has been using similar photographs to create objects inspired by the country's pharaonic heritage, using photographs of Luxor Temple taken by Antonio Beato, which have been incorporated into coaster designs (Fig. 3.12). These prints, which were once sold as collectables and postcards for Western travellers, have been adopted today by Egyptian professionals to cater for a growing Egyptian taste for 'heritage and vintage style'. In such ways the nineteenth-century photographs of ancient Egypt that fuelled 'Egyptomania' are reclaimed, reappropriated and re-inscribed by contemporary makers in Egypt. ⊙

◁ FIG. 3.11: Gabriel Lekegian, Sphinx, after 1886. Griffith Institute, University of Oxford.

▷ FIG. 3.12: Dina Hafez, Coaster design showing the Temple of Luxor (using a photograph by Antonio Beato), 2018. Private Collection.

4 DECOLONISING MY GAZE

SARA SALLAM

Despite being born and raised in Egypt, my first encounter with the ancient Egyptians was through the television screen. I remember seeing them draped in gold, wearing heavy eyeliner, flying between the columns of temples and conjuring up fire by snapping their fingers. In movies, they were mystical beings. In everyday conversations, they were a source of pride. Perhaps, then, it is not surprising that before seeing the pyramids, I was already drawing them as the backdrop to any landscape that I painted at school. And perhaps it is only natural that before experiencing what it means to lose someone, I knew all about the process of mummifying human remains. I never questioned these experiences, growing up in Egypt, not until I travelled abroad.

It was not long ago that I read about an Egyptian ideological movement that emerged in the early 1920s called Pharaonism. One of its leading figures was Taha Hussein, an Egyptian writer who advocated an Egyptian national identity with pre-Islamic pharaonic roots. The movement's proposition for identifying with ancient Egypt was not only an attempt to unify and mobilise Egyptians against the British colonial occupation; it was also a way to reclaim the country's ancient heritage from a Western narrative.

What caught my attention, in particular, was that many of the movement's Egyptian artists had either studied in elite private schools or had pursued their education abroad – just like me. I, too, am part of the small social group of Egyptians that has access and the opportunity to visit such international institutions: I was mentored during my Bachelor's studies in Egypt by German educators. I then pursued my postgraduate education in England, after which I began exploring ancient Egypt in my artistic practice while preparing to immigrate to the Netherlands.

Upon returning from London, I began developing what became the first of a succession of works engaging with the ancient Egyptian past. *Playing in Fields of Reeds* is a series of photographic collages through which I reflect on the widespread culture in Egypt of avoiding any engagement with the topic of death. I had noticed how contemporary tombs are hidden out of sight from the living, behind high walls on the outskirts of cities. In contrast, we modern-day Egyptians talk with fascination about how our ancient ancestors conceived their cemeteries as gateways connecting

△ FIG. 4.1: Sara Sallam, *Sekhmet*, digital photographic collage from the series *Playing in Fields of Reeds*, Egypt, 2014–21. Private Collection.

the world of the living with the afterlife, which they envisioned as a blissful garden of reeds. Through my collages, I project this ancient attitude onto a burial ground in present-day Egypt, portraying it as an isthmus between two worlds, where life and death, as well as the past and present, coexist in harmony.

Curious to understand more about how Egyptians relate to death, I set out to document the different ways of experiencing an Egyptian tomb in my body of work entitled *The Fourth Pyramid Belongs to Her*. I saw archaeologists excavating in the name of science; tourists wandering, immersed in visual delight; residents digging illegally, hoping to find buried treasures; and mourners weeping for the death of a beloved. My photographic observations reveal one of the ever-present implications of the Western archaeological framing of the ancient Egyptian past: a dichotomy between modern cemeteries and necropolises. I wondered why the latter had lost their aura as places of mourning. Why could I stare curiously at a mummy displayed in a museum while I struggled to visit my grandmother's tomb?

I still remember how much I suffered from homesickness during my first couple of years in the Netherlands. During that time I increasingly pondered this dissonance in treating the ancient Egyptians as archaeological artefacts while considering them as ancestors. Through a series of collages, I accentuate this contradiction by portraying my grandmother as an ancient Egyptian. On the one hand, I elevate her memory by placing her onto a pharaonic pedestal. On the other hand, I project my grief for her onto the ancient Egyptians, mourning them likewise as dear, departed loved ones.

That same year a blockbuster Hollywood film was released. The latest in a long line of mummy monster-movies portrayed, yet again, an ancient Egyptian mummy accidentally coming back to life and bringing chaos upon the world. In these films, mummies behave like animalistic predators, running on all fours, growling and killing for sustenance. They are hunted down, drowned and burned alive without expressing

△ FIG. 4.2: Sara Sallam, *Plate 1*, digital photographic collage from the series *The Fourth Pyramid Belongs to Her*, Egypt, 2017. Tintera Gallery.

any sign of pain. I wondered: what would my ancestors say, if they were to watch along?

I began collecting and analysing these Western portrayals of mummies as monsters. As part of a postgraduate thesis discussing the mechanisms of dehumanisation in these films, I put together my film essay, *You Died Again on Screen*. While my thesis criticises the impact of this film genre on the way the ancient Egyptians are perceived, my film essay accentuates how mummies are systematically vilified to elicit fear and disgust in spectators. By juxtaposing scenes from more than ten widely distributed films with my voiceover addressing the portrayed mummies, I invite the viewers to identify with them and see the problematic nature of their continuous dehumanisation onscreen.

I am often asking myself whether I would have developed an interest in questioning how we modern-day Egyptians perceive our ancient past, had I not left Egypt. I often wonder to what extent I have internalised the Western colonial gaze that I am seeking to criticise. Would the pharaonist artists have resorted to ancient Egypt even if they had not been mentored by the pupils of Napoleon Bonaparte's scholars [*savants*]? Am I unconsciously responding to a Western curiosity for local narratives engaging with ancient Egypt? With these questions in mind, I see my work as a reflection of my ongoing journey of unlearning the exoticism of my own ancient heritage, reclaiming the representations of my ancestors and finding ways of decolonising my gaze. ⊙

▽ FIG. 4.3: Sara Sallam, *Her Hand Made of Granite*, grid of archival photographs from the series *The Fourth Pyramid Belongs to Her*, Egypt / The Netherlands, 2017–22. Private Collection.

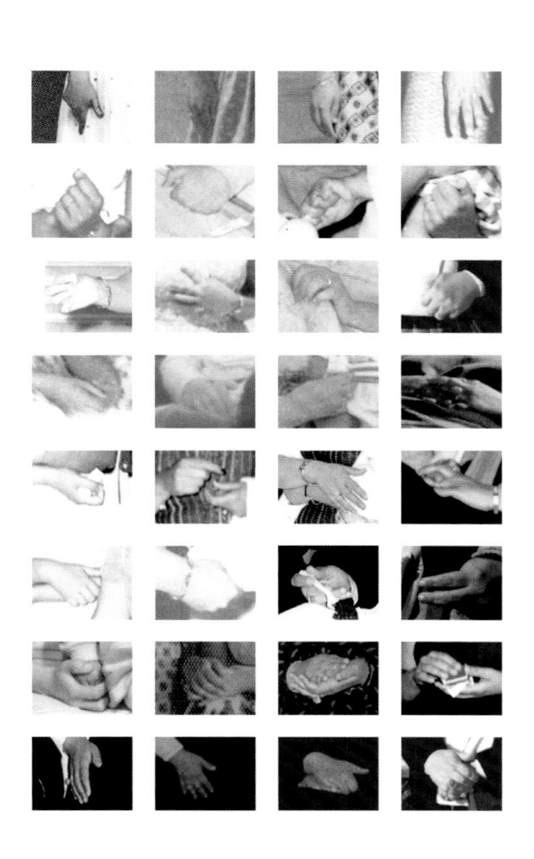

5 VISIONS OF ANCIENT EGYPT IN NINETEENTH-CENTURY PAINTING

ELIZABETH PRETTEJOHN

Lawrence Alma-Tadema is now best known for his scenes of everyday life in Classical Rome, replete with sumptuous white marble, Mediterranean sunshine and flowers in abundance. Yet he made his first international success with a darker and stranger scene, set in a more distant past: *Pastimes in Ancient Egypt 3,000 Years Ago* (Fig. 5.2). First exhibited in Brussels in 1863, it won a medal the next year at the Paris Salon, and again at the vast *Exposition Universelle* of 1867, where the art of all nations vied for critical attention.[1] In this painting the young artist, still in his twenties, established the hallmarks of his later practice: subject matter from everyday life, enacted by ordinary people, in settings of dazzling complexity, every detail of which was informed by careful research. Scholars have identified dozens of sources for motifs in this painting – museum objects, illustrations in books on Egyptian antiquities, previous paintings or photographs of ancient sites, and literary descriptions of Egyptian customs, from ancient texts to contemporary historical novels.[2] Yet the viewer experiences the scene not as a compendium of references, but rather as a coherent whole, a vivid slice of ancient life.

Two female dancers are caught in mid-air, ribbons flying in a shaft of sunlight. The dancers, the musicians who accompany them and their audience make up a varied community whose skin tones range from ivory to deep black. The implied social hierarchies are not correlated with skin colour: the two darkest figures are a prominent guest, seated at extreme right, and the player of an Egyptian harp. This is anything but a familiar social world, for a nineteenth-century European viewer; it is a scene of revelry and opulence, but not obviously of decadence or excess. A servant holds a cup to the lips of a white-robed figure, who drinks deep and holds a lotus flower, but like the other guests sits upright, after the fashion of Egyptian art. Gender is muted, and one wonders whether the white-robed figure is male or female. The dancers are female, but their movements seem more stylised than sexualised; in this respect they are unlike the figures in many nineteenth-century 'Orientalist' paintings.

◁ FIG. 5.1: Lawrence Alma-Tadema, *An Egyptian Widow in the Time of Diocletian*, Opus XCIX, 1872 (detail). Rijksmuseum, Amsterdam. Gift of Mr and Mrs Drucker-Fraser, Montreux.

▷ FIG. 5.2: Lawrence Alma-Tadema, *Pastimes in Ancient Egypt 3,000 Years Ago*, Opus XVIII, 1863. Harris Museum & Art Gallery.

A strange scene, then, for a European viewer of the 1860s, but also a highly coherent one. Partly that is due to the consistently Egyptian styling of figures, architecture and accessories, but it is nonetheless a feat of the artist's imagination to persuade viewers that this assemblage of unconventionally posed figures, amidst a riot of different patterns, constitutes a real, living world. It convinced the distinguished Egyptologist Georg Ebers, who wrote: 'When the Egyptians forgot life's cares in holiday pleasures, they must have appeared as he represented them in his first Egyptian picture.'[3] Those words, 'must have', signal the persuasiveness of the image, and they recur like a leitmotif through critical responses to Alma-Tadema's imagined scenes of ancient life.

Ebers was both a scholarly Egyptologist, professor at Leipzig, and the bestselling author of historical novels set in ancient Egypt; he became fast friends with Alma-Tadema and wrote the first book-length study of the artist's work. Thus he was particularly well placed to evaluate the artist's turn to Egyptian subject matter in 1863 – 'the portal', as he put it, 'of his road through antiquity'. When Ebers asked his friend how this came about, the artist replied:

> 'Where else should I have commenced when I first began to make myself familiar with the life of the ancients? The first thing the child learns of ancient times leads it to the court of the Pharaohs, to Goshen in Egypt, and when we go back to the source of the art and science of the other nations of antiquity how often we reach your Egypt!'[4]

Today's children still encounter ancient Egypt in their earliest schooldays, perhaps on museum trips to see the mummies or in children's storybooks (Amazon lists more than 1,000 titles under 'Ancient Egypt for kids'). Alma-Tadema's reference to Goshen (the land of the Israelites' exile in the books of Genesis and Exodus) suggests, however, that for a nineteenth-century European child the first encounter with ancient Egypt was likely to have been through the stories of Joseph and Moses in the Bible – approximately 3,000 years ago. Arguably, the paintings of Alma-Tadema and his generation played a crucial role in shifting the popular image of Egypt from the Bible to the excitement of archaeological discovery, which would continue to burgeon through to the twentieth-century craze for 'King Tut'. For a time, however, these two visions of ancient Egypt were in creative interplay.

△ FIG. 5.3: Hector Horeau, *Karnak: Great Temple: Hypostyle: Section showing columns*, c.1841–46. Griffith Institute, University of Oxford.

Alma-Tadema's *Pastimes in Ancient Egypt* made a striking impact at exhibition partly because it was unlike anything seen before. Paintings of everyday life in modern settings were common enough, including those set in modern Egypt, such as the compelling scenes by the British artist John Frederick Lewis, who lived in Cairo for a decade in the 1840s. Lewis' immersion in Egyptian life was unusual, but he was one of many European artists who found a ready market for pictures featuring the colourful scenery and people of the Middle East; such paintings are often called 'Orientalist'.[5] Artist-travellers also represented the ruins of ancient monuments, both for scholarly purposes and as sublime scenes in their own right.

The French architect Hector Horeau and the British landscape painter David Roberts were among the first to make extensive tours of Egypt, at the end of the 1830s, and both published their sketches and studies in impressive volumes, which served as sources of information about Egyptian monuments as well as introducing them to wide audiences. Horeau's *Panorama d'Égypte et de Nubie* (thirty-seven plates, 1841–46) and Roberts' *Views in the Holy Land, Syria, Idumea, Arabia, Egypt and Nubia* (six volumes, 1842–49) appeared almost simultaneously, in Paris and London respectively. The works of the two artists demonstrate different possibilities for representing Egyptian antiquities. Horeau's careful watercolour study of the columns at Karnak has an obvious documentary function (Fig. 5.3). It records the colour schemes and decoration, as well as the proportions of the columns – so different from the standard 'orders' of Greco-Roman architecture. At the same time the monumentality of the columns, which dwarf the figural representations, and the play of light and shade convey mystery and grandeur, even on the small scale of the watercolour drawing. The large oil paintings that Roberts derived from his Egyptian sketches are staged in quite different, more theatrical ways, yet they too make the most of the striking shifts of scale so characteristic of the Egyptian monuments. This is not just a matter of the topographical artist's standard device, reducing the scale of the figures to emphasise the grandeur of the monument, in a work such as *Ruins of the Temple, Kom Ombos, Upper Nile, Egypt* (1842–43, Fig. 5.4). The positioning of the half-buried columns against the sky, the expanse of sand, even the hot sunlight convey what made the Egyptian landscape appear sublime. Roberts himself found this disconcerting. In a letter to a friend, enlivened by his idiosyncratic spelling, he wrote:

> [T]here is a tottal absence of that which constitutes the great charm of all other ruins, vegetation and picturesque foliage. Ponderious as are the dimensions of those glorious remains

▽ FIG. 5.4: David Roberts, *Ruins of the Temple, Kom Ombos, Upper Nile, Egypt*, 1842–43. Touchstones Rochdale Art Gallery.

> there wants something beside the deep blue of an Eastern Sky the arid granite rocks, and the white sand of the Desert – they strike the beholder with wonder, but not pleasure, an ivy mantled tower with a brawling burn conveys I rather think more pleasurable sensations than the Land of the Pharaohs with all its wonders.[6]

In the event, Roberts produced some of the nineteenth century's most memorable evocations of Egyptian ruins, but his longing for something more conventionally picturesque shows just how alien such landscapes could appear to European eyes.

By the 1860s, then, artist-travellers had developed varied ways of representing contemporary Egypt, in addition to the long-established traditions for biblical and historical subjects, such as pharaoh's daughter discovering the infant Moses or the death of Cleopatra, both of which remained favourites throughout the century. However, it was a novel idea to bring the ancient Egyptians to life, and to represent their manners and customs with all the fullness of material detail that one would expect to see in the real world of the present day, as Alma-Tadema did in *Pastimes*. Interestingly, an experiment along similar lines appeared at London's Royal Academy exhibition in the same year, 1864, that Alma-Tadema's picture was first exhibited in Paris. *On Guard in the Time of the Pharaohs* was the work of another artist at the beginning of his career, Edward John Poynter (Fig. 5.5). Although the training of both young artists had been unusually cosmopolitan (Alma-Tadema in Antwerp and Brussels, Poynter in Paris and Rome), there is no evidence that they knew one another, or that either was aware of the other's interest in Egypt. They seem independently to have hit upon the idea of presenting an episode from everyday life amidst a panoply of *realia* (real-life material objects known from archaeological or artistic sources). The axe in Poynter's painting is based on a specific object in the British Museum, also illustrated in books such as J. Gardner Wilkinson's *Manners and Customs of the Ancient Egyptians* (first published in 1837), just as objects in Alma-Tadema's painting – harps, footstools, collars, cups and even the elaborate wigs – can be traced to both kinds of source.[7] Poynter depicts an ordinary soldier, nameless, but gives him considerable dignity through his confident stance and alert gaze. The figure is plausible as a living example of the soldiers seen in Egyptian bas-reliefs and wall paintings.

▽ FIG. 5.5: Edward John Poynter, *On Guard in the Time of the Pharaohs*, 1864. Private Collection.

Why did both the Dutch artist, Alma-Tadema, and the English one, Poynter, suddenly display interest in re-creating ancient Egyptian life in modern paintings? Perhaps the two artists were inspired, independently, by recent experiences of the same Egyptian antiquities. On his first visit to London, in 1862, Alma-Tadema became fascinated with the Egyptian collections at the British Museum and by the spectacular displays of the Crystal Palace, the vast iron-and-glass structure originally designed for the Great Exhibition of 1851 in Hyde Park, re-erected in 1854 as a magnificent tourist attraction and educational facility at Sydenham in South London. Among the new displays in the redesigned building were an Egyptian Court, composed of colourfully painted plaster casts that evoked a

▽ FIG. 5.6: Edward John Poynter, *Offerings to Isis*, 1866. Newport Museum and Art Gallery.

▷ FIG. 5.7: Edward John Poynter, *Adoration to Ra*, 1867. Private Collection.

variety of architectural spaces, and two colossal seated sculptures, twenty-one metres high, based on the remains at Abu Simbel and approached along an avenue lined by eighteen sphinxes. Everything in the Crystal Palace was a reproduction, and some purists sneered at the inauthenticity or accused the exhibits of vulgarity and sensationalism.[8] But for those who – like Alma-Tadema and Poynter – had not had the chance to visit Egypt itself, the simulated sculptures, pylons and colonnades revealed a grandeur of scale and magnificence of ornament for which there was no parallel in Europe. This was a new experience of extraordinary power for the hundreds of thousands who visited – a popular audience of remarkable, and perhaps unprecedented, diversity.

It was probably not until the very end of 1864 (after the first exhibition of *On Guard*) that Poynter moved into the rooms in Great Russell Street, immediately opposite the British Museum, that had just been vacated by Edward Burne-Jones and his family (two years later Poynter would marry Agnes MacDonald, the sister of Burne-Jones' wife Georgiana).[9] His Egyptian subjects of the next few years surely display the benefits of such proximity to the Museum's collections.[10] Specific objects from the Museum, such as the box carried by the girl and the altar in the right distance, appear in *Offerings to Isis* of 1866 (Fig. 5.6).[11] Perhaps more important, though, is the development in Poynter's style and approach. Whereas the soldier in *On Guard* assumes the contrapposto pose of the

European tradition or of Greco-Roman statuary, the girl in *Offerings to Isis* stands straight, hips and shoulders aligned. Her pose is contained and formal, yet she moves naturally; one feels that this is how the people represented in Egyptian statues or bas-reliefs might walk. One of her breasts is exposed, but there is no sense of the titillation so often encountered in European Orientalist pictures. We are witnessing a world with different customs and different rituals from ours (as seen in the figures worshipping at the background altar), even though it is one in which every detail is lucid and legible.

In *Offerings to Isis* and its successor the following year, *Adoration to Ra*, the artist has imagined a material environment, complete in every detail. The later painting repeats the row of red columns, and also includes two wooden jar-stands, based on British Museum objects (Fig. 5.7).[12] Stands of this kind caught on; not only did they become stock objects in Egyptianising and biblical paintings by a number of artists, but they were also imitated in modern furniture designs (see Chapter 7). An example recurs again, together with the characteristic red columns, in *Feeding the Sacred Ibis in the Halls of Karnac* of 1871 (Fig. 5.8). Here a more dramatic sunlight effect, and more vivid colouring on the colossal columns, accompanies the sweeping gesture of the figure. She is engaged in a ritual that once again appears strange to a European viewer, feeding the birds within a temple interior (a figure is similarly employed in the distant background of *Offerings to Isis*). It is not, then, only the material environment that the artist has imagined. Crucially, he also reveals the religious observances that European viewers might be tempted to consider 'primitive'. There is no sense, however, of condescension, and although again we see the bare breasts of the female figure, there is no particular emphasis on the sexualised aspects of the body; indeed, the body in shadow is somewhat upstaged by the painter's tour de force, the light permeating the white drapery from the rear.

▽ FIG. 5.8: Edward John Poynter, *Feeding the Sacred Ibis in the Halls of Karnac*, 1871. Private Collection.

The works considered so far can be described as 'genre paintings', scenes in which figures of no special historical importance enact the business of everyday life. A work of 1872 by Alma-Tadema follows suit, but also deepens the emotional import of the scene: *An Egyptian Widow in the Time of Diocletian* (Fig. 5.1). Like *Pastimes*, this includes a row of musicians, of colour ranging from light brown to deep black, with shaven heads and exotic instruments, seated on the ground. Lost in their lament, they are irregularly grouped around the decorated case of a mummy, its head obscured on the right by a cluster of objects including canopic jars for preserving the internal organs of the dead. The composition gives the sense that the scene is unfolding independently of the observer, who seems to come upon it by chance, or even to intrude on the scene. The widow's face is unseen, but her pose expresses profound grief, even while it imitates, more naturalistically, the angular, twisting forms of figures in Egyptian wall paintings.

In the decade since *Pastimes* and *On Guard*, Alma-Tadema, like Poynter, had internalised his understanding of Egyptian style. Both artists seem to have graduated from an almost schoolboyish fascination with the artefacts to respect for the world they come from. For Ebers, this meant a deeper understanding of Egyptian art itself:

> Besides, there was something in the grandeur and peculiarity of Egyptian art, and the original, orderly, and profoundly moral civilization of

> the Egyptian nation, which awed, attracted, and fascinated [Alma-Tadema]. Like all true artists and lovers of art, his eyes were open to the beauty of the works, not only of the architects, but the sculptors of ancient Egypt ...[13]

In *An Egyptian Widow* the individual artefacts are still identifiable, but they are smaller in scale relative to the whole than in Alma-Tadema's previous work; the muted colours and diffused light help to subordinate the objects to the overall mood and effect.[14] As both contemporary and subsequent critics have noted, the setting is reminiscent of the Egyptian displays at the Crystal Palace: the half-wall linking the columns behind the musicians recalls the entrance to the Egyptian Court, and the colossal statues in the background are interspersed with the green foliage that Roberts missed in Egypt itself, but which made the Crystal Palace resemble a greenhouse. The painting does not exactly reproduce any of the spaces in the Palace, but it gives some idea of the visitors' experience of being enveloped or immersed in its fantasies of past worlds.

The sounds of music formed a vital part of the sensory experience at the Crystal Palace, and perhaps it is interesting that Alma-Tadema's Egyptian scenes almost invariably include musicians and musical instruments. Indeed, musicians became a frequent element in the Egyptian visions of later artists, including the sculptor Edward Onslow Ford, whose mesmerising bronze *Singer* accompanies herself on an ancient harp (1889, Fig. 5.9). Almost as celebrated as the fine-art displays of the Crystal Palace were the

△ FIG. 5.9: Edward Onslow Ford, *The Singer*, 1889. Tate.

▽ FIG. 5.10: Edward John Poynter, *Israel in Egypt*, 1867. Guildhall Art Gallery.

Handel Festivals held biennially from 1859 onwards, with performances literally by casts of thousands. From the start, a staple feature was Handel's oratorio *Israel in Egypt*.[15] Can it be a coincidence that Poynter gave the identical title to the largest and most ambitious painting of his career so far, which also featured a giant lion, colossal seated sculptures and Egyptian architectural elements reminiscent of those at the Crystal Palace (Fig. 5.10)?

The idea for the picture originated in a sketching-club session of 1862, for which the theme was 'Work'.[16] This was at the beginning of Poynter's interest in Egypt, and he seems immediately to have connected the theme with the forced labour of the Israelites in the book of Exodus. When the final painting was exhibited at the Royal Academy in 1867, it was accompanied by a catalogue quotation drawn from the same passage in the first chapter of Exodus that provided the dramatic opening of Handel's oratorio: 'And the Egyptians made the children of Israel to serve with rigour.'[17] To bring home the point, Poynter exaggerated the size of the granite lion, based on an example at the British Museum also reproduced for the Crystal Palace, which the workers are dragging into position.[18] Although some critics carped at the liberties Poynter took, the discrepancy between the small figures of the labourers and the giant architectural forms corresponds to the extreme contrasts of scale that were such a conspicuous feature of the Egyptian monuments, as well as reinforcing the narrative. The tense and straining poses emphasise the 'rigour' of the labour, and an Egyptian 'task-master' wields a whip to drive the workers harder. P. G. Hamerton, the critic for the *Saturday Review*, hinted at the contemporary relevance of the theme:

> What we chiefly care about in Mr. Poynter's picture is the terrible impression which it conveys of the sort of work the Israelites had to do ... One great reason why it has become so famous is its readily felt allusion to the relation between the labour of masses and the masters who direct it, and the purposes, often apparently so useless, for which these masses toil and die.[19]

When Poynter conceived the composition, the American Civil War was under way, and slavery was a fiercely debated issue. Simultaneously the newspapers carried reports of forced labour on the Suez Canal, under construction in the same part of Egypt as the biblical Goshen, where the Israelites were kept captive. The Canal opened in 1869 after a decade of work and the deaths of perhaps tens of thousands of labourers;

◁ FIG. 5.11: Lawrence Alma-Tadema, *Joseph, Overseer of Pharaoh's Granaries*, Opus CXXIV, 1874. Dahesh Museum of Art.

Hamerton may well have been alluding to that scandal, as well as to more general debates about labour in the age of Karl Marx and Friedrich Engels. Poynter's ambitious canvas, more than three metres wide, fulfils all the requirements of the history-painting tradition, by drawing out the contemporary moral relevance of a time-honoured subject from the Bible. Yet the painting is also innovative in its elaboration of an Egyptian setting, informed by the latest archaeological evidence.

Alma-Tadema also turned to biblical subject matter for two of his final Egyptian scenes, which in different ways represent the culmination of his experimentation. *Joseph, Overseer of Pharaoh's Granaries* (1874) takes furthest the artist's project of imagining figures who appear both entirely realistic, within the scene they occupy, and plausibly like the figures in ancient Egyptian art (Fig. 5.11). Indeed, on this occasion Ebers thought that his friend had gone too far: 'he has allowed himself ... to be too much influenced by the mode of execution of the Egyptian artists, who were trammelled by their canons'.[20] Yet the seated pose, like that of an Egyptian statue, effectively conveys how the young Joseph has assumed authority as pharaoh's overseer, and there is a compelling visual harmony between the figures and their decorative surroundings.

Something similar applies, with greater emotional intensity, to the figures in the sombre night-scene, *The Death of the First-Born* (1872, Fig. 5.12). It has often been suggested that the death in 1864 of Alma-Tadema's own firstborn son inspired this moving painting. If so, the artist has persuaded himself to identify with one of the most rebarbative figures in biblical history, the pharaoh who hardens his heart, again and again, against the Israelites who toil and suffer in Poynter's painting. Not merely the clothing, but the poses, gestures and expressions are those of people who are strikingly different from modern Europeans: pharaoh in the pose of a seated colossal statue, the attendants at bottom right who clasp their shaven heads and raise their hands in some form of invocation, and those constant participants in Alma-Tadema's paintings, the musicians bending over their long pipes as they dance into the scene at top right. To make such strange and even alien figures appeal so strongly to viewers' sympathies is a true tour de force. Little wonder that cinematic presentations of the death of pharaoh's firstborn, from Louis Feuillade's *L'Exode* of 1910 through

▽ FIG. 5.12: Lawrence Alma-Tadema, *The Death of the Firstborn*, Opus CIII, 1872. Rijksmuseum, Amsterdam. Gift of the heirs of L. Alma-Tadema.

△ FIG. 5.13: Edwin Long, *The Gods and Their Makers*, 1878. Towneley Hall Art Gallery & Museum.

to Ridley Scott's *Exodus: Gods and Kings* of 2014, have drawn overtly on Alma-Tadema's composition.[21]

After the early 1870s both Poynter and Alma-Tadema turned away from Egyptian subject matter, and both achieved great success with paintings of everyday life set in Greco-Roman antiquity. In some respects, that was an easier option: the emphasis on the naturalistic human figure in ancient Greek and Roman art, and the human scale of the architecture in sites such as Pompeii or the Greek temples, meant that there was no stylistic disjuncture between the imaginary characters and the art or architecture of their surroundings. In their Egyptian scenes, however, the artists had to imagine human figures that appeared plausibly like the stylised figures in ancient Egyptian art. They also had to cope with the extreme discrepancies in scale between the human figures and the colossal sculptures, columns and pylons familiar from paintings and publications by artists such as Horeau and Roberts. The spectacular displays of the Crystal Palace, as well as museum displays such as those of the British Museum and other European museums of Egyptian antiquities, helped artists to imagine a re-created Egyptian world in all three spatial dimensions. A further effort of the imagination was needed to realise that re-creation, convincingly, on a canvas or panel of limited dimensions.

Although Alma-Tadema and Poynter turned their attention elsewhere, the pictorial category they had pioneered in the 1860s carried on in the work of other artists, notably Edwin Long, who made a journey through Egypt and Syria in 1874.[22] Despite this direct exposure to Egyptian people and places, Long's work depended heavily on the procedures established by his predecessors for integrating human figures into archaeologically specific environments. His popular paintings often featured alluring women or piquant episodes more overtly adapted to European taste. Viewers of *The Gods and Their Makers* (1878) are introduced to an imaginary workshop, populated entirely (and entirely implausibly) by women, for the production of images of the Egyptian deities (Fig. 5.13). In an amusing episode, a living cat is presented as the model for a statuette of the cat goddess Bastet. Here the social status of the figures is keyed to their skin colour, as the darkest figure is the servant who holds the cat, its fur a bright white for contrast, and the lightest is the sculptor, elegantly applying a finishing touch to her work. The painting is 'full of fun and charm', in the words of one contemporary critic, but it is difficult to avoid the sense that the joke is at the expense of the Egyptian figures and their religion.[23]

Alma-Tadema finally made the journey to Egypt in 1902, for the opening of the Aswan Dam, the building of which had been overseen by his patron, the engineer Sir John Aird, who commemorated the occasion by commissioning that most traditional of Egyptian subjects, *The Finding of Moses* (Fig. 5.14). At more than two metres wide, this is Alma-Tadema's largest Egyptian painting and he duly includes the landmarks of Egyptian travel: the Nile, the expanse of sand and the pyramids in the background. Yet the slaves bearing the litter recall the musicians of *Pastimes* or *An Egyptian Widow*, and perhaps it is those figures who read most convincingly as Egyptian, in a painting that otherwise resembles a more conventional tourist's vision.

The material environment of ancient Egypt, as seen in the paintings of Alma-Tadema, Poynter and Long, appears entirely realistic or 'normal' to today's viewers. And yet the history of the works shows that the artists were creating a new way of representing ancient Egypt, with its own distinctive style and iconography. This was an iconography, to be sure, that was based on artworks and artefacts of 3,000 years ago, and was fascinating precisely because of their antiquity. But it was also one that needed to be imagined in a thoroughgoing fashion. If it still looks familiar today, that is partly because it served as a crucial visual source for the Egypt of cinema. More importantly, it successfully created a vision of Egypt that was not merely novel, but also beautiful. ⊙

▽ **FIG. 5.14:** Lawrence Alma-Tadema, *The Finding of Moses*, Opus CCCLXXVII, 1904. Private Collection.

6 VISIONS OF ANCIENT EGYPT IN THE MUSEUM

BENJAMIN HINSON

Museum displays do not passively reflect knowledge about ancient Egypt; they create it.[1] Today, the influence of museums in shaping perceptions of Egypt is most apparent in thematic displays that delineate 'daily life' and 'death' and emphasise the latter, which perpetuates tropes of Egyptians as death-obsessed.[2] However, displays of Egyptian material, and their power to influence, are no modern phenomenon. Orientalist artists like Edward Poynter and Lawrence Alma-Tadema incorporated artefacts from the British Museum into their paintings, to lend their romanticised visions of Egypt academic 'authenticity'; decades earlier, Percy Bysshe Shelley, inspired by the 'Memnon Head' and its impression of ancient, decayed power, penned 'Ozymandias'. With an emphasis on museums, this essay outlines how the collection and display of artefacts have shaped public perceptions of ancient Egypt.

◁FIG. 6.1: View through the Egyptian Room, in the Townley Gallery at the British Museum, c.1820 (detail). British Museum.

THE FIRST MUSEUMS

Egyptian artefacts first found a place within the 'cabinets of curiosities' (*Wunderkammern*) that emerged from the sixteenth century. These cabinets housed eclectic assemblages of natural and man-made objects (*naturalia* and *artificilia*), arranged alongside one another in specific contexts. The purpose of owning a *Wunderkammer* was not just for collecting's sake, but for self-definition, showing cultivation and sophistication. These collections were in some ways precursors to modern museums, as the taxonomy and organisation of objects helped to form and disseminate early understandings of ancient cultures.[3] Funerary figurines and animal mummies were often represented, but were treated as curios, understood as much as *naturalia* as *artifcialia* and displayed alongside other rarities and natural specimens, linking them by association.[4]

In the eighteenth century British and French elites also began collecting Egyptian objects. In November 1741 an Egyptian Society was formed in London, by four members who had been to Egypt – Lord Sandwich, Richard Pococke, Charles Perry and Frederick Norden – alongside interested antiquaries such as Charles Lennox, the 2nd Duke of Richmond. The society lasted only two years, but promoted a fashion for collecting Egyptian objects.[5] Artefacts traded hands; George Sandys acquired objects that he gave to John Tradescant, whose collection in turn formed a nucleus of the Ashmolean Museum in Oxford, and Pococke similarly sent items to the Duke of Richmond.[6] This collecting also promoted a market for 'aegyptiaca', with imitation artefacts drawing primarily from print sources. One of the earliest examples is a forgery shabti now in Oxford's Bodleian Library.[7]

These collections continued the *Wunderkammer* tradition, with animal mummies and smaller objects heavily represented. This is partly because they were easy to transport, relatively common and cheap, but also because the traveller's itinerary at this time focused on Cairo, Giza and Saqqara, where the largest-known cemeteries were located. Saqqara (known as 'the field of mummies') was particularly infamous for looting, to the extent that even contemporary travellers commented on the destruction.[8] In some cases, the looting biography of specific tombs can be traced. Shabtis from the tomb of Tarudj are today in several museums; the Bodleian received one from Archbishop William Laud in 1635, and the British Museum acquired several through the collection of Pitt Lethieullier in 1756, showing how early the tomb was plundered and the longevity of its exploitation.

NATIONAL MUSEUMS AND IMPERIAL POLITICS

These private collections often formed the core of national museums; the collections of both John Tradescant and Thomas Shaw are today in the Ashmolean.[9] Most famously, Hans Sloane bequeathed his collection of *c.*71,000 objects (including many Egyptian ones) to the nation in 1753, forming the core of the British Museum.[10]

Into the nineteenth century national museums gained increased significance. As European nations competed for political supremacy, so collecting became a shorthand for imperial strength.[11] Egypt was a key target – politically, as it was strategically positioned for access to India, but also culturally. Especially following the decipherment of hieroglyphs, Egypt became seen as the 'parent' of Classical Greece and Rome, and thus the origin of Western European civilisation more broadly. To Europe, ancient Egypt was rightful Western patrimony. European battles for political control of Egypt were played out through battles for material control. Although individuals could not conduct excavations, consular agents retained the freedom to collect, and European powers sent agents to acquire new objects to furnish national museums. Disputes between consuls acted as a microcosm of imperial rivalry.[12] How this material was displayed back home in turn also reflected changing beliefs in how knowledge should be imparted. Although early Egyptian holdings were a legacy of the *Wunderkammer* tradition, into the nineteenth century the museum's purpose became one of presenting a universal survey of aesthetic history. The nature of engagement with Egyptian objects thus changed, from interchangeable objects to unique, and increasingly monumental, pieces.[13]

Those with the closest ties to Egypt profited most in consular 'collecting', and the French led the way, although many European powers were involved.[14] Even British agents initially found the Louvre more eager to purchase from them.[15] France was quick to celebrate Egyptian art; following the Revolution, it formed a counterpoint to Classical art, which was closely associated with the Catholic Church.[16] The very architecture of the Louvre makes French attitudes apparent: ancient Egypt is depicted alongside Greece, France and Italy as one of the four great 'schools' of art.[17]

British appreciation, however, was slower to form. Until the mid-century Egyptian material occupied a strange position at the British Museum. Through Hans Sloane, it had been part of the collections since its beginning, and following the British victory over Napoleon in 1802 antiquities seized from the French – infamously including the Rosetta Stone – were brought and triumphantly displayed. However, whilst they made a great public impact, they were celebrated as political booty; on aesthetic grounds, they were derided.[18] Entrenched biases towards Greece and Rome as the origins of European art and civilisation, and a lack of basic knowledge about ancient Egypt, meant that it was separated from Classical 'fine art'.

These biases were reflected in the display space afforded to Egyptian objects. The British Museum's Townley Gallery, opened in 1808, housed both the Greco-Roman and newly looted Egyptian sculptures. However, compared to the Classical rooms, the Egyptian rooms were dimly lit, painted grey and the material was placed along the walls to avoid obstructing views. This created an impression of Egypt as 'shadowy, angular, and at odds with' the surrounding Classical material and architecture (Fig. 6.1).[19] Similarly, the preponderance of funerary remains and large-scale sculpture fostered views of Egypt based around monumentality, ruination and the passage of time.[20] A review of the Townley

△ FIG. 6.2: The British Museum: The Egyptian Room, with visitors. Engraving by Radclyffe after B. Sly, 1844. Wellcome Collection.

Gallery in 1810 objected to the very idea of placing Egyptian art near the 'elegant Greek and Roman sculptures', suggesting that instead they suited 'the solemn recess of a catacomb'.[21] By contrast, after the decipherment of hieroglyphs enabled greater understanding of Egyptian history, Egypt was reconsidered as the origin of Greek and Roman art, and thus the beginning of art history. In 1834 Egyptian material was relocated to a dedicated, prominent gallery space (Fig. 6.2). Over the course of several decades, Egyptian objects went from impressive but unknowable curiosities to the most important objects in the museum.[22] At each point, gallery display did not only reflect, but also influenced, public perceptions of Egypt.

The destruction of archaeological heritage wrought by Europeans became such that, in 1835, Egypt's ruler Muhammad Ali was pressured to enact legislation outlawing the export of antiquities. As European access to monuments became threatened, European attitudes changed, to frame looting in terms of 'preservation'. European accounts painted Egyptians as poor caretakers of Egypt's pharaonic legacy, and a danger to its sites.[23] This wrapped a desire to legitimise European claims to Egypt within a rhetoric of 'conservation'. European belief that Egypt remained Western patrimony therefore meant a need to de-legitimise native claims to that heritage. However, in practice, this legislation did little to prevent consular looting.[24] Inspired by European models, a museum facility (*al-antiqakhana*) was also created in Cairo, overseen by Rifa'a al-Tahtawi, who believed that artefacts should remain in Egypt. However, his enthusiasm that this museum should be primarily for Egyptian benefit was not shared. Muhammad Ali's legislation mentioned only foreigners as an audience; the museum was poorly resourced, actively condemned by Europeans and Americans and lasted only briefly.[25]

In 1858 a new antiquities service was created; however, French influence meant that it was run by the Frenchman Auguste Mariette, effectively as a French enterprise. This was accompanied by a newer museum built in 1863; whilst Mariette wanted it to be accessible to Egyptians, Egyptian audiences were not presumed to understand or be interested in academic knowledge, and many displays were therefore arranged on what Mariette called 'useless' aesthetic grounds.[26] The museum subsequently moved to its current site on Tahrir Square in 1902, with a neoclassical façade visually acting as a monument to Western imperialism.[27] Three further museums were subsequently founded, each dealing with a specific period of Egypt's past: Greco-Roman, Coptic and Islamic. This four-part schema solely reflected European divisioning of Egyptian history. Furthermore, the Pharaonic Museum was (and still is) commonly referred to as 'The Egyptian Museum', again representing European priorities and suggesting that the only 'true' Egypt is pharaonic.[28] In only one of the four museums – the Coptic – was its founder Marcus Simaika a native Egyptian; there was no Egyptian empowerment of the other branches.

In short, although by the end of the nineteenth century Egypt had established museums displaying its ancient heritage, they were result of colonialism and the diplomatic pressures of European powers, and European influences were embedded in their structure.[29]

THE 'EXCAVATED ARTEFACT'

In the late nineteenth century both museum curatorship and archaeology became established professions, and the recursive relationship between museums and Egyptology became more pronounced. Changes in excavation practice and antiquities legislation affected the material available to museums. However, the growth of regional museums and changing attitudes to the display of ancient Egypt in turn influenced excavations.[30]

This change is embodied by the Egypt Exploration Fund (EEF), now Society, founded in 1882 as the first foreign body officially permitted to excavate in Egypt.[31] The impetus for its founding was the continued concern of destruction of archaeological sites, and the need for a body to study and record places at risk. However, its aims also tied squarely into Victorian Christian values, in that it initially excavated at sites linked to biblical narratives and continued earlier imperial rhetoric of 'preservation'.[32]

The porous 1835 legislation preventing antiquity exports had been strengthened in 1869, 1874 and 1880. Theoretically therefore, at the point of the EEF's foundation, it remained impossible to remove material from Egypt. However, the legal and political framework surrounding these rules did little to impact European exploitation. In 1882 the Department of Antiquities remained French-run, and Britain's 'veiled protectorate' meant that it was embedded throughout Egyptian governance. There was therefore great pressure on the government to loosen its stance. After the EEF's first season at Tell el-Maskhuta, two statues were given to the British Museum as a personal gift from the Khedive (Viceroy of Egypt), an echo of the earlier looting of monumental objects linked to international politics. In subsequent years a system of 'partage' was established.[33] Each season, all the artefacts discovered were presented to the Antiquities Service, which took first pick. The remainder were allowed to be shipped to London, where they were displayed and subsequently divided amongst the institutions that had funded that year's work.[34] This arrangement was the exception to the otherwise continuing prohibition on export. However, whilst legal on paper, this system only existed through pressure from the colonial powers wielding influence in Egypt. Indeed, perhaps there was no clean break between the imperial collecting of the early nineteenth century and the 'legitimate' museum collecting of the latter half.

The development of systematic site excavations, and the establishment of partage, meant that the meaning of Egyptian objects again changed, from individual artworks to their place within a network of other material culture from a specific site, and embedded in social relations with specific institutions – an 'excavated artefact'.[35] Attention increasingly turned from temples to cemeteries and, where possible, settlement archaeology. Smaller objects – pottery, textiles, amulets – were discovered en masse and filled foreign museums. Partly this shift was due to a growing understanding of 'mundane' items as important evidence, but also to opportunism. Smaller items were easier to export and had more frequently fallen outside the interests of the Antiquities Service, which was focused on retaining monumental pieces.[36] As such, legislation was slow to keep up with changes in excavation.

Museums were not simply passive recipients of material, however; they recursively influenced excavation. The EEF's development coincided with the growth of regional museums, so there was an ever-increasing pool of institutions that were willing to support, but had limited funds.[37] This new material suited them perfectly. By the end of the century both local and national museums were EEF subscribers, looking to expand their collections. It is estimated that some 140 museums worldwide hold EEF-excavated material.[38] The importance of museum sponsors to the EEF's work is shown by the fact that its remit broadened by 1886, with its annual reports now stating three objectives: to organise excavations; publish findings; and preserve antiquities by presenting them to public institutions.

Ancient Egyptian material was now widely accessible to public audiences worldwide. Alongside this, the nature of its presentation changed again. As archaeological knowledge grew, so Egyptian objects were increasingly arranged and displayed through a filter of Western-developed material typologies, irrelevant to the ancient Egyptian mind. This reflected Victorian ideals of the taxonomic museum – masses of material, organised by type and with increasingly detailed labelling, to educate the public. However, as much as reflecting increased knowledge, the very classifying and ordering of material acted as a form of physical control over Egypt, and as a process of 'othering'.[39] This reflected Britain's broader imperial context of power over Egypt. Viewing objects on display, organised and 'understood', gave visitors a feeling of power over them – framing them as something to be looked at and positioned against a (Western) viewer.[40] This linked to the broader Victorian cultural 'exhibitionary complex', which cemented links between visual display, power and knowledge relations.[41] Museum displays were just one strand of the public display of ancient Egypt, which also included theatre and world fairs like 1851's Great Exhibition, which likewise 'exhibited' Egypt for the public.[42]

This organised – effectively colonialised – Egypt was further reflected in what information was *missing* from display. The EEF's excavations relied entirely on

▽ FIG. 6.3: Egyptian labourers waiting to be paid, Balabish, 1915. The Egypt Exploration Society.

mass labour by native Egyptians, who have historically been forgotten or ignored in Western accounts of the discipline that prioritise the 'heroes' of Egyptology (Fig. 6.3). Recent projects have aimed to recentre these Egyptian excavators and, where possible, to identify them from archival sources.[43]

As archaeological knowledge developed, so museum displays were increasingly turned to by artists, who copied actual objects into their paintings to lend their Orientalist visions a sense of reality (see Chapter 5).[44] Artists working from museum collections were nothing new; centuries earlier, Charles Percier and Hubert Robert had drawn the Egyptian rooms in Italian collections at the Villa Albani and the Capitoline Museum whilst on the Grand Tour, and printed illustrations of Rome's artefacts were crucial in disseminating ideas of Egypt across Europe (Fig. 6.4). Now, however, jewellery designers, furniture and interior manufacturers also began looking to objects for domestic design (see Chapters 7 and 8). The colonised ancient Egypt, as presented within museums, was carried through into the home and became a symbol of domestic consumption. With the discovery of Tutankhamun in 1922, this would reach a zenith.

In summary, the image of Egypt presented through museums in the late nineteenth century was idealised – a neatly organised display lost in time, and divorced from both the country itself and the context of its discovery. However, at the same time it was inexorably politically and colonially embedded, and reinforced broader political aspirations of control over contemporary Egypt. ⊙

▷ FIG. 6.4: Charles-Joseph Natoire, *Artistes dessinant dans la cour intérieure du Musée du Capitole à Rome* (Artists drawing in the inner courtyard of the Capitol Museum in Rome), 1759. RMN-Grand Palais (Musée du Louvre).

CLEMENS
C. NATOIRE.
1759.

7 REFORMISTS, AESTHETICS AND PRE-RAPHAELITES: NINETEENTH-CENTURY EGYPTIANISING FURNITURE

BENJAMIN HINSON

Egyptian-style furniture had existed in Britain since Thomas Hope's Duchess Street house (see Chapter 2). However, it remained a niche taste until the latter half of the nineteenth century, when the opening of the Suez Canal in 1869, the premiere of *Aida* in 1871 and ongoing archaeological discoveries kept ancient Egypt in the public consciousness. Paired with the development of mass-manufacture and an increasing consumer market, there was a growing taste for domestic objects inspired by ancient Egypt.

To meet this demand, furniture makers looked to ancient Egypt for inspiration, and in particular to the objects on display in museums. Two schools of design emerged, although both ultimately looked to the same source material: one, popularised by the reformist and Aesthetic movements, adapted the principles of Egyptian design, often alongside other 'exotic' influences such as Japanese, to create new forms. The other school more faithfully replicated Egyptian objects wholesale. This chapter explores how some of the most important movements and figures of the nineteenth century were influenced by Egyptian design, and looks at the sources they turned to.

◁ FIG. 7.1: Christopher Dresser, Designs for a 'scarab' jardinière, *c.*1870. Minton Archives at Stoke-on-Trent City Archives.

THE LEGACY OF THE THEBES STOOL

One of the earliest and most 'faithful' examples of Egyptian-inspired furniture was a chair designed by William Holman Hunt *c.*1857 and manufactured by J. G. Crace, for Hunt's house at Draycott Lodge, Fulham (Fig. 7.2).[1] Hunt had travelled to Egypt in 1854 during the painting of his *Finding of the Saviour in the Temple* and designed the chair immediately following this. Made of mahogany and sycamore and inlaid with ivory and ebony, its seat and legs were closely modelled on an ivory-inlaid New Kingdom stool in the British Museum (Fig. 7.3). Additionally, however, Hunt's chair incorporated a back with an inlaid lotus pattern, inspired by another chair in the Museum (EA2480). In his memoirs, Hunt wrote of how he was inspired by the British Museum's stool as a counter to the 'vulgar furniture of the day', and also of the effect it had on his Pre-Raphaelite companions.[2] Ford Maddox Brown subsequently designed a simpler version of this chair for Morris & Co. when it was founded in 1861.

◁ FIG. 7.2: William Holman Hunt, 'Egyptian' chair, c.1855–57. Birmingham Museum and Art Gallery.

▷ FIG. 7.3: 'Thebes Stool', Egypt, XVIIIth dynasty. British Museum.

Interestingly, Dante Gabriel Rossetti also designed a (now-lost) sofa and chaise-longue in 'Egyptian style', which featured in his 1860 painting *Joseph Accused before Potiphar* and was exhibited at the 1862 International Exhibition.[3] However, Hunt ultimately objected to how popular the design became.[4] Indeed, in 1866 it appeared in John Everett Millais' *Jephthah*; only a year afterwards it also appeared in Holman Hunt's own *Il Dolce far Niente*.

The most famous examples of the 'archaeological' school of furniture design, however, are the two variants of 'Thebes' stool patented by Liberty & Co. from 1883 onwards, two of the earliest products of its Furnishing and Decorating Studio. The first was based on a three-legged stool in the British Museum (EA2481). By the time the Liberty imitation was designed, the original had become well known and appeared frequently in Orientalist paintings.[5] The second example was based on the same four-legged stool that inspired Holman Hunt's chair.[6] These stools remained perennially popular, in production until 1912. The four-legged example especially was available in walnut, mahogany or oak, with either a leather, string or rosewood seat and an optional back or 'Egyptian' cushion.[7]

THE DESIGN REFORMISTS

Other designers took a more stylised interest in ancient Egyptian furniture. Perhaps the most well-known proponent of this was Christopher Dresser. A reformist, Dresser's work was highly rational, scientific and informed by a moral vocabulary that sought 'truth, beauty and power' through design. To Dresser, good design used appropriate and inexpensive materials and eschewed unnecessary ornamentation, with decoration abstracted to simplified conventionalised forms. These principles were informed by those set out by Owen Jones in his 1856 publication *The Grammar of Ornament*.

Dresser was highly complimentary of ancient Egyptian crafts, writing of their 'simple dignified severity'.[8] He summarised the merits of Egyptian art as 'length of line, firmness of drawing, severity of form, and subtlety of curve', which mirrored a 'dignified bearing' of ancient Egypt as a society.[9] This take on Egyptian art was fully in keeping with reformist tastes; in *The Grammar of Ornament* Owen Jones similarly noted that 'the ideas and the teachings it conveys to us are of the soundest' and dedicated eighteen plates to Egyptian ornament.[10] The reform movement promoted 'good' design amongst British manufacturers and the public at large – *The Grammar of Ornament* itself being intended as a sourcebook of the best of design – and thus ancient Egyptian art was valid for promotion. This is typified by a series of large-scale, portable cloth-printed panels from c.1853, designed by the Working Men's Educational Union, King William Street, London (Fig. 7.4). The Union was founded to provide education

△ FIG. 7.4: The process of mummification: scenes taken from New Kingdom tombs at Deir el-Medina. Working Men's Educational Union panel no. 447, *c.*1853. Private Collection.

to the working classes; these panels were available made-to-order, as touring lecture aids. The Egyptian series depicted scenes of mummification, crafts and architecture taken from tomb paintings, to accompany lectures such as 'The Monuments of Egypt'.

Dresser had visited Egypt in the 1890s, and his publications actively encouraged the first-hand study of Egyptian design.[11] However, rather than directing readers to original artefacts, it was to sources like *The Grammar of Ornament* and the Egyptian Court at the Crystal Palace. Reformists did not advocate direct copying of Egyptian ornament; Dresser wrote that Egyptian decoration itself was 'not suited to our wants. Yet the severity and dignity of the drawing we may well copy, for they are noble qualities.'[12]

During his career, Dresser provided designs for manufacturers of ceramics, metalwork, textiles and wallpapers, and from 1880 until its bankruptcy in 1883 he was founder and art manager for the Art Furnishers' Alliance, which marketed his and others' designs alongside imported works directly to the public. Egyptian influences, particularly floral motifs, are apparent in many of these media, most prominently Dresser's designs for Minton and Wedgwood ceramics.[13] In many instances, however, they showcase a blending with other cultural influences. For example, Dresser applied the scarab across multiple vessel forms, yet despite its Egyptian origin, his execution was indebted to Chinese design (Fig. 7.1).[14]

Dresser also employed Egyptian elements on furniture. *Principles of Decorative Design* illustrated an 'Egyptian-style' chair; its shape, and specifically the rounded braces linking seat to back, were inspired by the same chair emulated by Holman Hunt. Dresser noted that this feature was the one part of Egyptian chairs that was structurally less than ideal in wood.[15]

△ Fig. 7.5: Christopher Dresser, 'Egyptian-style' wardrobe, *c.*1880–83.
Private Collection.

The legs of Dresser's imitation chair were decorated with incised and gold-stencilled decoration of stylised and rigidly upright lotuses. Very similar patterning to this chair occurred on wardrobes made for the Art Furnishers' Alliance. Here, Egyptian lotuses are paired with Greek key-patterning and zigzag designs, another design synchretism (Fig. 7.5). As with his ceramic designs, this furniture is as much Asian as it is Egyptian; the black ebonised pine with gold stencilled detailing speaks strongly to Japanese lacquer-work, even if the motifs are Egyptian. Dresser had visited Japan as an agent of the then South Kensington Museum in 1867–68, to research Japanese manufacture and design – the first European designer to do so – and this visit strongly influenced his subsequent work.[16]

FROM REFORM TO AESTHETICISM

The Aesthetic movement was another design school popular in the later nineteenth century. One branch of a wider movement that also influenced painting, poetry and literature, Aestheticism in the decorative arts was a conscious reaction to the increasingly industrial nature of manufacture. Its core tenet was that art should not have to impart a moral message; rather, beauty for beauty's sake was valid. Aesthetic designers aimed to create beauty in utilitarian objects, to elevate them to the same level as 'fine arts' and to transform the everyday home into, in Oscar Wilde's words, 'the house beautiful'.[17] In this regard, Aesthetics stood in contrast to reformists like Dresser. However, in certain practical aspects they overlapped greatly. Aestheticism was characterised by eclecticism, looking to decorative elements from many cultures. Within this mixture of inspirations, Japan and China were particularly prominent. However, Aesthetic designers also looked to historical styles, English as well as Greek and ancient Egyptian.

In the case of Egypt, inspiration came most frequently from close study of museum artefacts. This was not just true of Aesthetic crafts designers, but also artists and writers; just as Shelley's 'Ozymandias' was a reaction to the 'Younger Memnon' statue of Ramses II, so in Oscar Wilde's 1894 poem 'The Sphinx' its descriptions of ruined Egyptian statues were clearly inspired by the rose-granite head and arm of a colossus of Amenhotep III in the British Museum (EA15 and EA55).[18] However, it is in furniture that the study of Egyptian design comes through most strongly.

Edward William Godwin is known for his 'Anglo-Japanese' furniture, but several of his designs are indebted to ancient Egypt.[19] Godwin studied first hand artefacts in the British Museum; his interest was in construction, and specifically the lattice-bracing and turned-wood elements of ancient Egyptian furniture. These feature in many of his otherwise 'Anglo-Japanese' or 'English' designs, showcasing a melding of styles that incorporated Egyptian influences, but turned them into something new. Like Dresser, Godwin preferred not to copy Egyptian objects directly, but to create 'a modern treatment'.[20] One particular table proved Godwin's

▷ FIG. 7.6: Edward William Godwin, Drawing of an 'Egyptian-style' table. Sketchbook 1865–80, fol. 38. Victoria and Albert Museum.

most popular Egyptianising design, first produced by William Watt in 1867.[21] Godwin described it as is 'Anglo-Japanese' in style, and in *Art Furniture* it occurs amongst examples of 'Old English or Jacobean' furniture, but the lattice-bracing and angled stretchers draw directly from the Egyptian furniture that Godwin studied.[22] The popularity of this table meant that its design was much imitated; in the Preface to *Art Furniture* Godwin criticised those who made 'unauthorised' copies.[23] The design was even copied by American firms, with a version illustrated in C. Cook's 1878 *The House Beautiful*.

Another table indebted to ancient Egyptian furniture is a black and gold example, very close to an image in Godwin's 1865–80 sketchbook (Fig. 7.6). The table has been variously attributed both to Godwin and T.E. Colcutt, but it again shows Godwin's distinctive melding of styles: the black-and-gold palette draws from Japanese lacquer, as with Dresser's furniture, and the curled scroll pattern recalls archaic Greek patterning. However, both the turned-wood legs and lattice-bracing are again Egyptian-inspired. At first glance the table is far removed from anything Egyptian, yet it showcases how Aesthetic furniture makers subtly enmeshed multiple cultural influences to make something new.

A PICTURE IS WORTH A THOUSAND WORDS

Although nineteenth-century furniture designers looked to actual ancient Egyptian objects for inspiration, they did not always look at the objects first hand. Rather, a key source was books, and in particular John Gardner Wilkinson's *Manners and Customs of the Ancient Egyptians*. This monumental work combined both a detailed text aimed at a general audience with hundreds of line drawings of tomb scenes and Egyptian objects, many taken from museum collections; all of the Egyptian furniture discussed was illustrated there. Owen Jones helped with the images, which proved particularly useful for designers because they were in black and white, stripped of extraneous detail.[24] The influence of *Manners and Customs* can be seen through its continual reissuing: after its first edition in 1837, totalling three volumes, it was republished as five volumes in 1841, 1847 and 1878.

Lawrence Alma-Tadema is known to have owned a copy, and Egyptian details within Dresser's works became much more pronounced at the same time as the book's 1878 reissue, suggesting that he likewise had access to a reference copy.[25] Furthermore, Holman Hunt had a copy of *Manners and Customs* whilst in Egypt in 1854, which may well have inspired him to look to the British Museum furniture for his chair.[26]

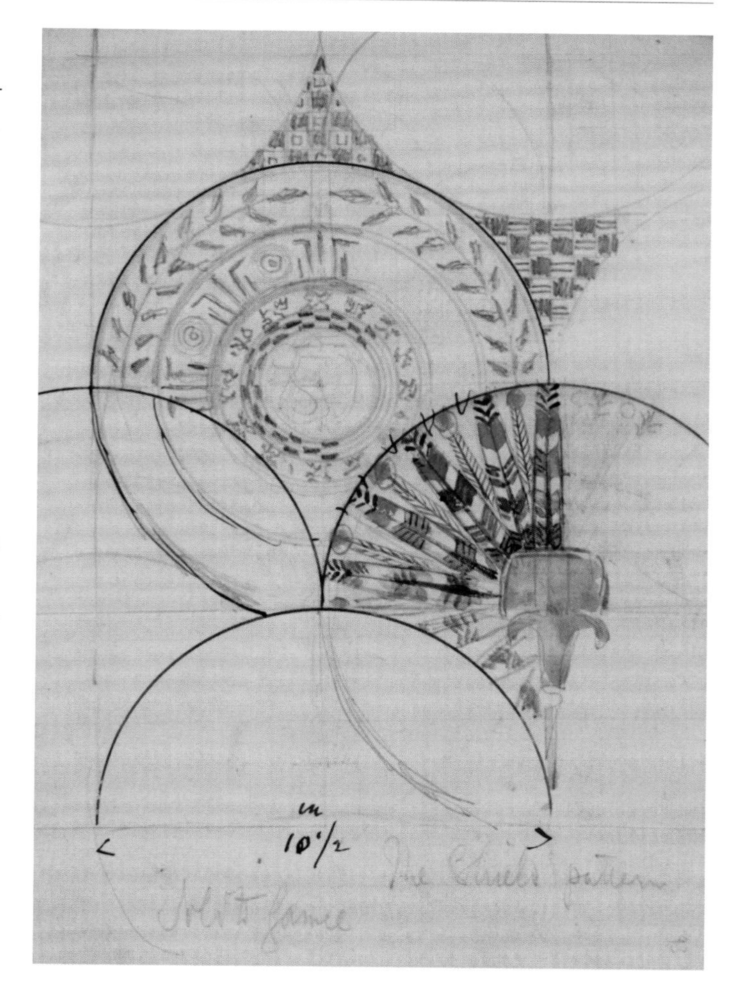

Artists looked to art books as a primary source material as much as the objects themselves, even when original artefacts were viewable in the British Museum. Godwin's sketchbooks contain drawings of Egyptian art taken directly from them; in one instance, his design for a 'shield' pattern incorporates an Egyptian fan taken from the image on plate V of *The Grammar of Ornament*, which copied a detail from the tomb of Ramses III (Fig. 7.7). Just because artefacts were increasingly visible, it did not end the continued importance of print material for designers looking to Egypt for inspiration. ⊙

△ FIG. 7.7: Edward William Godwin, 'Shield pattern' incorporating an Egyptian fan taken from *The Grammar of Ornament*. Sketchbook 1876–78, fol. 93. Victoria and Albert Museum.

8 JEWELLERS, GOLDSMITHS AND THE EGYPTIAN TASTE c.1867

ANNA FERRARI

... who would have believed that the Egyptian taste would be discovered once again and be the innovation we so admire today?... The Egyptian influence could be seen in the majority of jewelers' and goldsmiths' showcases, including those of Baugrand, Boucheron, Mellerio, Froment-Meurice and Duponchel.[1]
Henri Vever, *French Jewelry of the Nineteenth Century*

The Paris *Exposition Universelle* in 1867 was a crucial moment when jewellers and goldsmiths looked to ancient Egyptian forms and motifs. While the earlier nineteenth-century Egyptian revivals had inspired relatively little jewellery, the last decades of the century saw international – and especially French – jewellers and goldsmiths design highly inventive Egyptianising works.[2] The jeweller and historian Henri Vever offered two reasons for this renewed interest in ancient Egypt in the 1860s: the first was the construction of the Suez Canal, which was launched in 1859 by the international (largely French-owned) Suez Canal Company and was eventually inaugurated in 1869; and the second was the extraordinary finds of the French archaeologist Auguste Mariette which captured the public's imagination.[3] Mariette, who in 1858 had been granted the right to excavate in Egypt by Mohamed Sa'id Pasha, organised large digs that uncovered the coffin and mummy of Queen Aahotep in the necropolis of Dra Abu el-Naga in Thebes, as well as an extraordinary group of jewels and weapons. These were swiftly displayed at world fairs in London (1862) and Paris (1867), where they caused a sensation.[4] French Empress Eugénie even tried to acquire them for her collection, although she was rebuffed by Mariette.

The phenomenon of international world fairs also played a major part in popularising visions of ancient Egypt, with dramatic painted-plaster reconstructions of ancient monuments at the Crystal Palace re-erected at Sydenham in 1854 (see Chapter 3), and spectacular pavilions such as the Egyptian temple at the 1867 Paris exposition.[5] Mariette was heavily involved both in the design of the pavilion, which he suggested modelling on Emperor Trajan's kiosk at Philae, and in the selection of antiquities on display, which

◁FIG 8.1: Gustave Baugrand, Brooch with an enamelled profile likely representing the goddess Isis, c.1867. Wartski Ltd.

included Queen Aahotep's authentic ancient jewellery, blurring the distinction between real antiquities and staged spectacle.

The taste for Egyptianising jewellery was not an isolated fashion, however. It was part of a wider vogue for archaeological jewellery, spurred on by spectacular finds from excavations across Europe and the Middle East. The Campana Collection assembled by the Marchese di Campana was a vital influence: a vast collection, including almost a thousand Greek, Etruscan and Roman pieces of jewellery, it was acquired by Napoleon III and promptly exhibited for the benefit of jewellers and goldsmiths. This archaeological style was itself part of a broader revivalism that encompassed other more recent styles, such as Renaissance or Louis XVI. Crucially, this fashion for historical styles signalled a shift in the appreciation of jewellery design over intrinsic value or precious materials.[6] It also took on political associations: ancient Egypt, for instance, held particular significance for France since Bonaparte's invasion and Jean-François Champollion's decipherment of the hieroglyphic script.

The Castellani family were pioneering goldsmiths working in the archaeological style in Rome.[7] From the late 1840s the firm became best known for reproducing Italian jewellery (from Etruscan to Roman and Byzantine), which, in the context of the Risorgimento and calls for Italian unification, promoted the sense of a shared national past.[8] Despite this focus, Castellani produced a small number of ancient Egyptian-inspired jewels, testifying to the popularity of the style in the 1860s and 1870s. For example, one Castellani brooch incorporated an ancient faience scarab, mounted on a swivel to reveal its inscription, and framed by delicate micromosaic wings in a palette evoking the lapis lazuli, garnet and turquoise used in ancient Egyptian jewellery (Fig. 8.2). The brooch may originally have been part of a parure including a necklace, earrings and a larger brooch in the same design, which also associated ancient scarabs with colourful micromosaics.[9] The Castellanis appropriated this eighteenth-century technique, which was itself indebted to Classical sources, creating a hybrid archaeological style. The Egyptian style coincided with Castellani's rising international fame in the 1860s and 1870s when Alessandro, son of the founder Fortunato Pio Castellani, promoted the firm abroad, opening a branch in Paris and organising the firm's display at the 1862 London exposition, and establishing the Castellani pupil, Carlo Giuliano, in the London branch.

After Etruscan jewellery's revival at the 1862 London exposition, Egyptianising jewellery predominated

▽ FIG. 8.2: Castellani, Scarab brooch, c.1860. Private Collection.

▷ FIG. 8.3: Gustave Baugrand's showcase at the Paris 1867 *Exposition Universelle* included pharaonic-inspired objects and jewellery (reproduced in Vever, *La Bijouterie au XIXème siècle*). Bibliothèque nationale de France.

at the Paris 1867 *Exposition Universelle*. The French jeweller Gustave Baugrand, who had established himself in the early 1850s, rapidly becoming jeweller to Napoleon III and the imperial court, exemplified this shift in fashions. Praised for his Etruscan-inspired jewellery in London in 1862, he presented a spectacular showcase with pharaonic-inspired objects and jewellery five years later in Paris (Fig. 8.3). The case contained an abundance of diadems, necklaces and brooches, as well as remarkable Egyptianising decorative objects: a tea service, an enamelled mirror, a jade cup carried by Egyptian figures wearing *nemes* (striped headcloths worn by pharaohs); a gilded and enamelled silver jewellery box in the form of a temple supported by four sphinxes, which, according to a contemporary critic, 'one would believe had belonged to an Egyptian queen'; and a scintillating chased and enamelled sculpture of the goddess Isis, described as the 'Egyptian Venus', which presided over the display.[10] Pursuing the theme of Isis in jewellery, the display also included a rock-crystal pendant featuring the Egyptian goddess in profile. The jewel Baugrand presented in 1867 was illustrated by Henri Vever and is very similar in iconography and materials to another pendant (or brooch), which likely also represents Isis (Fig. 8.1).[11] The figure wears a feathered headdress and a broad necklace depicted in diamonds, rubies and emeralds, with three larger emeralds carved in the form of scarabs. The firm's presentation at the exposition was so admired that Baugrand was awarded the *Légion d'honneur*.

Mellerio also shone at the 1867 exposition, where the jeweller won a gold medal. The prestigious firm, jeweller to the kings and queens of France since its foundation in 1613 under Marie de' Medici, was renowned for its designs inspired by nature. Among the most noted jewels were a bejewelled peacock feather, which proved an instant success with Empress Eugénie who commissioned a version; and a *rocaille* diadem purchased by Queen Isabel II of Spain.[12] However, the firm also participated in the archaeological fashion between the 1850s and 1870s, producing Etruscan, Roman and Byzantine-inspired jewellery as well as a few Egyptianising objects. The French imperial jeweller successfully reinterpreted the ancient motif of the scarab, which was here carved from a large garnet encircled with diamonds and mounted with pearls, both of which were fashionable in nineteenth-century jewellery (Fig. 8.4).[13]

By 1867 Émile Froment-Meurice was a renowned Parisian goldsmith, perhaps best known for sumptuous

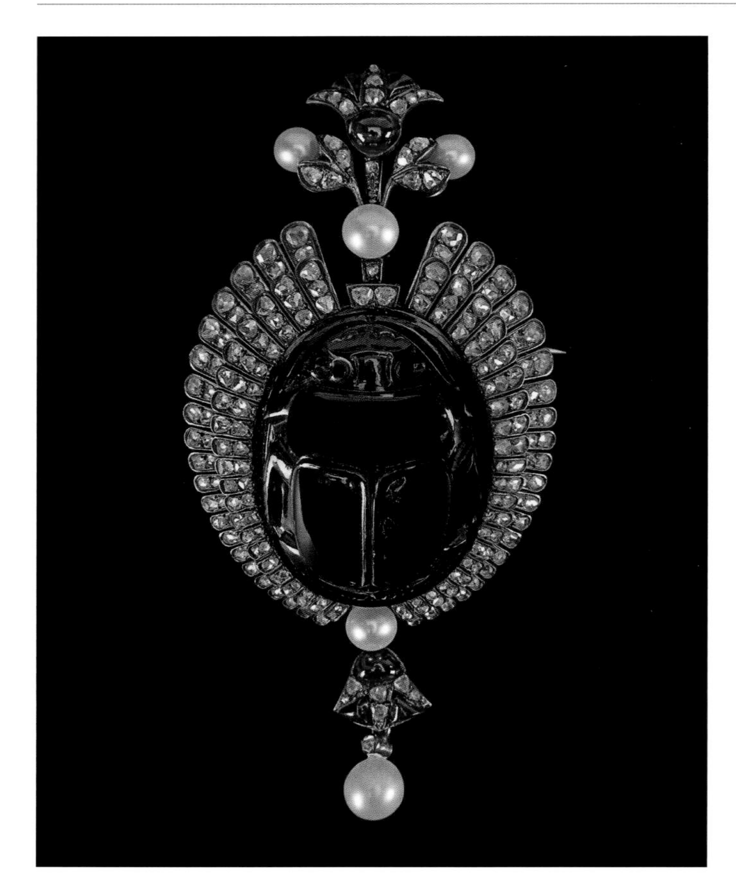

◁ FIG. 8.4: Mellerio dits Meller, Scarab brooch, *c.*1860–70. Private Collection.

△▷ FIGS. 8.5 and 8.6: Émile Froment-Meurice, Louis Audouard (designer), and Ambroise Dumoulin (goldsmith), *Garniture de cheminée*, 1865. P&O Heritage Collection.

decorative objects, although he also participated in the Egyptianising fashion, presenting 'many chased and enamelled bracelets, several of which were in the Egyptian taste'.[14] Émile had taken over the firm following the death of his father, François-Désiré Froment-Meurice, in 1855. The firm had won many awards at fairs, including at the 1851 World Fair in London, and its clients included international royalty and aristocracy.[15] Prestigious commissions included official gifts such as the ceremonial cradle marking the birth of the French imperial heir, presented by the City of Paris in 1855, and an important silver service for 100 guests in the Louis XIV style for the Viceroy of Egypt, Muhammad Sa'id Pasha, in 1855.[16] In 1865, his successor, Isma'il, commissioned Froment-Meurice to create a lavish neo-pharaonic silver *garniture de cheminée* as a gift to the board of directors of the shipping company P&O (Figs. 8.5 and 8.6). The central clock is designed in the shape of an Egyptian temple pylon, supported by four sphinxes resting on porphyry bases, which also recalls pharaonic sculpture. It is flanked by two classically shaped amphorae on tripod stands. The surfaces are covered in low-reliefs evoking ancient Egyptian sculpture and in stylised motifs such as lotus flowers.[17] A near-contemporary publication recorded the designer as Louis Audouard and the goldsmith as Ambroise Dumoulin.[18]

The garniture was a diplomatic gift. P&O's interest in Egypt went back to 1840 when it secured a contract for a mail service to Egypt, extending its route beyond the Iberian Peninsula to Alexandria and developing infrastructure that facilitated the crossing of Egypt to reach India via the Red Sea – a crucial route for the British Empire. The company's influence in Egypt continued in the 1850s with contracts permitting the transit of P&O passengers and loans for the construction of the railway between Alexandria and Suez via Cairo, which was a vital part of the country's travel infrastructure, especially before the opening of the Suez Canal.[19] The relationship was undoubtedly important to P&O, as less than a month after Sa'id's death in January 1863, P&O sent members of its board of directors to meet his successor, Isma'il. In August 1865 the garniture was sent to P&O with a letter from Mohamed Sherif Pasha, Isma'il's foreign minister,

△ FIG. 8.7: Émile Philippe, Brooch and earring parure, *c.*1869. Private Collection.

▷ FIG. 8.8: Necklace and earrings, late nineteenth century. Private Collection.

acknowledging the relations between P&O and the Egyptian government and describing the garniture as 'a token of his [Isma'il's] esteem and affection to the distinguished gentlemen who are managing the Company so skilfully, and at the same time to say how important he feels it is for the excellent relationship to be continued and developed in the future.'[20] Isma'il's choice of Froment-Meurice for this important commission reflected his Europeanised taste, as well as his interest in promoting Egypt's ancient past and harnessing it to his programme of modernisation.[21] The garniture also illustrates how British companies succeeded in gaining influence and power in Egypt, before Britain established a 'veiled protectorate' in 1882.

Pharaonic motifs remained current in jewellery design into the last decades of the nineteenth century. Émile Philippe, who was a student of Jules Wièse (a onetime collaborator of François-Désiré Froment-Meurice), also looked to ancient Egypt from the 1860s, when he designed a brooch and earrings featuring simplified crystal scarabs and enamelled vulture motifs set with turquoises (Fig. 8.7). At the Paris 1878 *Exposition Universelle* he presented a necklace, brooch, bracelet and earrings using pharaonic and modern scarabs – a recurrent motif in Egyptianising jewellery of the late nineteenth century – interspersed with cartouches.[22] A similar necklace by an unidentified maker reused Egyptian scarabs in a similar parure of a necklace and earrings (Fig. 8.8). The scarabs, with dates spanning more than a thousand years, and with inscriptions including both royal names and common good wishes, were likely chosen for their appearance and their harmonious tones of turquoise, greens and browns. They are linked by enamelled winged sphinxes and winged *uraei* (cobras) with human and animal heads, which sit on the hieroglyph for 'gold', that becomes a decorative motif.[23]

Although Egyptianising jewellery receded at the turn of the century, it did not disappear and at the 1900 Paris *Exposition Universelle* the Art Nouveau designer René Lalique exhibited an Egyptian tiara made for the actress Julia Bartet for her performance of *Bérénice*.[24] Lalique, who was personally interested in Egyptian antiquities, reinvented the ever-popular motif of the Egyptian scarab, casting in green glass four large scarabs that became the focus of an original necklace (Fig. 8.9). ⊙

△ FIG. 8.9: René Lalique, Necklace, *c.*1905. Wartski Ltd.

G. Rochegrosse, Pinx. E. Decisy, sc.

9 NINETEENTH-CENTURY MUMMY FICTION

ELEANOR DOBSON

In her film *You Died Again on Screen* (2018–20), in which she directly addresses the mummy in an intimate whispered voiceover, the artist Sara Sallam insists, '[c]ontemplating the fictional re-animation of your decaying limbs was a nineteenth-century invention'.[1] Indeed, when we think of the reanimated mummies familiar to us from horror films and Hollywood blockbusters, we are engaging in the afterlives of the imaginative fancies dreamed up by teenage girls of the nineteenth century, who pioneered this narrative seam. Jane Webb, orphaned at the age of seventeen, turned to writing to support herself. She produced a three-volume novel entitled *The Mummy!: A Tale of the Twenty-Second Century* – published in 1827, the year she turned twenty – at the heart of which is a thrilling description of the pharaoh Cheops (Khufu), reawoken in his pyramid tomb:

> Edric's senses swam, yet he could not move from the spot; he remained fixed, chained, and immoveable, his eyes still riveted upon the mummy, and every thought absorbed in horror. [A] fearful peal of thunder now rolled in lengthened vibrations above his head, and the mummy rose slowly, his eyes ... fixed upon those of Edric ... The thunder pealed louder and louder. Yells and groans seemed mingled with its roar; ... Edric saw the mummy stretch out its withered hand as though to seize him. He saw it rise gradually – he heard the dry, bony fingers rattle as it drew them forth – he felt its tremendous gripe – human nature could bear no more – his senses were rapidly deserting him; ... and then all was darkness![2]

In this now little-read text Webb conceived of the first reanimated mummy in English literature, often held to have been inspired by Mary Shelley's *Frankenstein*, conceived when Shelley herself was just eighteen. Frankenstein's creature is likened to a mummy in appearance twice in her text, and these similes may well have taken root in Webb's imagination when envisioning her own take on an inert body returned to life. Webb's novel is far from Shelley's eerie precedent, however. *The Mummy!*, set centuries

◁ FIG. 9.1: Georges Rochegrosse illustration, in Théophile Gautier, *Le Roman de la momie* (The Romance of a Mummy), Paris, 1920, frontispiece. Private Collection.

△ FIG. 9.2: 'Mr Grubbe Dancing', in 'Mr Grubbe's Night with Memnon', *Illuminated Magazine*, May 1843, p.34. Private Collection.

in the future, delights in satirising its present moment. Cheops first emerges as a figure of horror, though it quickly becomes apparent that he is no typical Gothic antagonist, instead wryly dishing out sage political advice in this advanced world. Mummies were more often used as comic rather than horrific devices in the years following the publication of Webb's novel.

Edgar Allan Poe's 'Some Words with a Mummy' (1845), in which the reanimation is effected by the application of an electric current to the tip of the individual's nose, is likely the best-known comic mummy story. Upon receiving this shock, the mummy of Allamistakeo (whose name foretells that the endeavour is not going to yield the results that the group of men undertaking the experiment are looking for) 'opened its eyes and winked very rapidly for several minutes', 'sneezed', 'sat upon end' and 'shook its fist', before 'address[ing]' the group.[3] Allamistakeo, so rudely awoken, underlines the cultural and scientific superiority of ancient Egyptian civilisation when compared to that of the modern United States. Webb's and Poe's ancient Egyptians both invite us to poke fun at the idea of linear human progress from Antiquity to the present, and undermine Western assumptions of cultural superiority.

Such early mummy tales were probably inspired by the mummy-unwrapping demonstrations (most famously undertaken by Thomas 'Mummy' Pettigrew in Britain, and George Gliddon in the US) that were drawing in audiences who were keen to observe what lay beneath the bodies' bandages. In the 1840s, at the peak of the unwrapping craze, narratives of a distinctly romantic flavour emerged. In Albert Smith's 'Mr Grubbe's Night with Memnon' (1843), for example, the eponymous Grubbe becomes enthralled with all things Egyptian after watching a mummy unrolling. Finding himself locked inside the British Museum at midnight, having fallen asleep in the Egyptian Gallery, Grubbe is confronted with magically enlivened artefacts, including a procession of mummies who 'lifted up the covers of their painted tombs ... stretching forth their pitched and blackened limbs'.[4] As the animated Egyptian collection dances, spurred on by copious amounts of punch, Grubbe is especially taken with 'a fair young daughter of the Nile', 'whose soft downy cheeks, roguish kissable lips, and supernaturally-sparkling eyes ... for a time made him forget his age' (Fig. 9.2).[5] The irony, of course, is that the Egyptian woman is vastly older than Grubbe.

This scenario, of slipping into unconsciousness only to encounter ancient Egyptians restored to life – and being particularly enthralled with an ancient Egyptian woman – had appeared a few years earlier, in the French author Théophile Gautier's 1840 short story 'Le Pied de momie' ('The Mummy's Foot'). All that is left of the Egyptian woman in Gautier's narrative is the titular appendage, but a dream reveals the princess in full; when Gautier's protagonist seeks to marry her, her father denies the union because of the extreme age gap. Similar situations were to be imagined decades later in Grant Allen's 'My New Year's Eve Among the Mummies' (1878) and H. Rider Haggard's novella 'Smith and the Pharaohs' (1912–13). In Haggard's text it is the mummy's hand that has survived rather than her foot, but as in Gautier's original, this remnant is the bodily trace of an enthralling whole, which appears to the protagonist in spirit form (Fig. 9.3).

From Gautier's short story through to the mummy fiction of the early twentieth century, one significant strand of mummy literature centres on the female mummy as an object of desire. Gautier was to revisit this theme in his 1857 novel, *Le Roman de la momie* (*The Romance of a Mummy*), editions of which often featured sensual illustrations of ancient Egypt. A particularly lavish edition of the text published in 1920 is explicit in its politics of looking: the unwrapped ancient Egyptian woman, Tahoser, stands subject to the male gaze of the younger of the text's two modern archaeologists, modestly attempting to cover herself in a pose reminiscent of Botticelli's *The Birth of Venus* (Fig. 9.1).

Gautier himself witnessed a mummy unrolling, though it was after the publication of his two mummy-themed texts. His account of the spectacle is noteworthy for its lack of comedy and romance. His observations of the unwrapping of the body of an ancient woman called Neskhons contrast starkly with the beautiful revived women he had earlier imagined: 'Strange indeed was the appearance of the tall rag-doll ... moving so stiffly and awkwardly with a sort of horrible parody of life, under the hands that were stripping it, while the bandages rose in heaps.'[6] Gautier infuses his description of the event with a Gothic frisson, taking time to describe the atmospheric effects of the weather on proceedings:

> a sudden storm was lashing the windows with heavy drops of rain that rattled like hail; pale lightnings illumined on the shelves ... the old yellowed skulls and the grimacing death's-heads of the Anthropological Museum; while the low rolling of the thunder formed an accompaniment to the waltz of Nes Khons ... as she pirouetted in the impatient hands of those who were unwrapping her.[7]

In this stormy setting (redolent of the awakening of both Shelley's creature and Webb's Cheops), the mummy appears reanimated in a kind of *danse macabre*.

After the century's midpoint a more spine-tingling strand of mummy fiction emerged, and again it was women writers who were to inject horror into their fictional depictions of the ancient Egyptian body. Unlike the perfectly preserved Sleeping Beauties conjured up by Gautier and Smith, and later by Allen and Haggard, the mummies at the centre of these texts were often instead sinister crones.[8] Their retaliation to the penetration of their tombs by male explorers might be read as vengeance for a metaphorical act of sexual violence in men's encroachment upon the most sacred of feminine spaces.[9]

Just a year after the publication of her celebrated *Little Women* (1868), Louisa May Alcott published one such mummy's-curse story entitled 'Lost in a Pyramid' (1869). Alcott's narrative appeared swiftly after her friend Jane Goodwin Austin's 'After Three Thousand Years' (1868), which, along with the earliest-known curse tale – the anonymously authored 'The Mummy's Soul' (1862) – comprises a modest American corpus of 1860s mummy horror.[10] Alcott's story opens with two men exploring a pyramid, who choose to burn a woman's mummified body to produce light, in a bid to find their way out (Fig. 9.4). They retrieve mysterious seeds buried with her and bring these back with them from Egypt. Germinating the seeds produces 'one ghostly-white flower, shaped like the head of a hooded

▽ FIG. 9.3: Alec Ball, 'He Stretched out his arms to clasp her, and lo, she was gone', in H. Rider Haggard, 'Smith and the Pharaohs', *The Strand Magazine*, 45 (266), February 1913, p.122. Private Collection.

▷ FIG. 9.4: 'Life was dear to me. A few dry bones might save us', in 'Lost in a Pyramid', *The New World* 1 (1), 16 January 1869, p.8. Private Collection.

"Burning her! Oh, Paul, what do you
iean?" asked the girl, sitting up with a face
all of excitement.
"I'll tell you. While busied with Madame
a Momie, our fire had burned low, for the dry
ase went like tinder. A faint, far-off sound
aade our hearts leap, and Niles cried out:
Pile on the wood; Jumal is tracking us; don't
et the smoke fail now or we are lost!'
"'There is no more wood; the case was
ery small, and is all gone,' I answered, tear-

of rest in the country will give us back ou
blooming Eve again. Have you no curiosit
to learn my surprise?" he asked, to change he
thoughts.
The vacant look stealing over the girl's fac
gave place to one of interest, but as she lis
ened it seemed to require an effort to fix he
mind upon her lover's words.
"You remember the day we rummaged i
the old cabinet?"
"Yes," and a smile touched her lips for
moment.

LOST IN A PYRAMID.—"LIFE WAS DEAR TO ME. A FEW DRY BONES MIGHT SAVE US."

snake, with scarlet stamens like forked tongues'.[11] When the fiancée of one of the men plucks the flower to wear at her breast on her wedding day, the mysterious flower saps her life and she is left a state of perpetual un-death. The men are punished for the violence enacted on the body of an ancient Egyptian woman by a reciprocal act of destruction.

In a reversal of this gender dynamic, H. Rider Haggard, in his historical novel *Cleopatra* (1889), sees a male body plundered of its valuables by a woman. Egypt's last pharaoh, Cleopatra, rifles through the mummified body of Menkau-ra, searching for jewels that have been hidden within (Fig. 9.5). The jewels are secreted in his chest cavity in case of a time of Egypt's great need, and are protected with a 'curse of the Dead' to ensure that they are never removed for selfish purposes.[12] That the spirit of the king appears in the form of a gigantic white bat when Cleopatra approaches the pyramid indicates that although his spirit has exited his body, Menkau-ra still guards his corpse and its treasures. Likewise, when she plunges a dagger into the mummy's chest the groaning of her servant can be heard; his lifeless body is later found with the bat hanging from his chin. The treasures that Cleopatra retrieves are a wealth of emeralds and two enormous pearls, one of which she dissolves in wine and drinks in a display of opulent indulgence. In Haggard's novel, Cleopatra's tragic end is thus reimagined as the fulfilment of a curse that she has brought upon herself through her own extravagance.

▽ FIG. 9.5: Maurice Greiffenhagen, 'She held it to the light and gave a little cry', in H. Rider Haggard, *Cleopatra*, London, 1889, p.188. Private Collection.

'She held it to the light and gave a little cry.'

It was at around the time of Haggard's novel that mummy fiction truly flourished, with hundreds of such tales appearing across the next couple of decades. Arthur Conan Doyle published two mummy stories in the 1890s: 'The Ring of Thoth' (1890) and 'Lot No. 249' (1892). The former is a tale of love that spans millennia: an ancient Egyptian who discovered the chemical secret to extreme longevity seeks the antidote that will reunite him with his beloved, whose mummified body resides in the Louvre. The latter is the haunting tale of a mummy reanimated by an Oxford undergraduate who uses this sinister body to do harm to his enemies. Like many of these texts, 'Lot No. 249' enjoyed an afterlife beyond its original republications, in reissues and translations. It was retitled 'La Momie vivante' ('The Living Mummy') after it was republished for French readers in the aftermath of the discovery of the tomb of Tutankhamun. While in Doyle's original the mummy's reanimation was revealed in a horrifying denouement (and illustration) late in the story, 'La Momie vivante' made clear from its cover that a supernormal threat would be encountered between its pages (Fig. 9.6).

The mummy's potential physical threat and its sexual allure were brought together in Bram Stoker's turn-of-the-century horror novel *The Jewel of Seven Stars* (1903). In this text, little of the mummy's more comic origins is discernible. Queen Tera leaves a trail of injury and death behind her. When her body is unwrapped, the protagonists are shocked to discover that she is the doppelgänger of the daughter of the Egyptologist who brought her body from Egypt to Britain. An experiment to revive her leaves the novel's various characters dead (aside from the narrator) and Tera herself at large. In 1912 a version of the text with a revised ending was published; the experiment fails to return Tera to life and the narrator marries the Egyptologist's daughter, but, as the double of Tera – who increasingly channels the queen as her psychic powers grow – it is unclear whether this is in fact a spiritual rather than physical revival of the mummy.

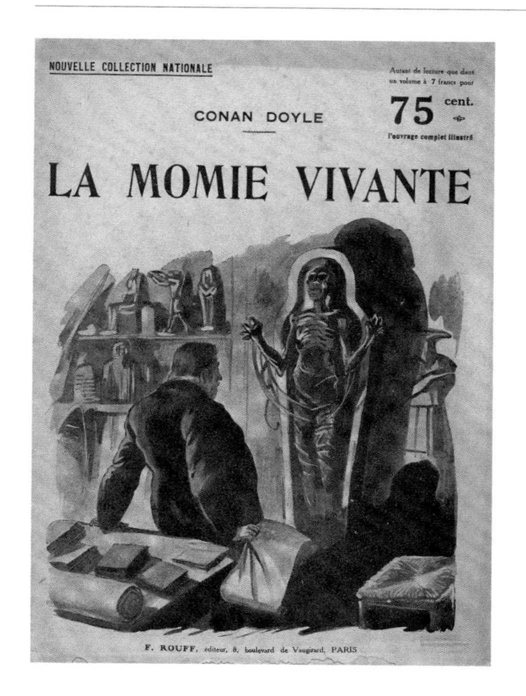

△ FIG. 9.6: 'La Momie vivante' (The Living Mummy), Paris, 1923–24. Private Collection.

▷ FIG. 9.7: Philips Brothers, Marie Corelli's 'cursed' necklace, late nineteenth century. Victoria and Albert Museum.

While the mummy stories that are today best remembered, and most frequently anthologised, are the writings of Doyle, Haggard and Stoker, the giants of late nineteenth-century Gothic and adventure fiction – novels such as Henrietta Dorothy Everett's *Iras: A Mystery* (1896, published under the pseudonym Theo Douglas) and Charlotte Bryson Taylor's *In the Dwellings of the Wilderness* (1904) – underscore women's continued contribution to the two most potent varieties of mummy fiction by the close of the nineteenth century: the romance on the one hand, in which the restored Egyptian mummy is an unattainable object of desire, and the horror story on the other.

The woman who undoubtedly contributed the most to our modern understanding of the mummy's curse, however, is Marie Corelli. Corelli was a bestselling novelist in her own time, whose books were read and enjoyed by the likes of Queen Victoria. Her novel *Ziska* (1897), while dealing with an embodied ancient Egyptian spirit rather than a mummy, combines desire and horror, culminating in a transformation scene inside a pyramid in which the titular character fades from solid woman to translucent ghost: 'her form grew thin and skeleton-like, while still retaining the transparent outline of its beauty; and he realised ... that no creature of flesh and blood ... clung to him, but some mysterious bodiless horror of the Supernatural'.[13] Ziska kills the man who is the modern reincarnation of her lover from her previous life, as he had murdered her in a moment of passion.

Ziska was one of the many nineteenth-century texts reissued as publishers sought to capitalise on the Tutankhamun discovery in the 1920s, the narratives of which Corelli undoubtedly shaped. It was she who wrote to *The New York Times* in 1923 suggesting that something other than natural causes was to blame for the 5th Earl of Carnarvon's illness. Proposing that the ancient Egyptians had secreted mysterious poisons in their tombs to guard against grave-robbers, Corelli, in her anticipation of Carnarvon's death, was integral in cementing the place of the mummy's curse in the early twentieth-century press. Her Egyptian necklace is a physical emblem of her respect for – and fear of – ancient Egyptian forces, beliefs that narratives of mummies encouraged far more broadly in the wider population (Fig. 9.7). While she claimed it brought her luck, she asserted that she would never bring herself to wear it.[14] The necklace had, according to Corelli, been discovered around the neck of a figure that metamorphosed fluidly across categories of comedy, romance and horror across the nineteenth century and beyond: the mummy. ⊙

10 DOMESTIC TOURISM II

MAHA MAAMOUN

Domestic Tourism II combines scenes from Egyptian films featuring the pyramids as backdrop, examining narratives of recent history.

In *Domestic Tourism II* my interest is not in the issue of tourism per se, but in generic visual representations of Cairo in a broad sense, and where this intersects with, and is negotiated by, personal experiences ...

In *Domestic Tourism II* my starting point was the representation of the pyramids in Egyptian cinema. My interest in the pyramids actually started when I realised how weird it is, though we see them all the time without really being conscious of them, to have these huge minimalist structures overlooking a city as labyrinthine and complex as Cairo. And also how strange it is to have these icons so physically close to the city but in touristic representations banished from the present time and place, shown mostly with the endless desert as their background and referring only to ancient Egyptian civilisation. I then started getting interested in how different their cinematic representations are. How in the latter they are implicated in the city's ongoing negotiations and active struggle over its past and present.

◁ FIG. 10.1: Stills from Maha Maamoun's film, *Domestic Tourism II*, 2009.

In the research phase for *Domestic Tourism II* I started looking for films that had a scene with the pyramids as the backdrop. I asked people if they remembered any such scenes. The result was a collection of some of the most memorable scenes, which also tend to be some of the most dramatic. Yet I also came across many banal ones. Looking through this large database of scenes, I ended up with a sort of line-up of symbolic meanings attached to these icons, or 'a continuous flow of references to a single icon', as curator Bassam El Baroni described it in an interview we did recently and from which this text has evolved.

A lot of the scenes by the pyramids, or at least the ones that people remember, are quite politically charged, and are tied to distinct chapters in Egypt's modern history. The pyramids are commonly used as a symbol of Egypt, a constant against which the Present is brought into focus, as contrastingly different from a magnificent Past. These are mostly nostalgic lamentation scenes, more prevalent from the 1970s onwards, which compare the corrupt Present (read government or sometimes society at large) to an imagined glorious Past. Alternatively they provide a continuum of that glorified Past, mostly in scenes from the 1950s and 1960s, when the schism between the 'nation' and the 'state' was briefly suspended and a rhetoric of national unity prevailed.

Working on *Domestic Tourism II*, I tried not to have a heavy hand with the material, so I kept to what I felt was the least interventionist method and composition, a chronological structure that is not totally linear. So the film starts with the most recent scenes I had, descends back to the oldest scene, and then ascends up again to the present, in what can be seen as a pyramidal structure. The timeline is: 2000s–90s–80s–70s–60s–50s–60s–70s–80s–90s–2000s. I wanted to start and end with the present so that the film does not end up as a celebration of a romantic past vs a rough present. Instead, it visits the past and shows its various formulations by a changing present. Of course I chose what scenes to include or exclude. These choices basically excluded what I considered repetitive scenes.

To give the film such a chronological/pyramidal structure was not only a (dry) conceptual preference. For this historical chronology is at the same time an emotional chronology and brings with it an emotional structure and rhythm for the film, as the drama engulfing the pyramids gradually rises and falls with time. The film starts with scenes from the 2000s, with their lighter and more superficial engagement with social and political issues, then the tone of the film heightens as we move backwards through the 1990s, 1980s and 1970s, with cinema's deeper engagement with the harshness of political and social realities. The tension is then released with the celebratory scenes of political and social glee from the 1960s and 1950s, where the pyramids act mostly as a backdrop to a celebrating and celebrated middle class. Here we reach the oldest scene I have, the turning point, after which the tension gradually builds up as we move up again through the traumatic political and economic upheavals of the late 1960s, 1970s and 1980s, phasing out to the present [2000s]. The gradual rise and fall in the intensity of the scenes structures the film in a way that makes the whole viewable, in the sense that the film feels like it has an introduction, middle and end.

'But it's really interesting,' says Bassam El Baroni, 'that you mentioned the minimalistic nature of Egypt's best-known icon and the schism between the mathematical metaphysical nature of its weight and presence and the seemingly loose and unbinding structure of Cairo's socio-politics. Would you say that there is a strange sort of metaphysics going on when the pyramids are the backdrop in scenes in Egyptian movies?'

My revised answer is: I find it interesting that you see some of the 'mathematical and metaphysical' aspects of this icon addressed in Western films, where the pyramids are a subject of a lot of sci-fi films, for example, or films that dabble, however superficially, with the philosophical underpinnings of ancient Egyptian civilisation; whereas in Egyptian cinema, as well as in other forms of mass knowledge production, these aspects are hardly touched, and the only narrative in which the pyramids most prominently appear, and are conveniently fixed, is a nationalist historiography.

However, bringing together the various and numerous cameo appearances of the pyramids in Egyptian cinema, where they are made to speak the language of the day, whether it is social and political celebration or frustration, may end up accenting their constant, 'mathematical and metaphysical' presence in the background over their changing socio-political foreground. And maybe the tables are turned then, and the background recasts, or reinterprets, the foreground, not vice versa.

'So *Domestic Tourism II* somehow exposes this niche where a kind of suppressed or rather latent metaphysics creates friction and plays out against a scheme of nationalism?'

My revised answer is: I feel that to have such abstract minimalist structures looming over and part of the urban fabric of this megalopolis is almost surreal, visually at least. And yes, that would be nice. ⊙

This text is based on an interview of Maha Maamoun by Bassam El Baroni for *Past of the Coming Days*, the catalogue of the Film and Performance Programme curated by Tarek Abou El Fetouh for the Sharjah Biennial 9. It was originally published in September 2009 on the website of Universes in Universe – Worlds of Art (UiU); see: www.universes.art/en/nafas/articles/2009/mahamaamoun

▷ FIG. 10.2: Stills from Maha Maamoun's film, *Domestic Tourism II*, 2009.

11 MODERNISM AND ANCIENT EGYPT: HARLEM, PARIS AND LONDON

ANNA FERRARI

Between the 1920s and 1950s, modernist artists reinvented ancient Egyptian culture, adopting it to reflect their own formalist and political interests.[1] In doing so, they departed from the Romantic visions of landscapes and Egyptian ruins or the erotic fantasies conjured by nineteenth-century artists. The Swiss sculptor Alberto Giacometti visually articulated a perceived connection between ancient Egyptian and modern art in 1937 when he copied on the same sheet of paper a bust of a pharaoh, often identified as Senusret III, and a self-portrait by Paul Cézanne (Fig. 11.2). With Cézanne considered a father figure of avant-garde movements of the beginning of the century, including Fauvism and Cubism, Giacometti's pairing suggested a formal parallel between ancient Egypt and French modern art and effectively bridged the millennia between both works and traditions.

Artists were not alone in drawing such connections. Indeed, the German Egyptologist Hedwig Fechheimer explicitly discussed this perceived relationship in her book *Die Plastik der Ägypter* (*Egyptian Sculpture*, first published in 1914 and translated into French in 1920), invoking a 'kinship' between the Cubist aesthetic and Egyptian conceptions of art.[2] She further argued that ancient Egyptian art had preceded modern art in applying Cézanne's oft-quoted advice to 'treat nature by the sphere, the cylinder and the cone.'[3] As such, Fechheimer supported the association between ancient Egyptian and modern art, and may in fact have prompted Giacometti to pair an Egyptian bust with Cézanne's self-portrait.[4]

Before the First World War, the avant-garde and its critics frequently invoked ancient Egyptian art as part of wider global artistic traditions to which they looked, reacting against the academic emulation of Greco-Roman Classical art. The idea that art from beyond the Classical canon could reinvigorate a Western artistic tradition that was seen to be exhausted and obsessed with the pursuit of naturalism was a powerful belief among modernists. Crucially, though, while subverting the Western hierarchy of artistic traditions, the idea of regenerating modern art placed non-Western arts in a secondary position to modern art. In the late nineteenth and early twentieth centuries,

◁ FIG. 11.1: Alberto Giacometti, *Standing Woman*, 1958–59. Sainsbury Centre.

△ FIG. 11.2: Alberto Giacometti, Copies after A Head of Senusret III and after Cézanne self-portrait, 1937. Fondation Giacometti.

the problematically called 'primitive' arts included arts from European traditions such as Cycladic and Romanesque art, as well as non-Western art from Japan, China, India and ancient Egypt, and also African and Pacific art.[5] However, by the 1920s 'primitive' art was identified primarily with African and Pacific arts, distinguished from other traditions by their then little-understood historical development and apparent absence of narrative subjects.[6] Ancient Egyptian art was therefore part of modernist artists' wider visual landscape, but was typically divorced from other artistic traditions from the African continent.

Ancient Egyptian art was a malleable concept and different artists invoked it for different reasons. The painter Paul Gauguin, who fashioned himself as the 'savage' artist and drew from the French medieval tradition as well as Japanese prints and Polynesian art, also invoked the study of ancient Egyptian art, in which he found 'a healthy element', and which he contrasted with 'decadent' Greek art, positing it as anti-academic.[7] In 1908, the self-taught painter Henri Rousseau also referred to Egyptian art when he reportedly remarked to Pablo Picasso, 'We are the two greatest painters of our age – you in the Egyptian style, I in the modern.'[8] Picasso had then just painted his seminal work *Les Demoiselles d'Avignon* (1907) and was developing what became known as Cubism, neither of which today seems particularly close to ancient Egyptian art. Rousseau's comment, however, suggests that he saw 'the Egyptian style' as part of Picasso's radical innovations. Among the Parisian avant-garde, Amedeo Modigliani was also particularly enthused by ancient Egyptian art, as well as by ancient Cycladic, Khmer, African and early Italian art, all of which informed his stone sculptures. The Russian poet Anna Akhmatova recalled accompanying him to the Louvre's Egyptian galleries in 1911:

> Modigliani was crazy about Egypt. He took me to the Louvre to look at the Egyptian section; he assured me that everything else, 'tout le reste', didn't deserve any attention. He drew my head in the attire of Egyptian queens and dancers, and he seemed completely carried away by the great Egyptian art. Obviously Egypt was his last passion.[9]

On the other hand, Guillaume Apollinaire, the critic who championed the Parisian avant-garde, claimed in 1913 that the Cubists' study of Egyptian, African and Pacific sculpture had encouraged the movement's tendency towards abstraction, or what he called the fourth dimension.[10] Meanwhile, in London it was the Indian, Assyrian and Egyptian collections of the British Museum that prompted Jacob Epstein and Henri Gaudier-Brzeska to carve directly into the stone block.[11] The practice of 'direct carving' (cutting into stone or wood, rather than the academic process of modelling in clay and transferring the figure into the block) was more than a technique and became a central tenet of British modern sculptors in the interwar years.

That artists such as Modigliani and Epstein specifically associated ancient Egyptian art with the great imperial collections of the Louvre Museum and the British Museum was not incidental. The colonial context shaped the way in which modern artists encountered non-Western arts, including ancient Egyptian art: they visited imperial collections extensively developed in the nineteenth century, saw private collections and acquired photographic reproductions in books and periodicals – all of which mediated European and American artists' engagement with ancient Egypt, as did colonial exhibitions and popular culture. The frequency and vagueness with which pharaonic art was cited reveals its significance for modern artists, but also its flexibility. It was both distinct from the Classical tradition and from African art, occupying a liminal position that allowed artists to reinvent and interpret it according to their agendas, whether for African American artists of the Harlem Renaissance making powerful political statements, for sculptors such as Henry Moore and Ronald Moody looking to it for its formal or spiritual qualities, or for Giacometti's and Francis Bacon's expressive representations of the human figure.

At the centre of the art world, Paris extended its influence across the Atlantic and spurred artists to look to African art. While before the First World War the Parisian avant-garde distinguished ancient Egypt from Africa, in the United States several African American artists and intellectuals reclaimed it as part of their African heritage, tracing their culture to an august ancient civilisation reaching back millennia. The cultural movement that emerged in the 1920s and 1930s, known as the Harlem Renaissance, celebrated the black experience and its creative contributions to music and jazz, literature, theatre and art. It sought to inspire pride in African American culture at a time when, despite emancipation, many remained oppressed, disenfranchised and segregated. Drawing on pan-Africanist ideas, philosophers such as W.E.B. Du Bois and Alain Locke exhorted African American artists to look to African art.

African American sculptor Meta Vaux Warrick Fuller initially trained at the Pennsylvania Museum and School of Industrial Arts before studying in Paris between 1900 and 1902, where she was deeply impressed by her visit to Auguste Rodin's studio.[12] Fuller was championed by Du Bois, a co-founder of the National Association for the Advancement of Colored People in 1909, who commissioned her to sculpt an allegorical figure of 'Ethiopia' for the African American booth at the *America's Making Exposition* in 1921.[13] *Ethiopia* is a powerful figure of a standing black woman wearing a pharaonic *nemes*-headdress, who appears to emerge from unravelling mummy wrappings, turning her head as if coming back to life (Fig. 11.3). The sculpture occupied a prominent place in the booth, which pursued the ancient Egyptian theme and was modelled on an Egyptian temple. Fuller herself explained the importance of the ancient Egyptian reference in symbolising African American emancipation when she wrote:

> Here was a group ... who had once made history and now after a long sleep was awaking, gradually unwinding the bandage of its mummied past and looking out on life again, expectant but unafraid and with at least a graceful gesture. Why you may ask the Egyptian motif? The answer, the most brilliant period, perhaps of Egyptian history was the period of the Negro kings.[14]

Fuller's association of ancient Egypt with black pharaohs echoed Du Bois's views expressed in his 1915 book *The Negro*.[15] In this survey history of Africa, Du Bois reclaimed Egypt as part of the African continent, refuting the white narrative that linked Egypt to Greco-Roman history and therefore to Europe. Du Bois argued that the origins of the Egyptian civilisation lay in Africa and highlighted the period in the eighth century BC when black Africans from Nubia ruled Egypt. Du Bois called Upper Nubia by its Greek name, Ethiopia (although it is distinct from the modern-day country), and in doing so associated Ethiopia with ancient Egyptian history.[16] The country Ethiopia held particular appeal for African Americans as an independent African nation that was not under European colonial power, and was also home to one of the oldest Christian communities going back to the fourth century AD. Finally, Ethiopia could also suggest the late nineteenth-century African religious movement known as Ethiopianism. It drew on the biblical references to Ethiopia and invoked Psalm 68:31 – 'Princes shall come out of Egypt; Ethiopia shall soon stretch out her hands unto God' – which African American thinkers interpreted as a prophecy announcing black people's freedom from enslavement.[17] By titling her work *Ethiopia*, Fuller drew on these rich associations, casting contemporary African Americans as the heirs of a successful Nubian dynasty that had ruled Egypt, while simultaneously invoking political independence and a long Christian tradition.[18]

From the mid-1920s, Aaron Douglas also called upon ancient Egyptian visual culture to create powerful representations of the modern African American experience, while simultaneously drawing on Cubism's flattened pictorial space, Art Deco's graphic simplification of form and Precisionism's sharp lines and muted palette. Originally from Kansas in the Midwest, Douglas arrived in the creative effervescence of Harlem and was swiftly commissioned to provide illustrations for *The Crisis* magazine edited by Du Bois, as well as for Alain Locke's seminal anthology *The New Negro* (1925), which celebrated the creative force of African American artists.

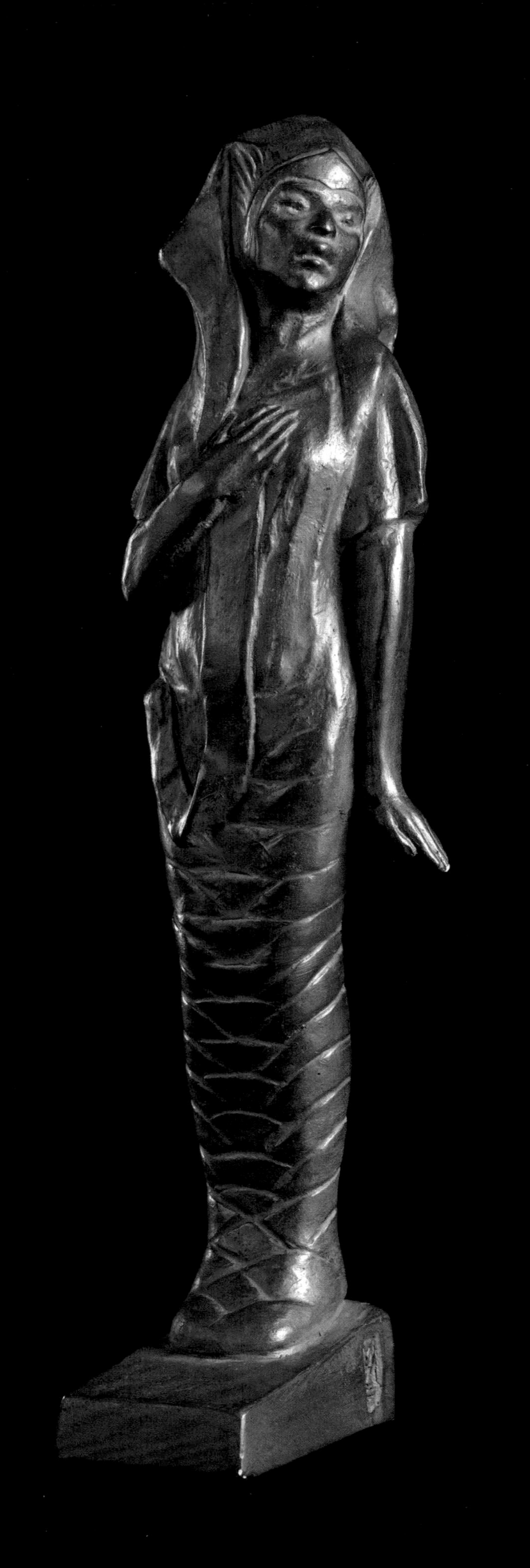

◁ **FIG. 11.3:** Meta Vaux Warrick Fuller, *Ethiopia*, 1921. Collection of the Smithsonian National Museum of African American History and Culture. Gift of the Fuller Family.

▷ **FIG. 11.4:** Aaron Douglas, *Building More Stately Mansions*, 1944. Rhode Island School of Design.

Douglas's 1920s designs for *The Crisis* focused on silhouetted figures with heads in profile, reminiscent of ancient Egyptian reliefs and paintings, while motifs such as pyramids, lotus flowers and sphinxes became shorthand for a great ancestral African culture. He drew on this visual vocabulary in his 1944 painting *Building More Stately Mansions*, a rousing vision of African American labour set against ancient Egyptian achievement (Fig. 11.4). In the foreground, silhouetted figures wielding tools are viewed against the backdrop of monumental and awe-inspiring arches, church spires and modern skyscrapers, while beyond loom a gigantic profile of a pharaoh and a pyramid. Douglas seems to collapse the centuries, drawing a connection between ancient Egypt's great architecture and modern African Americans' achievements. This places African Americans at the centre of a global narrative, visually suggested by the mother and children gathered around a globe from which radiate concentric circles of light or energy, conveying dynamism, modernity and a sense of optimism.

If ancient Egypt conveyed a powerful message about emancipation for African Americans, in Paris and London modernist sculptors saw it as an anti-academic tradition and admired its formal qualities, its economy of form, its figures' hieratic poses and its use of materials. Significantly, ancient Egyptian sculpture was often carved in stone or wood and could therefore be seen to support the technique of direct carving, which became central to the artistic identity of sculptors such as Henry Moore. In contrast to academic sculpture, where a clay model was scaled and reproduced by a skilled craftsman, direct carving stood for originality and authenticity. In London the British

◁ FIG. 11.5: Henry Moore, *Woman with Upraised Arms*, 1924–25. Henry Moore Foundation.

△ FIG. 11.6: Striding figure of Meryrahashtef, 2345 BC–2181 BC. British Museum.

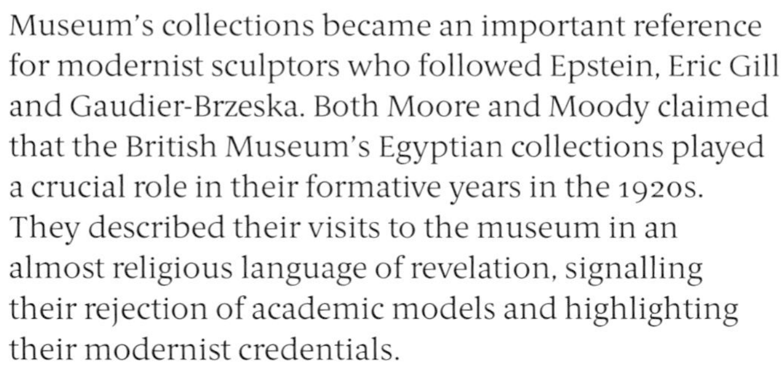

Museum's collections became an important reference for modernist sculptors who followed Epstein, Eric Gill and Gaudier-Brzeska. Both Moore and Moody claimed that the British Museum's Egyptian collections played a crucial role in their formative years in the 1920s. They described their visits to the museum in an almost religious language of revelation, signalling their rejection of academic models and highlighting their modernist credentials.

Moore was a sculpture student from Yorkshire when he first visited the British Museum in 1920, the same year he began carving in stone. He excitedly reported to his friend, the sculptor Jocelyn Horner, 'Yesterday I spent my second afternoon in the British Museum with the Egyptian and Assyrian sculptures – An hour before closing time I tore myself away from these to do a little exploring and found ... in the Ethnographical Gallery – the ecstatically fine negro sculptures.'[19] Aside from his keen enthusiasm, Moore's letter reveals his perception of ancient Egyptian sculpture as part of a vast breadth of decontextualised global artistic traditions that encompassed Assyrian art and other African art, echoing the non-Western traditions invoked by pre-war modernists.[20]

In 1921, he moved to London and enrolled at the Royal College of Art, giving him further opportunities to explore the British Museum. *Woman with Upraised Arms* of 1924–25 reveals Moore engaging with the formal qualities of ancient Egyptian sculpture while also departing from them (Fig. 11.5). Carved directly into a single block of grey Hopton Wood stone, the figure has a compact quality, even though space flows between the arms. Moore may have been inspired by a monumental three-metre-long red granite arm in the British Museum, believed to be from a statue of Amenhotep III (XVIIIth dynasty). Later in his career, he remembered the impact this sculpture had made on him, recalling that:

> When I first visited the British Museum's Egyptian sculpture gallery, and saw the 'great arm' and imagined what the whole figure was like; which it had only been part of – then I

realised how monumental, how enormous, how impressive a single piece of sculpture could be. Though it wasn't just the size alone which impressed me. Size and monumentality are not always the same thing. What I found in the Egyptian pieces was a monumentality of vision.[21]

Moore reinterpreted his sources, however, and the sculpture's expressive face and pierced form are clearly departures from pharaonic sculpture. Ancient Egyptian objects, and particularly the British Museum's collections, remained important to Moore for formal purposes rather than for their archaeological significance. In 1981, he published *Henry Moore at the British Museum*, which focused on the sculptures he most admired and included ancient Egyptian works such as a wood-carved striding figure, which he praised for conveying a sense of tension (Fig. 11.6). Towards the end of his career, in 1978, Moore sculpted two small works, *Egyptian Figures I* and *Egyptian Figures II* (Fig. 11.7). Standing on raised bases, the figures evoke pharaonic pair statues, which represented a husband and wife, either standing or sitting, depicted from a strict frontal view. Despite their diminutive size, they embodied the 'monumentality of vision' that Moore associated with ancient Egyptian sculpture.

▽ FIG. 11.7: Henry Moore, *Egyptian Figures I*, 1978. Henry Moore Foundation.

Ronald Moody recalled his own discovery of the British Museum's collection in 1928 (eight years after Moore's) in almost identical terms to Moore. Born in Jamaica in 1900, Moody arrived in London in 1923 to learn dentistry, bowing to family pressure to join a medical profession.[22] However, he was rapidly drawn to sculpture and frequently recalled a life-changing encounter with Egyptian art in the Museum, where 'while in the Egyptian Room ... a sudden revelation came to me and I felt that sculpture was my real medium.'[23] In another account in 1951, Moody elaborated:

> I often went to the British Museum, National Gallery and other Art Galleries, coming away, I am afraid more puzzled than pleased, until one day I discovered Egyptian sculpture all for myself. It was an amazing experience and I haunted that room for a long time after. The use of the material, the massive forms treated with such amazing skill, sensitiveness, delicacy and daring, and lastly, the spirit behind it was strangely sympathetic. From that moment I felt I wanted to do sculpture.[24]

In drawing a contrast between the National Gallery – guardian of the national Renaissance collections – and the Egyptian sculpture at the British Museum, Moody echoes the modernist rejection of the Classical tradition. His perception of Egyptian sculpture's spiritual dimension was especially important for the artist, who also developed a profound interest in Indian and Chinese art and philosophy.

Moody was a self-taught sculptor, and his first series of works in the mid-1930s consisted of monumental wood-carved figures, which gained critical attention at exhibitions in Paris and Amsterdam. Buoyed by these successes, he moved to Paris in 1938 and established himself in the city that was perceived as the centre of the art world. There he carved the *Male Standing Figure – The Priest* in 1939, a figure conveying a sense of stillness, whose draped clothing and restrained hieratic posture evoke pharaonic sculpture (Fig. 11.8). Moody's choice of rosewood, a tropical timber, was most likely intentional given its rarity and cost, and

MALE STANDING FIGURE
RONALD MOODY (JAMAICA)
1208 CARVED FROM PALISANDRE

◁ FIG. 11.8: Ronald Moody, *Male Standing Figure – The Priest*, 1939. UK Government Art Collection.

▽ FIG. 11.9: Ronald Moody, Drawing of an ancient Egyptian lotus-shaped lamp, undated. Tate Archive.

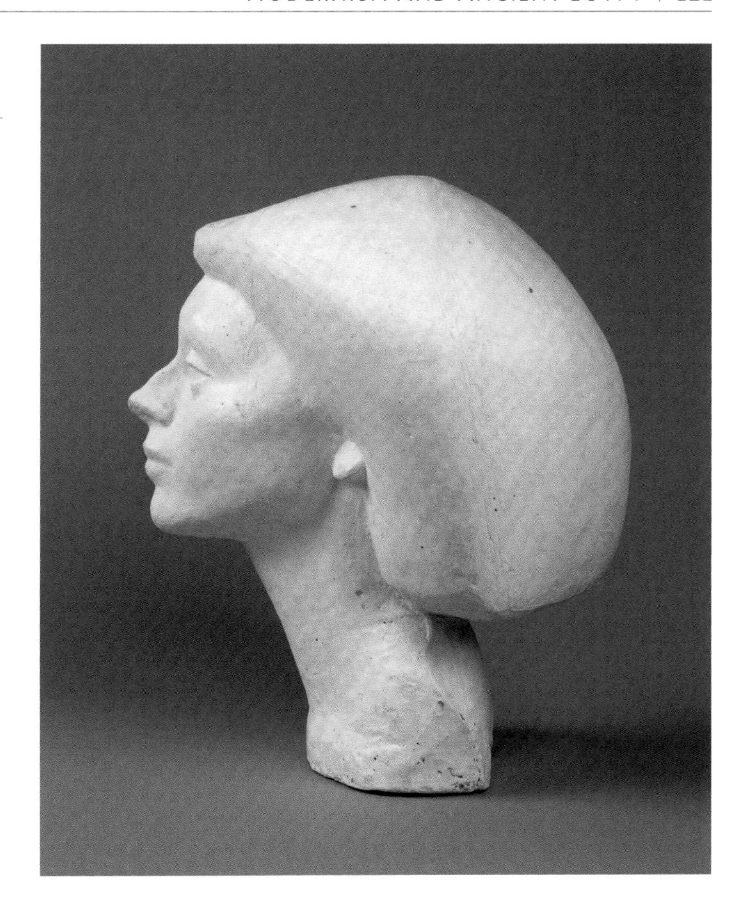

△ FIG. 11.10 Alberto Giacometti, *Head of Isabel*, 1936. Fondation Giacometti.

further emphasises the figure's association with non-Western art. Moody continued to study pharaonic art throughout his life; in a BBC radio lecture about the history of Egyptian art, given in 1950, he delighted in the 'perfect craftmanship shown in a wooden comb', while his archives reveal a sketch of a lamp in the form of three lotus flowers, which is closely related to a delicately carved alabaster lamp from Tutankhamun's tomb (Fig. 11.9).[25]

Both Moore and Moody attributed a revelatory role to the Egyptian sculpture collections of the British Museum in the 1920s, manifesting their modernist approach to sculpture. Each saw different qualities in Egyptian sculpture; Moore praised its 'monumentality of vision', while Moody invoked its materials and spiritual dimension.

Ancient Egyptian art also informed Giacometti's and Bacon's approach to representing the human figure. For Giacometti, ancient Egypt was a major visual reference that was reflected in his sketches of pharaonic sculpture and in his own sculpture.[26] Giacometti first came face-to-face with ancient Egyptian art when, as a young artist in 1920, he travelled to Italy and visited the archaeological museum in Florence. When he settled in Paris, Giacometti became an assiduous visitor of the Louvre Museum and its Egyptian galleries. Illustrated books were also a crucial source, particularly Fechheimer's *Die Plastik der Ägypter* and Ludwig Curtius's *Ägypten und Vorderasien* (*Egypt and the Near East*), copies of which he acquired in 1920 and 1923 respectively.

The early 1930s were a pivotal moment in Giacometti's career, during which his engagement with Egyptian art came to the fore just as he returned to figuration. In 1935, Giacometti met the British artist Isabel Nicholas (later Rawsthorne), who was part of the artistic circles in Montparnasse and who became his muse. She sat in 1936 for her bust, *Head of Isabel*, which later acquired the nickname '*Tête égyptienne*', most likely because it depicts Isabel in a strictly frontal view, her delicate features framed by her voluminous hair, visually evoking wigs worn by women in ancient Egyptian art (Fig. 11.10). The frontality, simplification of form and serene expression recall Egyptian busts, while her elegant profile with her long neck extended forward suggests the limestone and plaster bust of Queen Nefertiti excavated at Tell el-Amarna by the German archaeologist Ludwig Borchardt in 1912. Transported illegally to Germany, the bust was first publicly exhibited in 1924, propelling it to instant fame and simultaneously prompting Egyptian restitution claims that continue to this day.[27]

In an interview with Pierre Schneider in 1962, Giacometti discussed his sustained interest in 'primitive' arts, explaining that:

> The works of the past that I find resemble reality most are those which in general one deems most distant from it ... Chaldea, Egypt, Byzantium, Fayum, some Chinese objects, Christian miniatures of the high Middle Ages. It is not at all what one calls realism ... Any one of us resembles an Egyptian sculpture far more than any other sculpture ever made.[28]

The standing or walking human figure, which became a focal point of Giacometti's post-war oeuvre, also reflects his interest in pharaonic sculpture. The restrained pose, lithe limbs and block-like base of *Standing Woman* (1958–59) draw parallels with the hieratic standing figures of ancient Egyptian sculpture (Fig. 11.1). Giacometti shared his admiration for such art with his patrons, Robert and Lisa Sainsbury, who purchased *Standing Woman*. When Giacometti gave them three sketches of their son David in 1955, the Sainsburys offered the sculptor a 'small, beautiful, ancient Egyptian head they knew he would love' as a token of their gratitude.[29]

That same year, Francis Bacon painted *Sketch for a Portrait of Lisa* when the Sainsburys became lifelong patrons (Fig. 11.11).[30] Although Bacon was a few years younger than Giacometti and lived in London, they shared mutual friends, such as Isabel Rawsthorne. *Sketch for a Portrait of Lisa* was one of the last portraits Bacon painted from life before he chose to work from photographs. Even when he invited his subjects to sit for him, Bacon is known to have drawn from photographs of other subjects. Lisa Sainsbury's portrait has evoked comparisons with ancient Egyptian sculpture, particularly photographs of busts of King Akhenaten and Queen Nefertiti, both of which were reproduced in Kurt Lange's 1951 book *König Echnaton und die Amarna-Zeit* (*King Akhenaten and the Amarna Period*) which Bacon owned (Fig. 11.12).[31] The portrait shares Akhenaten's heavy eyelids, hollow cheeks and sensual mouth, while Lisa's elongated neck evokes Nefertiti's elegant bust, conflating Lisa with two famous Egyptian royal figures who had instigated an artistic revolution.

Ancient Egypt offered Bacon a source of powerful images to manipulate and absorb for his own expressive purposes, in addition to the wealth of sources on which he drew from across the Western canon of art, which included Nicolas Poussin, Edgar Degas, Vincent van Gogh, but also Eadweard Muybridge's photographic motion studies and Sergei Eisenstein's films, and photographs from books on subjects ranging from history to medicine. In the late 1920s, Bacon developed a friendship with the Egyptologist Guy Brunton, who specialised in Predynastic Egypt and was a frequent visitor to Bacon's home in South Kensington.[32] Between 1953 and 1954, prior to meeting the Sainsburys, Bacon executed a series of four works based on the Sphinx at Giza, which are perhaps his most direct references to ancient Egypt, while simultaneously invoking the Greek hybrid creature of Oedipus' legend. Although Bacon claimed that his work was not political, such images may have surfaced because of the Egyptian Revolution of 1952, when the British-supported monarchy was overthrown and Britain's control of the Suez Canal ended, placing Egypt at the forefront of current affairs.

Bacon's extensive collection of books relating to ancient Egyptian art, however, is perhaps most revealing. Following the painter's death in 1992, his South Kensington studio, which was stacked with hundreds of books, magazines and loose leaves, was thoroughly catalogued, offering an insight into his interests and working processes.[33] The hoard of material includes nearly forty books about ancient Egypt and its art, as well as many loose leaves with photographs of Egyptian works.[34] Most of the books were published between the 1960s and the 1980s, which is unsurprising given Bacon's peripatetic lifestyle until he moved to Reece Mews in 1961. However, there are notable earlier books, including Lange's *König Echnaton*, which Bacon may have acquired in the 1950s, and *The Art of Ancient Egypt: Architecture, Sculpture, Painting, Applied Art*, which was published in 1936 and became an important source book.

Bacon articulated his admiration for ancient Egyptian sculpture in an interview with David Sylvester in 1974, stating:

> I think that perhaps the greatest images that man has so far made have been in sculpture. I'm thinking of some of the great Egyptian sculpture, of course, and Greek sculpture too. For instance, the Elgin Marbles in the British Museum are always very important to me,

◁ FIG. 11.11: Francis Bacon, *Sketch for a Portrait of Lisa*, 1955. Sainsbury Centre.

▽ FIG. 11.12: Bust of Akhenaten illustrated in Kurt Lange's book *König Echnaton und die Amarna-zeit* (*King Akhenaten and the Amarna Period*), 1951.

> but I don't know if they're important because they're fragments, and whether if one had seen the whole image they would seem as poignant as they seem as fragments.[35]

Within a century of Gauguin contrasting the 'healthy' ancient Egyptian to the 'decadent' Greek, Bacon reversed the modernist dichotomy between Classical Greek and ancient Egyptian arts, instead absorbing both into his visual repertoire as malleable sources of emotive forms open for his reinterpretation. Between the 1920s and the 1950s, few of the modernist painters and sculptors who engaged with ancient Egyptian art travelled to Egypt, and their encounter with the ancient culture was therefore mediated through publications, private collections and imperialist museums in Britain, France and the United States. Modernism reinvented ancient Egypt, transforming it from the Romantic and Orientalist visions of the nineteenth century and investing it with new meanings that suited twentieth-century agendas. From Gauguin to Giacometti, ancient Egyptian art was part of geographically and chronologically disparate arts promoted in reaction to the Classical tradition. European modernist sculptors in particular saw in Egyptian sculpture different facets that chimed with their rejection of Classicism: a sense of monumentality, a reference for hieratic poses, a spiritual dimension or a standard for carving technique. At the same time, among African American intellectuals and artists of the Harlem Renaissance, ancient Egypt played a significant role in transforming the narrative about African Americans from enslavement to emancipation and in rooting their history in a brilliant culture. ⊙

12 MODERN VISIONS OF ANCIENT EGYPT

NADIA RADWAN

In 1945 the artist Ramses Younan, a member of the Art and Liberty Surrealist group (Art et Liberté), presented his work entitled *Tropique du Cancer* at the Art Foyer of the Lycée français in Cairo (Fig. 12.2). The painting depicts three flayed female figures in front of a classical torso, set in an architectural landscape opening onto an uncanny desert recalling Giorgio de Chirico's emblematic enfilades of porticoes. Younan also clearly alludes to the Surrealist works of Yves Tanguy and Salvador Dalí, and in the centre, as if to highlight the ultimate paradigm of modernity, he figures an easel supporting a portrait by Picasso. This significant work embodies the Egyptian avant-garde's self-definition as being a part of the narrative of modern art and its claim to be at the same time universal, transnational and Egyptian.

The members of the Egyptian Surrealist group Art and Liberty, founded by the francophone writer and poet Georges Henein in 1939, were deeply concerned by the realities of Egyptian society as well as by its past. While they explored the worlds of dreams and the subconscious, psychoanalysis and the uncanny of everyday life, these artists also expressed their social concerns, their revolt against the rise of Fascism in Egypt, colonisation, the inequalities of the feudal agrarian system and the extreme poverty of the Egyptian peasant, the *fellah*.

It was also in reaction to a former generation of artists commonly called the pioneers (*al-ruwwad*) or the *nahdawi*, because they engaged with a cultural renaissance movement called the *nahda* (awakening) – and which I rather call the 'moderns' – that these avant-gardes were able to assert themselves. And because Egypt witnessed a precipitation of modernity in the field of visual arts, these modern artists engaged with European media and genres by simultaneously emancipating themselves from them to engage with local references, including ancient Egypt.[1]

The turn of the twentieth century in Egypt was marked by transcultural exchanges with Europe and by the institutionalisation of art and art education. From that perspective, three major aspects can be underlined in the formation of Egyptian modern art. The first is the transfer of knowledge through the creation of cultural and artistic institutions and the

◁ FIG 12.1: Mahmoud Mokhtar, *Le Réveil de l'Égypte* (Egypt Awakening), c.1928. Photo, archives Emad Abou Ghazi.

△ FIG. 12.2: Ramses Younan, *Tropique du Cancer* (Tropic of Cancer), c.1945. Collection May Moein Zeid & Adel Youssry Khedr, Cairo.

migration of institutional models from Europe to Egypt, but also the tensions that this migration created – for instance, by defining a hierarchy between fine arts and applied arts. The second aspect is the impact of the trans-Mediterranean circulations of artists not only on their artistic practice, but also on the construction of the modernist discourse. The third significant point is the role played by intermediaries, patrons or diplomats in the formation of Egyptian modern art.

FINE ARTS VS APPLIED ARTS

The institutionalisation of art education was first envisioned in Egypt in the field of applied and decorative arts to answer an increasing demand for local specialised craftsmen. Since the nineteenth century, education in the field of industrial art had been part of the modernisation reforms (*tanzimat*) established under the rule of the viceroy Muhammad Ali, who set up practical schools (*madrasat al-amaliyyat*). Later, in 1868, during the rule of his grandson Khedive Isma'il, engineer Ali Mubarak established the Sultanal School of Industrial Arts (*madrasat al-funun wa al-sina'i al-sultaniyya*). Although the School included a special section for decorative arts, it was at first mainly intended to train military and hydraulic engineers.

These first institutions opened the way to the establishment, in 1919, of a School of Decorative Arts (*madrasat al-funun wa al-zaghrafa*) in Cairo to answer the need for a local labour specialised in the fields of tapestry, woodwork, metalwork and ironwork. The students of this School were regularly sent on scholarly missions to Great Britain, and these exchanges would later give birth to an increasing interest in Egypt for artistic pedagogy and the revival of arts and crafts.

The School was dominated by British professors, who were heirs of the Arts and Crafts movement, such as the Scottish interior designer and architect John Ednie, a follower of Charles Rennie Mackintosh. It is noteworthy that while the domain of applied arts was dominated by the British, the administration and teaching of the School of Fine Arts in Cairo would remain in the hands of French and Italian artists for almost half a century. There was thus, after the establishment of these art schools, a cultural and geopolitical division of the artistic field between European presences.

However, although by the 1920s the institutional domain of applied and decorative arts was well established and was perceived as the continuation of a local tradition, the establishment of a School of Fine Arts in Cairo would appear, on the contrary, totally experimental and alien. It was created by the patron and art collector Prince Yusuf Kamal and officially opened its doors in May 1908, a date that marks the canonic beginning of Egyptian modern art.[2] Based on the model of the Académie des Beaux-Arts in Paris, the School was free of charge and was open to all young boys without distinction of origin, religion or social class.

For almost thirty years it was headed by European artists, until 1937 when foreign public officials were progressively replaced by Egyptians after the retreat of the British troops and the declaration of independence. Women, on the other hand, would have to wait until the 1950s to gain access to the School. This did not, however, stop them from making art, exhibiting and engaging in the local art scene.

Prince Yusuf Kamal appointed a French sculptor named Guillaume Laplagne to head the institution. Little is known about his life and career, except that Laplagne was trained at the École des Beaux-Arts in Paris, as a pupil of the sculptor Louis-Ernest Barrias, and that he probably arrived in Egypt as artistic adviser to the Khedive Abbas Hilmi II. He produced Orientalist bronzes and Africanist ethnographic sculptures that he may have executed during the *Croisière Citroën*, also known as the *Croisière Noire* (Black Cruise) in 1924–25, which was dispatched by France as a colonial expedition in sub-Saharan Africa. This raises the question not only of the models that were transmitted by the teachers of the School, but also of the representation of sub-Saharan Africa and Sudan by Egyptian artists and, to a certain extent, of a colonial attitude transposed into the visual arts of this period.[3]

The declared goal of the School was to train young Egyptians in the field of the European fine arts as a part of a civilising project. The programme implied the practice of Western techniques, such as easel oil-painting, and genres such as portraits, landscapes and nudes. Thus knowledge of the fine arts (*al-funun al-jamila*), as defined by the West, would become a prerequisite for engaging with a national artistic modernity.

However, this project was received with much scepticism, leading to an intense debate among intellectuals, part of which was published in the local press. Underlying this debate was persistent resistance to the hierarchy between the so-called 'minor' or decorative arts, associated with a local practice, and the so-called 'major' arts, associated with colonial presence. Besides, two main questions lay at the heart

▽ FIG. 12.3: Mahmoud Mokhtar, Relief for the pedestal of the Sa'd Zaghlul Monument in Cairo representing the blacksmiths, *c.*1930. Photo, archives Emad Abou Ghazi.

of the discussion. The first was whether it made sense to introduce European artistic practice into a country that was primarily in need of skilled craftsmen and technical expertise, and where the practice of applied and decorative arts was rooted in a local tradition. The second question was to determine what the roots of this new art would be: Arab, Islamic, Egyptian?

During the first quarter of the twentieth century ancient Egypt would principally be chosen as the most adequate creative source to engage with a national style that was capable of reflecting Egyptian identities and complying with the decolonial political project of the *nahda* (awakening). This cultural 'renaissance', primarily formulated by nationalist intellectuals, was reflected in literary and visual imagery. Based on the idea of a search for authenticity (*asala*), the intertwinement of peasantry, ancient Egypt and popular traditions would be expressed in art and literature (Fig. 12.3). Consequently the first graduates of the School of Fine Arts who practised easel oil-painting would remain exclusively committed to figuration, until the shift towards pan-Arabism and the first experiences of abstraction in the early 1950s under the regime of Gamal Abdel Nasser.[4]

▽ FIG. 12.4: Mahmoud Saïd, *La Fille aux yeux bruns* (The Girl with Brown Eyes), 1943. Al-Ahram Collection, Cairo.

Moreover, the reception of the legacy of the Orientalist tradition played a significant part in this definition of authenticity, notably through depictions of the feminine figure and the genre of the nude. A representative of this approach was the Alexandrian artist Mahmoud Saïd, who was certainly one of the most prolific and renowned painters of his generation.[5] If he did not radically break away from gendered stereotypes, his feminine portraits relocate certain Orientalist tropes to serve a discourse of rootedness. By translating the feminine figure into a well-defined space, his portraits mark a distance from the archetype of the secluded, secretive and prohibited interior of the harem or the Turkish bath, to depict modern Egyptian women with agency, often from the working class (Fig. 12.4).[6] Mahmoud Saïd had travelled regularly to Italy and was profoundly marked by the Italian painters of the Quattrocento.

Such journeys were significant in the careers of Egyptian modern painters like Mahmoud Saïd. And while European artists came to work in Egypt as art teachers or to set up their studios in Cairo and Alexandria, young artists made the reverse journey to complete their studies in Paris, Rome or Florence.

CIRCULATIONS

The mobility of young Egyptian artists who received scholarships to study in Europe had a major impact on the redefinition and relocation of their own practice. In addition to artistic training, these scholarly missions were an opportunity to build or consolidate international networks. It was also a chance to approach the materiality of artworks that the artists had studied, prior to their journey, from reproductions in books. It is significant that during the first thirty years the study of ancient Egyptian art was excluded from the curriculum of the School of Fine Arts in favour of copying Greco-Roman statuary, mainly from casts imported from European museums. This would lead to artists visiting the archaeological sites of Upper Egypt on their own initiative, alongside their official training.

The sculptor Mahmoud Mokhtar, who was born in a small village of the Nile Delta called Tombara, was the first to receive a scholarship to study in Paris (Fig. 12.5). Guillaume Laplagne, who saw in his pupil a talented

sculptor, had convinced Prince Yusuf Kamal to finance Mokhtar's stay in Paris. Upon his arrival, Mokhtar frequented the atelier of the sculptor Jules Coutan (Prix de Rome and a member of the Académie des Beaux-Arts) before successfully passing the entry exam of the École des Beaux-Arts in October 1912. It was also in Paris that Mokhtar executed the model for his famous sculpture *Nahdat Misr* (*Egypt's Awakening*), which was to become a national monument and the visual embodiment of the cultural renaissance. Nevertheless, it was only after his model was admitted to the Salon des Artistes Français that an Egyptian delegation from the *wafd* (National Party) visited Mokhtar in his studio and decided to erect it as a monument in a public square in Cairo (Fig. 12.1).

It is noteworthy that the first Parisian model for the monument had been considered inauthentic and was criticised for this reason by Egyptian nationalist intellectuals. While it is true that Mahmoud Mokhtar had been inspired by Ptolemaic statuary of Greco-Roman influence, which he had probably seen at the Louvre, critics perceived the model as being 'too European'.[7] On the contrary, the final monument – officially inaugurated on 20 May 1928 in Bab al-Hadid Square in front of Cairo's Central Railway Station – was acclaimed as a creation in line with the purest tradition of ancient Egyptian statuary.[8] This reception was due not only to the subjects of the monument representing a sphinx and a peasant unveiling, but also to the traditional material used by the sculptor, which was pink granite from Aswan.[9] Nonetheless, it is ironic that the final monument owes much more to Mokhtar's Parisian training and the Mediterranean Modernism of Antoine Bourdelle and French Art Deco than to his original sculpted model, which was in fact closer to existing ancient statuary. This anecdote shows how the discourse of Egyptian artistic Modernism and authenticity was constructed through these trans-Mediterranean exchanges and mobility.

◁ FIG. 12.5: Mahmoud Mokhtar in Paris *c.*1912–13. Photo, archives Emad Abou Ghazi.

▽ FIG. 12.6: Mahmoud Mokhtar posing beside his sculpture for the pedestal of the Sa'd Zaghlul Monument in Alexandria representing Lower Egypt, *c.*1930. Photo, archives Emad Abou Ghazi.

The same fear of Westernisation is also obvious in a letter written by Prince Yusuf Kamal to Mahmoud Mokhtar, in which he urged the artist to come back to Egypt:

> You are Egyptian and you must come back to us Egyptian. You must work conscientiously in Paris, because we place all our hopes in you. We are looking forward to the results of your hard work to prove that Egyptians are not lacking in ideas and are not unable to succeed in the field of Art, which is one of the manifestations of civilisation.[10]

On his return, Mahmoud Mokhtar was at the service of the national movement and was commissioned to realise two monuments to the glory of the nationalist leader Sa'd Zaghlul – one for Cairo and the other for Alexandria. Both would be inspired by ancient Egypt, thus linking the leader and symbol of independence to Egypt's glorious past (Fig. 12.6).

During this period Mokhtar also conceived numerous sculptures of smaller dimensions in which he asserted his style in operating a synthesis between the Egyptian woman peasant (*fellaha*) and the figure of the queen-pharaoh. His *Bride of the Nile*, for instance, whose model was his Parisian partner, Marcelle Dubreil, is an example of this trans-Mediterranean style (Figs. 12.7 and 12.8). In 1929 he sculpted a whole series of peasant women, which are characterised by their simplicity of volume, gentle gestures and pure lines (Fig. 12.9).

While Mokhtar's career benefited from the creation of new art institutions in Egypt and from state scholarships, the career of the Alexandrian painter and diplomat Mohamed Naghi followed a different path, in

◁ FIG. 12.7: Mahmoud Mokhtar, *Arous El Nil* (The Bride of the Nile), 1929. Private Collection.

▽ FIG. 12.8: Marcelle Dubreil, date unknown. Photo, archives Emad Abou Ghazi.

▷ FIG. 12.9: Mahmoud Mokhtar, *Au Bord du Nil* (On the Banks of the Nile), 1931–39. Private Collection.

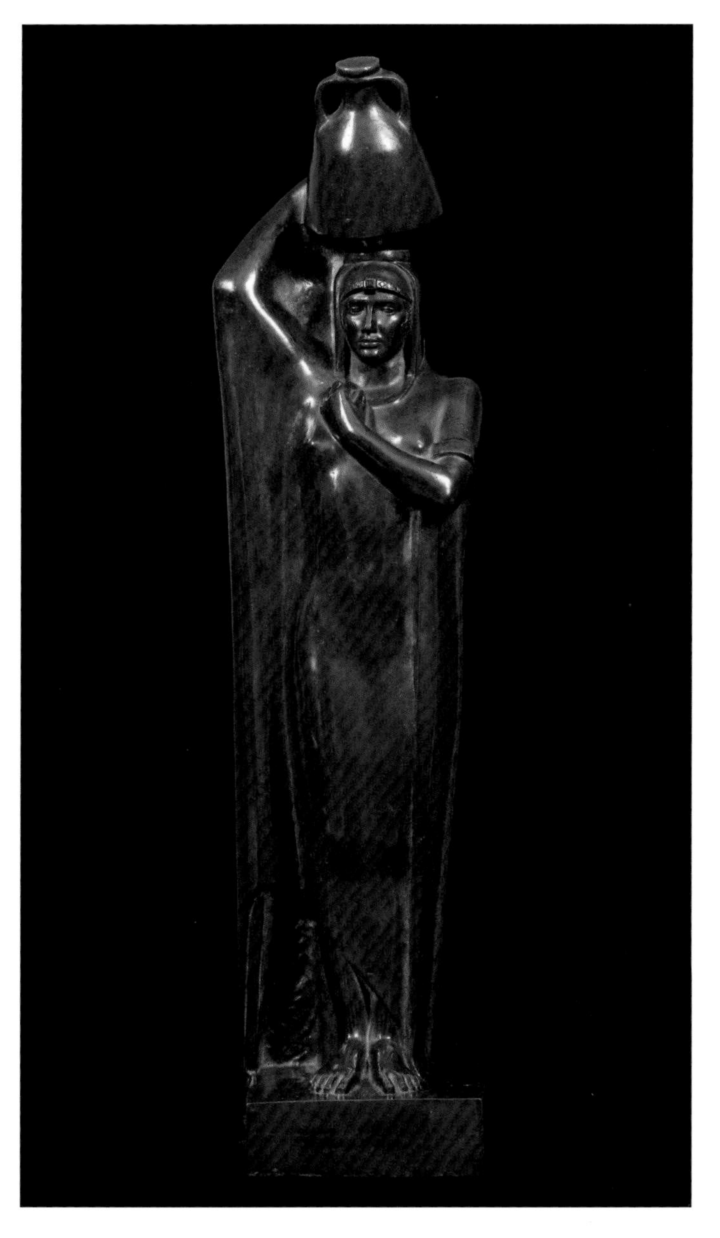

so far as he did not need this support because he came from a privileged background. Naghi studied at the Swiss School of Alexandria, where he befriended the Italian poet and Futurist essayist Giuseppe Ungaretti. He studied law, but very early on took drawing lessons in the studio of the Italian painter Alberto Piatolli in Alexandria. After graduating from the University of Lyon, Naghi enrolled at the Academy of Florence in the Scuola Libera del Nudo. During this period he painted Italian landscapes and Roman ruins that betray the influence of Divisionism and the Macchiaioli.[11]

He returned to Egypt, where he worked as a diplomat for the Ministry of Foreign Affairs while he continued to paint. In 1918 Naghi went to Giverny and studied under the elderly Claude Monet for a while. From then on, he affirmed his belonging to the Impressionist movement. Even though he was aware of the avant-gardes that dominated the Parisian artistic landscape, it was Impressionism that, according to him, could best meet the requirements of the cultural renaissance. He thus claimed his belonging to Impressionism at a time when the movement was completely outdated in Paris, and he questioned his own positionality by saying:

> Should I stay in Paris? Should I join one of the flourishing avant-garde groups, that fascinate me by their audacity and follow their example? I fear to break away from my own heritage by throwing myself in a flow of innovative pictorial movements while progressively distancing myself from Egyptian arts to which I feel a strong tie.[12]

His double career as a painter-diplomat enabled Naghi to get involved in cultural policies. In 1926, for instance, he took advantage of his position as attaché to the Royal Legation in Paris to represent Egypt at the first Congress of Popular Arts in Prague.[13] It was in Paris that he befriended the Cubist painter André Lhote, who would mark Naghi on a theoretical level; as well as the influential writer and feminist Juliette Adam, founder of *La Nouvelle Revue*, whose portrait he would paint in 1923. A fervent supporter of Egyptian independence and close to the nationalist leader Mustafa Kamil, Adam had notably expressed her anti-colonial ideas in her book *L'Angleterre en Égypte*, published in 1922.

During that time Mohamed Naghi conceived his *Renaissance of Egypt* (also known as the *Cortège of Isis*) to decorate the new Egyptian Parliament in 1923. The commission of this work was highly symbolic, as it was intended to celebrate the end of the British protectorate and the promulgation of a new Constitution. Naghi's large decorative painting represents Isis, the goddess of fertility and maternity, leading a triumphal cortège as a symbol of Egypt's rebirth. The inauguration of this decorative painting was also connected to the discovery of the tomb of Tutankhamun, excavated in 1922 by the British Egyptologist Howard Carter, whose impact in Egypt was unprecedented. As the official opening of the tomb coincided with the first freely elected Parliament, the link between ancient Egypt and contemporary politics was explicitly established.

In 1932 Naghi was sent by the Egyptian Ministry of Foreign Affairs to Addis Ababa, at a time when tensions were growing between the Ethiopian monarchy and the Italian government over the presence of its military troops in the country. This was the beginning of what is known as his Abyssinian period, a prolific production characterised by the use of warm colours and bright light to depict scenes of Ethiopian court life, including several portraits of Negus Haile Selassie (Fig. 12.10).

As a diplomat, Naghi did not clearly express his political opinions concerning Mussolini's Fascist regime and the invasion of Ethiopia. Nevertheless, he expressed his admiration for the Italian Futurists: for Ungaretti, his friend, but also for Filippo Tommaso Marinetti, who was born in Alexandria and did believe in a national art that would serve progress and modernisation. Naghi would become the first Egyptian to head the School of Fine Arts in Cairo in 1937, and after the Second World War he was appointed director of the Egyptian Academy in Rome in 1947. Because of his status as a diplomat, Naghi was, amongst others, an influential intermediary and participated actively in the implementation of cultural policies in Egypt.

INTERMEDIARIES

Among the intermediaries who played a significant part in promoting art in Egypt was the politician and art collector Mohamed Mahmoud Khalil, who headed the Society of the Friends of Art, as well as the annual Cairo Salon for nearly twenty years. Khalil spent his life travelling between Cairo and Paris, where he and his French wife, Emilienne Luce, acquired an important collection of French Impressionist and Post-Impressionist art, including works by Monet, Manet, Rodin and Gauguin (to name only a few), which are displayed in their former home in Giza (today the Mohamed Mahmoud Khalil Museum).

△ FIG. 12.10: Mohamed Naghi, *Religious Procession*, Addis Ababa, 1932. Tate.

His diplomatic ties with France led him to be appointed artistic director of the Egyptian Pavilion at the 1937 World Exhibition in Paris, called the International Exhibition of the Arts and Techniques of Modern Life, where Egypt was represented for the first time as an independent nation. This exhibition would enable him to import artworks from the Louvre and the Musée du Luxembourg the following year to Cairo for a large exhibition of French art.

The Egyptian Pavilion, designed by the architect Roger Lardat, was articulated around four main themes: agriculture, tourism archaeology and applied arts. Mohamed Naghi was commissioned to decorate the entrance hall with a large vertical panel called *The Tears of Isis* (Fig. 12.11). The panel represents Isis weeping and praying over the dead body of her husband and brother Osiris, who was murdered out of jealousy by her brother Seth, and fertilising the land of Egypt with her tears (Fig. 12.12).

Produced more than a decade after *The Renaissance of Egypt* for the Egyptian Parliament, Naghi refers, once again, to the Osirian myth. In the centre of this composition stands an imposing and majestic Isis, dressed in a white tunic, her hands crossed over her chest in a gesture of mourning. In the background a peasant nonchalantly drives his oxen in front of the funerary temple of Deir el-Bahari, entrenched in the mountainous landscape of the Valley of the Dead. At the feet of the goddess, two men carry a sarcophagus on the sly.

This scene could refer to Naghi's involvement in the field of cultural heritage and suggest an allusion to the looting of tombs in the Theban Valley, or to the restitution of Egyptian antiquities by European nations, which was then already part of the public debate. Indeed, in the 1920s the question of restitution arose not only in the context of antiquities but also of contemporary objects. For instance, the feminist Huda Shaarawi, who founded the Egyptian Feminist Union in 1923, and her colleague Saiza Nabarawi, with whom she established the monthly journal *L'Égyptienne*, had called for the restitution of Mahmoud Mokhtar's sculptures from France to Egypt after his death.

Egyptian feminists were also influential intermediaries and patrons politically committed to the nationalist cause and decolonisation. They had founded the feminine counterpart of Mohamed Mahmoud Khalil's society, called the Women's Committee of the Society of the Friends of Art. This branch of the Society was also committed to the revival of traditional crafts as an essential part of identity-building. These ideas were regularly published in *L'Égyptienne*, which often linked the revival of traditional crafts to the revival of the creative force of ancient Egypt.

◁ FIG. 12.11: View of the central hall of the Egyptian Pavilion of the *Exposition Internationale* in Paris, 1937, featuring Mogamed Naghi's panel *Les Larmes d'Isis*, a portrait by Mahmoud Saïd of his daughter Nadia (on the right) and Mahmoud Mokhtar's bronze *Head of Saad Zaghloul* (in the centre). From 'Egypt in Paris' published in *al-Musawar*, no. 356, 1937. Archives ArtTalks.

△ FIG. 12.12: Mohamed Naghi, *Les Larmes d'Isis* (The Tears of Isis), central panel of the Egyptian Pavilion for the *Exposition Internationale* in Paris, 1937. Mohamed Naghi Museum.

▷ FIG. 12.13: Inji Efflatoun, *Harvesting the Dates*, 1973. Private Collection.

In 1924 Huda Shaarawi established and financed a craft school in the poor neighbourhood of Rud al-Farag, located north of Cairo, to provide free training to young people in pottery and ceramics. The school's objective was to serve the discourse of authenticity by producing ceramics that were allegedly made 'by the children of the country in the purest Egyptian tradition', but that were, in fact, created by highly skilled artisans, some of whom had been trained in the manufacture of Sèvres at Shaarawi's expense.[14, 15] She had tried, not without difficulty, to present the ceramics of the school at the Cairo Salon. These craft schools thus proposed a counter-narrative to the claim that the fine arts, understood as having been imposed by the colonial presence, were superior to applied or decorative arts.

Egyptian feminists also claimed the right for women to access the School of Fine Arts in Cairo, invoking the example of Turkey and Mustafa Kemal Atatürk's reforms of the Academy of Fine Arts in Istanbul, which was open to women. They encouraged women artists, who – despite their exclusion from the School until the 1950s – took private lessons in artists' studios and actively participated in the Cairo Salon.

One of them was the artist, feminist and political activist Inji Efflatoun, who benefited from the support of the feminist elite even during her imprisonment under Gamal Abdel Nasser's regime for her political activities in the communist organisation *Iskra*. She continued to paint during her incarceration between 1959 and 1963, mainly portraits of her fellow detainees and views from the window of her prison cell. After her release her style evolved towards a lighter touch, often leaving parts of the canvas apparent, and she represented everyday scenes, life in the countryside and artisanal activities (Fig. 12.13).

Artists such as Efflatoun would mark a shift in Egyptian modern art, in the context of disillusion with the *nahda* project and the growing political tensions and social issues felt at the dawn of the Second World War and the beginning of the 1939 economic depression. It is in this context that the revolutionary avant-gardes such as the Egyptian Surrealist group would emerge and distance themselves from the illusion of ancient Egypt as an expression of collective identities. ⊙

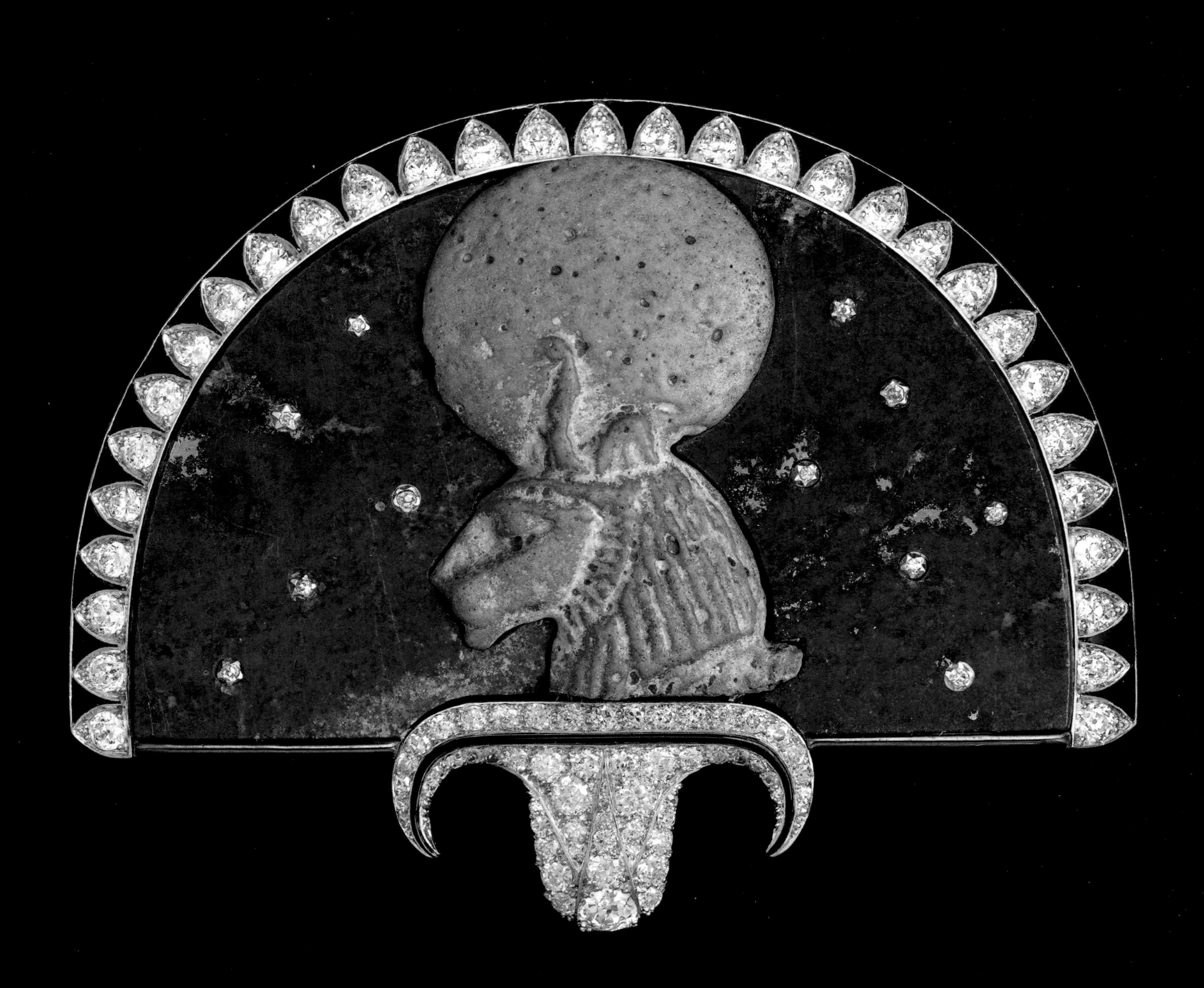

13 EGYPTO-DECO OR HOW TUT SHAPED MODERN LIFE

GHISLAINE WOOD

When Agatha Christie's *Death on the Nile* was published in 1937, it came towards the end of a period that had witnessed intense fascination with ancient Egypt. From the discovery of Tutankhamun's tomb in 1922, ancient Egypt had profoundly shaped notions of pleasure, escape, entertainment, consumption and, ultimately, the modern experience in the popular consciousness. With its elegant Art Deco cover, recalling historical views of the Great Temple at Abu Simbel, *Death on the Nile* used the backdrop of ancient Egypt for a very modern murder mystery (Fig. 13.2).[1] The novel's contemporary themes of travel, glamour, greed, deception, shifting identities and the disruption of wealth and class structures ensured that it became an enormous hit and further embedded Egypt under the skin of popular culture. By 1937 Egypt's influence could, of course, be seen across almost all spheres of life, from what people wore to where they lived and worked,

◁ FIG. 13.1: Cartier London, Brooch, 1923. Nils Herrmann, Collection Cartier.

▷ FIG. 13.2: Robin Macartney, Cover design for *Death on the Nile* by Agatha Christie, watercolour, *c.*1937. The Christie Archive Trust.

to what they did for fun or bought for their homes. It was a pervasive presence and often an active agent, as in Christie's novel, lining the fabric of modern life – a pylon here, a lotus or sun disc there. Paradoxically then, ancient Egypt came to represent the modern for many people for much of the interwar period.

TUT

Most of this fascination was spawned by the discovery of the tomb of Tutankhamun. Against the backdrop of a shifting political landscape as Egypt strived for independence from British control, Howard Carter found in the Valley of the Kings one of the only largely intact pharaonic tombs ever to have been discovered. It can fairly be described as one of the most significant moments in not just Western archaeological history but cultural history, and one that had the effect of dramatically collapsing time, as hundreds of near-pristine 3,000-year-old objects were removed from the tomb and recorded, for consumption by the world's media. The find transfixed audiences everywhere and accelerated change in many spheres. In Egypt, Tutankhamun became a nationalist symbol for a newly independent country, while the find transformed the field of Egyptian archaeological discovery and restructured colonial relations (see Chapter 12). But it followed a period when the mystique of Egypt had been growing steadily and when figures like Howard Carter were part of wider colonial networks and structures that helped to disseminate both knowledge and the material culture of ancient Egypt around the world.

Before the discovery of the tomb, Carter had been in Egypt for many years working at sites along the Nile and in various capacities. He was born in 1874 in Swaffham, Norfolk, into a family of artists, and his father Samuel John Carter was a well-known animal-portrait painter and taught his son to paint. Howard became a proficient watercolourist and, through his father's patrons, Lord and Lady Amherst (William Tyssen Amherst was a collector and supporter of several excavations in Egypt), he first encountered ancient Egypt. He was invited to record works in the Amherst collection at Didlington Hall in Norfolk and was then recommended by Amherst to Professor Percy E. Newberry. Newberry, a lecturer in Egyptology at the University of Cairo and on the staff of the Egyptian Museum of Antiquities, took Carter on and in 1890 the seventeen-year-old was employed at the British Museum for several months, before travelling to Egypt to record archaeological sites and objects as a junior draughtsman on the staff of the Egyptian Exploration Fund (EEF) (now Society).[2]

In Egypt, Carter became an assistant to one of the most influential archaeologists to shape the field, Sir William Flinders Petrie, and worked with him at Amarna and then on several sites, including the tombs at Beni Hasan and the mortuary temple of Queen Hatshepsut at Deir el-Bahari, recording the reliefs, decorations and inscriptions for the EEF. Carter's depictions of the painted wall scenes in the tombs at Beni Hasan remain important records, where the original decorations have since suffered extensive degradation, and his excellent draughtsmanship in documenting objects and sites was invaluable at a time when colour photography did not exist.[3] For instance, his watercolour of the dummy vases in the tomb of Yuya and Thuya reveals the vivid colours and skill employed by the ancient Egyptian craftsmen in creating the *trompe l'oeil* effect of precious materials (Fig. 13.3). His sensitive depiction of a hoopoe bird emerging from a gap in a wall reveals his interest in the natural world of Egypt. Beyond the pure recording and documenting of sites, Carter produced many studies of birds, animals and landscapes over his years in the field (Fig. 13.4).

By 1899 he had risen swiftly and was appointed to the post of inspector of monuments in Upper Egypt

▽ FIG. 13.3: Howard Carter, Dummy Vases of Painted Wood, watercolour, after 1905. Private Collection Rupert Wace.

△ FIG. 13.4: Howard Carter, *Under the Protection of the Gods*, watercolour, 1908. Private Collection Rupert Wace.

and Nubia. He continued to have a successful career with the Egyptian Antiquities Service until 1905, when a quarrel with visitors to Saqqara resulted in a diplomatic incident and he resigned from his post. Thereafter Carter made a living selling his watercolours and dealing in ancient Egyptian artefacts until, in 1907, he was introduced to Lord Carnarvon.

The 5th Earl of Carnarvon had developed a passion for archaeology after visiting Egypt to convalesce, and he employed Carter to lead his excavations, first at several sites near Thebes, until the concession for the Valley of the Kings became available in 1914. The inhospitable and barren rock valley, on the opposite side of the Nile from the ancient city of Thebes, had from the reign of Thutmose I become the burial site for the kings of the New Kingdom, who initiated the tradition of using hidden burial chambers to avoid grave-robbing. Carter's familiarity with the site and his admiration for the magnificent tombs of Seti I and Ramses II (robbed of their contents in Antiquity) led to his desire to excavate in the valley, believing that there were tombs of the New Kingdom that were unaccounted for.[4]

With the outbreak of the First World War, Carter did not start to dig until the autumn of 1917 and then employed a systematic methodology developed by Flinders Petrie in the 1890s. Digging to the bedrock in a grid system, he found little over the next few years, and in early 1922 Carnarvon was ready to give up the concession. With one area left to excavate, Carter convinced him to extend the dig for a further year. The steps to the tomb of Tutankhamun were found on 4 November 1922, and the riches within took Carter more than ten years to record, conserve and clear. His team meticulously, by the standards of the period, documented each step of the process, describing in notes, drawings and photography every object and its position.

Once the enormity of the discovery was clear, Carter assembled a group of specialists to work on the tomb and amongst these was the photographer Harry Burton, who was instrumental in framing how the tomb and its contents were seen.[5] Works from the tomb were documented in a series of Burton's photos sent to *The London Times* as part of a contract that Carnarvon signed. *The Times* had exclusive access to news of the discoveries and images and sold the rights on to publications including *The Illustrated London News*, which covered the finds in great detail. The selling of the exclusive rights to a British newspaper was contentious at a moment when issues concerning the 'ownership' of the tomb were being played out against a fraught political backdrop. As one of Carter's fellow archaeologists, Arthur Weigall, highlighted, the new political landscape of an independent Egypt was shifting perceptions:

> You have found this tomb, however at a moment when the least spark may send the whole magazine sky high, when the utmost diplomacy is needed, when Egyptians have to be considered in a way to which you and I are not accustomed, and when the slightest false step may do the utmost disservice to our own country.[6]

Retaining control of the Suez Canal remained uppermost in British political interests, but the perceived British 'ownership' and control of the tomb, and the dissemination of its imagery worldwide, was problematic for the Egyptian Antiquities Service and the newly independent nation. Harry Burton's dramatically lit and striking photos did more than

◁FIG. 13.5: Harry Burton, Photograph showing the sealed doorway to the Burial Chamber, after most of the objects in the Antechamber had been removed but with sentinel statues still in place. Published in *The Times*, 5 March 1923. Private Collection Rupert Wace.

bring the material culture of the tomb to audiences – they triggered a craze with enormous commercial repercussions, but one completely divorced from contemporary Egyptian identity or control. Every detail of every object was scrutinised and copied, and often copyrighted, for worldwide consumption (Fig. 13.5).

EGYPTO-DECO

Ancient Egyptian aesthetics were already being lauded in the fashionable circles of the Paris art world prior to 1922 and the discovery of the tomb (see Chapter 11). The French writer and critic Guillaume Apollinaire, writing in 1917, linked ancient Egypt to the contemporary fashion for Africa, connecting or eliding pan-African art forms in ways that fundamentally shaped approaches to contemporary design:

> It is ... impossible at present to assign a definite date to these beautiful wooden fetishes, some of which are of great antiquity (I am speaking here of the African idols). Their characteristic style attests to an unquestionable relation with Egyptian aesthetics, from which they derive; unless, on the contrary, it was the African works that influenced the Egyptian artists – which would also amply justify the current interest in them.[7]

The widespread interest in a range of non-Western cultures that was facilitated by the flow of objects arriving in Paris from her colonies created the particular conditions for the emergence of an eclectic new style in the decorative arts, which became known as Art Deco. However, the discovery of the tomb accelerated the appetite for Egyptian-styled fashions, interior design and architecture, and France's long engagement with Egypt provided a rich seedbed for the emergence of a new style that incorporated Egyptian forms into its decorative repertoire. Like the Empire style of a century earlier, which heavily utilised Egyptian decorative elements and in turn influenced a new generation of designers in the early twentieth century, Art Deco absorbed Egypt, becoming the modern decorative, commercially contingent style that dominated the Paris *Exposition Internationale des Arts Décoratifs et Industriels Modernes* of 1925 and then spread around the world, borne on a sea of greater global connectivity.

Egypt was easily assimilated into the eclectic language of Art Deco and could be traced not only in the forms and materials employed, but also through the influence of many of its early pioneers, including the designers Paul Poiret, George Barbier, Eileen Gray and Jean Dunand, amongst others. From Henri Sauvage's 1928 design for a low-cost block of flats that emulated the stepped pyramid at Saqqara, to Eileen Gray's or Jean Dunand's sensuous use of gold lacquer and direct borrowing of Egyptian forms, these designers did much to popularise the Egyptian decorative thread running through Art Deco, while the interconnected and interdependent worlds of fashion and interior design became the crucible both for the development of Art Deco and for the dissemination of Egyptian style during the 1920s and beyond.

The Parisian fashion designer Paul Poiret was a key figure in the early popularisation of Egyptian fashions, with his range of Egyptian-inspired clothes and his exotic Middle Eastern-themed parties, such as 'The Thousand and Second Night', held in Paris in June 1911. His eclectic beaded dresses, which incorporated Egyptian motifs alongside a range of other sources, were influential before the discovery of Tut's tomb, but after 1922 many designers rushed to issue Egyptian collections, with ancient motifs drawn from the iconography of the tomb now littering gowns and accessories. French designer Jeanne Paquin's *Momie* design for an evening dress for summer 1923, with its gold lamé and embroidered peplum front, was typical of the wave of Egyptian fashions. These designs were quickly disseminated from the Paris couture houses and were widely copied around the world (Fig. 13.6). With names such as the 'Luxor gown' or 'mummy wrap', they were distinguished by low waists, layering, fabrics falling to the ankles and the use of Egyptian motifs and colour combinations.

A range of embroidered evening jackets and coats, probably made in Britain in the late 1920s, employed hieroglyphs in cartouches and represented the more literal translation of Egyptian symbols into fashions, precipitated by the discovery of the tomb (Fig. 13.7).[8] More expensive beaded and embroidered examples of eveningwear were followed by printed fabrics with Egyptian patterns for daywear. Agatha Christie, for example, was photographed wearing her fashionable printed Egyptian-motif day-dress on several occasions, while a dress from the early 1930s used a pattern depicting an Egyptian landscape replete with pyramids and palm trees. Both spoke to the range of inventive

▽ FIG. 13.6: Paquin Ltd, 'Momie' gold lamé evening dress with Egyptian-style embroidered peplum in front, designed by Madeleine Wallis, 1923. Victoria and Albert Museum. Given by the House of Worth.

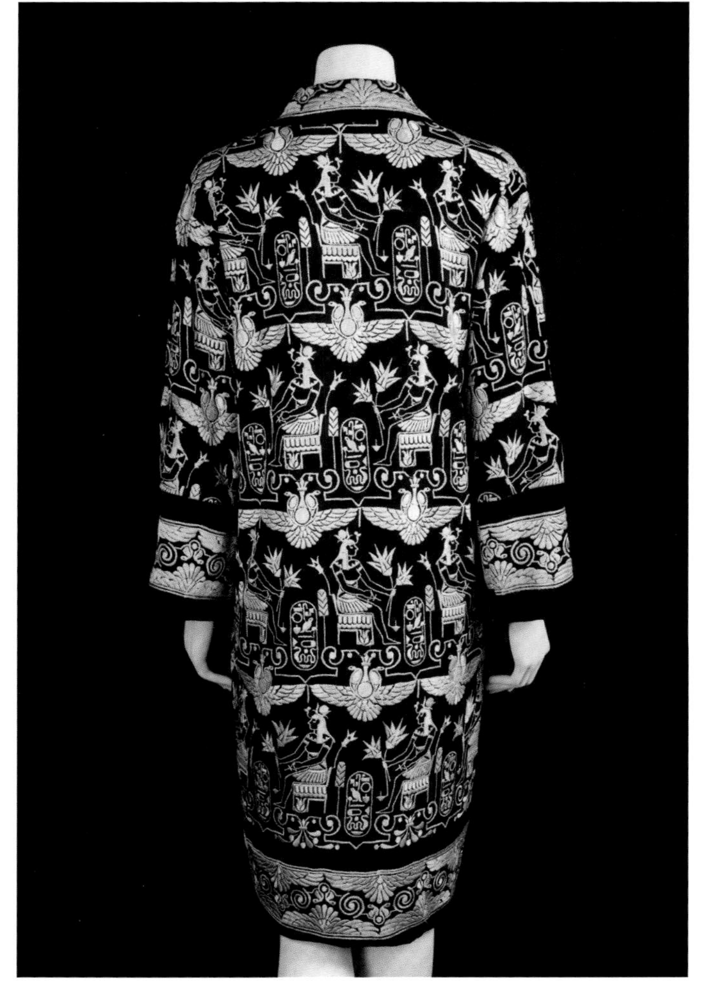

▷ FIG. 13.7: Evening coat with Egyptian-style embroidered decoration, late 1920s. Collection of Cleo and Mark Butterfield: C20 Vintage Fashion.

new patterns available (Figs. 13.8 and 13.9). Printed furnishing fabrics were produced alongside textiles for dress, with firms such as the Lancashire-based Steiner & Co. designing a number of patterns based on hieroglyphs.

The field of fashion illustration helped to establish the taste for Egyptian themes. George Barbier was one of the leading fashion illustrators of the period, who, with Paul Iribe and Georges Lepape, did much to promote early Art Deco style and the fashions of Paul Poiret in the pages of fashion magazines such as *Art, Goût, Beauté* and the *Gazette du Bon Ton*. Barbier's most overtly Egyptian project was for the illustrations of *Le Roman de la momie* by Théophile Gautier, which was republished by A. & G. Mornay in Paris in 1929 (Fig. 13.10). Gautier's text was first published in book form in 1858 and illustrated the mid-nineteenth-century preoccupation with the mysteries of Egypt and its appetite for the occult, but Barbier's illustrations were a thoroughly contemporary interpretation of the subject.[9] The book's highly stylised, decorative scenes employ strong colour and flat repeating patterns, and are reflective of the wider sphere of fashion illustration that Barbier came to define, although by the late 1920s this style of illustration was on the decline in fashion magazines. Barbier also worked for the popular entertainment review *Les Folies Bergère* and with the illustrator Erté, created Egyptian-themed sets, costumes and promotional material that did much to promote ancient Egypt in the sphere of popular entertainment.

◁ FIG. 13.8: Agatha Christie wearing a dress with printed Egyptian pattern. Setting off on a world tour aboard RMS Kildonan Castle from Southampton, January 1922. The Christie Archive Trust.

▽ FIG. 13.9: Day dress, printed rayon crepe, 1930s. Collection of Cleo and Mark Butterfield: C20 Vintage Fashion.

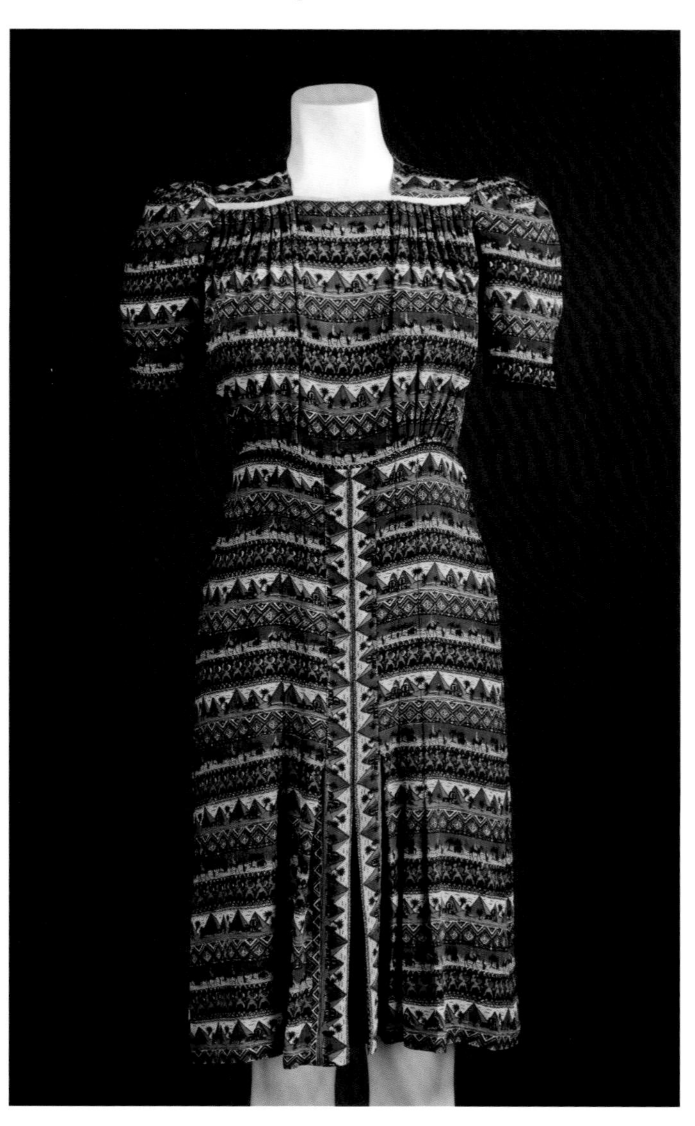

de perles d'or.
Pharaon parut sur le seuil de la salle; une vipère d'or ceignait son épaisse chevelure, et une calasiris, dont les plis ramenés par devant formaient la pointe, lui entourait le corps de la ceinture aux genoux. Un seul gorgerin cerclait son cou aux muscles invaincus.
En apercevant le roi, Tahoser voulut se lever de son siège et se prosterner; mais Pharaon vint à elle, la releva et la fit asseoir.

286

△ FIG. 13.10: George Barbier, Illustration from *Le Roman de la momie* by Théophile Gautier, 1929. Shapero Rare Books.

Paris as the centre of luxury consumption – a position that the city firmly re-established with the exhibition of 1925 – held sway over the perception and adoption of fashionable new trends, and many Parisian luxury companies launched products that were Egyptian-inspired. Cartier produced a range of Egyptian pieces that married a love of Egyptian style with the passion for acquiring real Egyptian antiquities. Louis Cartier, one of the three Cartier brothers, collected ancient Egyptian antiquities, bought from the dealers Kalebdjian Frères and Dikran Kelekian, both of whom opened businesses in Paris. Louis not only exhibited these works in his home, but also developed the idea of synthesising ancient and modern, by incorporating fragments of ancient faience into pieces of new jewellery. Mounting pieces in modern settings using platinum, diamonds and a variety of stones employed by the ancient Egyptians, such as carnelian, turquoise and lapis lazuli, Cartier created unique pieces that played on the allure of wearing ancient amulets. It is important to note that, while Cartier was buying pieces from Parisian dealers which may have come from legitimate sources, many antiquities left Egypt through unregulated trade.

The wearing of ancient grave goods was not a new idea; the Kalebdjian Frères had staged an exhibition in 1913 for which the catalogue stated, 'Today fashion decrees that the elegant Parisienne should wear ancient jewelry; and not merely stale imitations, but the very jewels themselves that once adorned the bosom of an Egyptian queen or a Greek empress.[10] Cartier's pieces became extremely popular, but were produced in relatively small numbers. One striking example of around 1923 incorporates an ancient green-glazed bust of the goddess Sekhmet set against a lapis-lazuli sky with diamond stars (Fig. 13.1). Pieces such as this helped Cartier establish a reputation around in the world, but particularly in Cairo, where it became supplier to King Fuad and the Egyptian court. During the 1920s another leading French jewellery company, Van Cleef & Arpels, produced a range of exquisitely constructed lightweight and flexible bracelets that incorporated Egyptian motifs (Fig. 13.12). Utilising precious stones, they exploited the colour contrasts of rubies, sapphires and other gems to create decorative friezes. The company also devised an adaptable clip that could be worn on a hat, belt or dress.

Beyond fashion, other luxury sectors to exploit the commercial potential of ancient Egypt included the perfume industry. The company Parfums Bichara was founded in 1896 by Bichara Malhamé – 'The Syrian Perfumer', as he described himself – and produced perfumes, cosmetics and hair products for markets in Europe and the Middle East. Using the actress Sarah Bernhardt to endorse his perfumes, the company became very successful at the turn of the nineteenth century, supplying perfumes to the royal Egyptian court. Bichara's perfume *Ramses II* of 1928 was sold in a striking obelisk-shaped bottle covered in hieroglyphs and was made by the French luxury glass manufacturer Compagnie des Cristalleries de Saint-Louis. It came in a similarly shaped and decorated cardboard box (Fig. 13.13). The symbolism of obelisks held particular resonance in France, as the first Egyptian obelisk to be erected in Europe since the Roman period was in the Place de la Concorde in 1831, given by Muhammad Ali Pasha, Vice-Regent of Egypt, to Louis XVIII.

Alongside Bichara, the Egyptian-French company Parfums Ramses had offices in Paris and Istanbul and was established in 1916 by M. de Bertalot with Orosdi-Back. It was best known for its luxury perfumes and

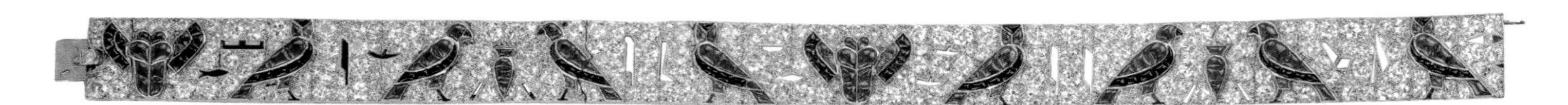

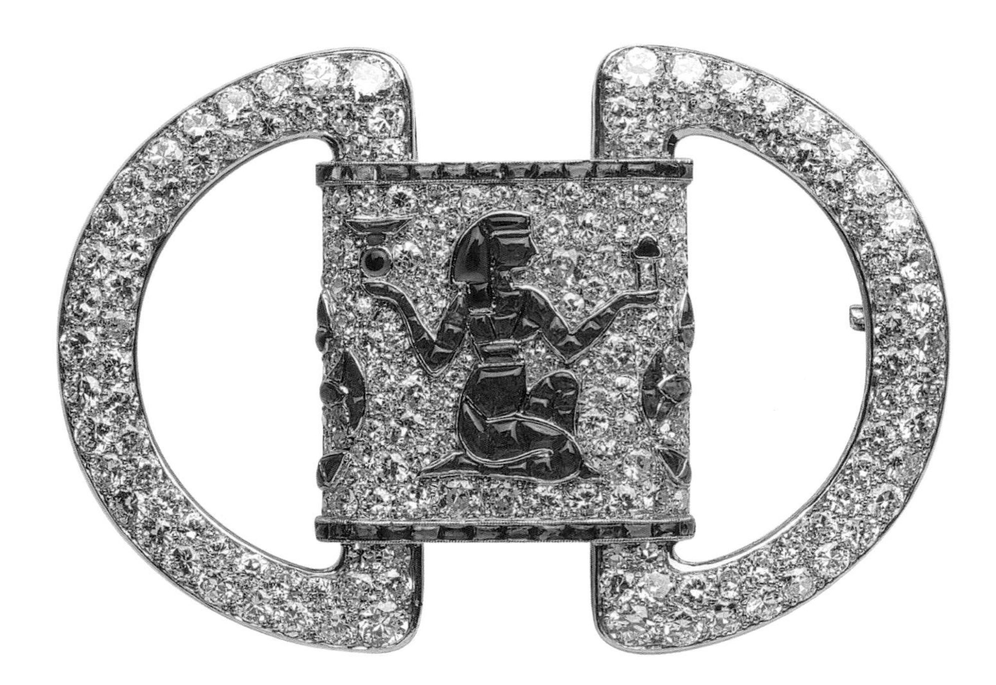

△ ◁ FIG. 13.12: Van Cleef & Arpels, Paris, 'Egyptian inspiration' bracelet and brooch, 1924–25. Van Cleef & Arpels.

▽ FIG. 13.13: Parfums Bichara, Ramses perfume bottle manufactured by Saint-Louis, France with box, 1928.

cosmetics with ancient Egyptian themes, and it became a major exporter to Africa and the Far East. The company's Paris shop had five monumental marble figures of pharaohs on the façade, which was sadly destroyed in 1929 after the company closed. Ramses produced a number of popular perfumes, including *Ambre de Nubie* and the *Sphinx d'Or*, which was launched in 1923 in a sphinx-shaped bottle. As with Bichara, the bottle was produced by a leading French crystal company, Baccarat. Of course the link between perfume and cosmetics, with their exotic and foreign ingredients, and Egypt, with its ancient association with beauty, was an easy one for the industry to exploit and promote. The allure of these products was that they were perceived to be from Egypt.

After the discovery of Tutankhamun's tomb, tourist travel to Egypt swiftly increased and a number of travel companies responded by developing the market for Egyptian travel. Thomas Cook, who had been established in Egypt for more than half a century, resumed steamboat Nile cruises and introduced new ships; but perhaps the most extraordinary statements

of 'Tutmania' were two new ships launched on the Marseilles-to-Alexandria line by Compagnie des Messageries Maritimes (MM). The Marseilles-based MM dominated the eastern Mediterranean and Indo-China lines during the 1920s, servicing the French colonies of North Africa and the Far East. During the 1920s the president of the company, Georges Philippar, injected a new vision and energy into the designs of the company's fleet that built on earlier traditions of ship decoration, which evoked a romantic vision of the destination country to which the ship travelled.

The two new ships running to Egypt spectacularly represented this trend. *Champollion* (1925) and the *Mariette-Pacha* (1926) embodied the passion for all things Egyptian, as spawned by the discovery of Tutankhamun's tomb. The public spaces were richly decorated, fusing neo-Egyptian motifs with modern elements and creating extraordinary fantasy spaces where Egyptian imagery ran through their design from the paintings, furniture and decorative metalwork of the lift cages and balustrades, to the richly patterned carpets with their interspersed lotus and papyrus patterns. Papyrus-form columns (copies of those found in the Great Aten Temple at Tell el-Amarna), Egyptian-style sculptures and a painting of an ancient Egyptian barge by the Orientalist painter Jean Lefeuvre adorned the extraordinary glass-roofed hall on board *Champollion*.[11] The MM ships were emblematic of a desire within the wider French cultural sphere of architecture and design to present a grander vision of France (and her colonial aspirations) – one that was fully exploited at the Paris Colonial Exposition of 1931.

WIDER MARKETS

Beyond the luxury markets of Paris, many companies around the world developed commemorative ware to mark the discovery of the tomb. A huge range of objects were produced, but one of the industries most quickly able to respond was ceramics manufacture. In Britain companies such as Wedgwood, which had historically produced Egyptian-inspired pieces, issued new ranges, while from 1921 Carter, Stabler and Adams (CSA) in Poole established a new range of highly fashionable modern pieces retailed through the department stores Liberty and Heal's. A dramatic papyrus-pattern design employed the bright colours and painterly style that became typical of CSA's output and made the company one of the most popular producers of wares in the Art Deco style.

Perhaps the most distinctive range produced to mark the discovery, though, was Carlton Ware's 'Tutankhamen' produced in Stoke-on-Trent from 1923 (Fig. 13.14).[12] Carlton Ware concentrated on the decorative giftware end of the domestic pottery market

▷ FIG. 13.14: Carlton Ware, vase, lidded jar and lidded dish, *c.*1923. Private Collection.

and produced decal and hand-painted tablewares. The 'Tutankhamen' range was decorated with gilt-transfer prints and enamel-painting. Inspired directly by objects from the tomb, the range incorporated moulded pharaoh heads on lids that were based on the sentinel statues, which were some of the first objects from the tomb to be widely disseminated in photographs and were extensively copied. The dramatic gold-and-black colours of the sentinel statues were reproduced in the Carlton Ware figure-heads and were applied to bodies in a number of colour combinations (Fig. 13.5).

The ceramics industry quickly developed patterns and manufactured new ranges in response to the demand for Egyptian-inspired works, and this was equally true for pressed glass and tin, and for other industries that could produce new moulds and adapt their manufacture. But attendant with the demand for new products was a growth in the manufacture of objects made in Cairo, for the tourist market and for export. Highly intricate marquetry work – using materials such as bone, straw and coloured woods, and applied to a range of decorative objects, including tables, benches, boxes and trays – had historically been produced in Cairo for export, and by incorporating ancient Egyptian motifs based on finds in the tomb, the Western market for these decorative objects increased.

ARCHITECTURE

For many people in the later 1920s Egyptian-style buildings were becoming a familiar sight on many high streets and were indelibly associated with modernity – newly built factories, office blocks and cinemas were the sites for modern industries, modern entertainment and modern consumption. Writing in the *Architects' Journal* (*AJ*) on 'Landmarks of the Year, A Retrospect of 1928', Professor C. H. Reilly singled out the bold new Egyptian-styled Carreras cigarette factory in London's Mornington Crescent for special comment:

> one must admit that the building has a certain strength and unity. It looks admirably suited to its purpose which is to be both an airy, clean factory and a good advertisement. It is the later quality one fears. We may have whole districts of our towns destroyed by advertising buildings in bright colours ... Poor old Mornington Crescent, I feel sorry for it with this highly made-up neighbour blocking the views it had enjoyed.[13]

Reilly was here rehearsing a well-worn discourse to be found in pages of the AJ: the architectural establishment's disdain for what was perceived as brash decorative Modernism, described in one article of 1929 as the 'Dressmaker's style', a nod to Art Deco's origins in Paris's fashion and design networks.[14] The Carreras cigarette factory did indeed prefigure a slew of industrial buildings and cinemas built during the late 1920s and 1930s in the Egyptian style, which were very consciously 'advertising buildings in bright colours'. In fact the Egyptian style became a preferred decorative idiom that was particularly selected for commercial and entertainment architecture.

▽ FIG. 13.15: Design for Ferry Engineering Works (Willans and Robinson Limited), Queensferry, 1901–06. RIBA Collections.

◁ FIG. 13.16: Greater London House, formerly the Carreras Cigarette factory, London, 1928.

△ FIG. 13.17: Carreras Cigarette factory, the Boardroom on the ground floor, 1928. RIBA Collections.

However, the forms of Egyptian-inspired architecture that used the pylon, amongst other elements (and was influenced by monuments such as the Temple of Edfu), had been utilised in earlier industrial buildings, such as the Willans and Robinson Ltd Ferry Engineering Works, designed by Harry Bulkeley Creswell (Fig. 13.15). Creswell had worked as inspecting engineer for the Crown Agents for the Colonies, and his factory at Queensferry in Flintshire (1901–06), with its huge pylon-like tower and battered Egyptianising piers articulating each bay, was a grand statement in ancient Egyptian massing and form. The factories of the late 1920s and 1930s, by contrast, often relied on colourful exterior decoration and Egyptianising motifs, these elements providing a sensuous skin to large-span concrete structures.

Egypt clearly signalled carefree commercial modernity, but also often expressed a colonial exoticism, and the Carreras cigarette factory was a case in point. One of the most dramatic buildings in the style, the factory was designed by Marcus Evelyn Collins and Owen Hyman Collins with A. G. Porri. In 1928, having outgrown previous sites, the Arcadia Works (as it was then called) opened in Mornington Crescent and was at the time the largest reinforced concrete factory in the country. Its monumental papyrus-form columns with red, green and blue decoration were based on the columns at the Tomb of Panehsy at Amarna, while the giant bronze black cats flanking the entrance referred both to the Carreras Black Cat brand of cigarettes and to the Egyptian goddess Bast. Indeed, the building was to have been called Bast House (Fig. 13.16).

Beyond the myriad Egyptian motifs on the exterior façade, such as the winged sun disc, exterior lamp fittings and Egyptian-inspired script, the decoration carried on into the interior. The boardroom was also richly decorated with Egyptian motifs – the painted ceiling and wall decoration included repeating lotus patterns and geometric forms. The boardroom chairs employed the fretwork of ancient Egyptian chairs and stools, emulating the Thebes stools produced by Liberty, while the side chairs featured animal-paw feet (Fig. 13.17). The careful coherence of the Egyptian theme running through the decorative scheme was also tied to the appropriateness of the Egyptianising decoration for the product being manufactured. The tobacco came from Turkey and was known as 'Egyptian tobacco', its association as a product from, and for, Empire being made clear in the decorative scheme. The opening events for the factory were a spectacle that reinforced Egypt as central to the company's identity. The road and pavements in front of the factory were covered in sand to evoke the desert, with actors in ancient Egyptian costume and a chariot being raced down Hampstead Road.

The Carreras was followed by a number of Egyptian-inspired factories as the style became expressive of modern industries and objectives. The architectural practice of Wallis Gilbert and Partners was one of the most successful firms to design industrial buildings in Britain and frequently adopted Egyptian forms. The firm was formed from a partnership between the US construction firm Kahncreet and the British architect Thomas Wallis and specialised in reinforced concrete producing large-scale industrial spaces. From the late 1920s it began to design a series of factories, many on London's arterial Western Avenue. The Firestone Factory (1928–29) was followed by the Pyrene Factory (1930–31), the India Tyre Factory at Inchinnan in Scotland (1930–31) and then the Hoover Building (1931–32), all with Egyptian elements.[15] Again, like Carreras, these buildings employed white cement façades with coloured decorative elements highlighted. The Pyrene Factory was described as a 'striking essay in white cement with highly coloured faience' and 'a gateway of industry in a rainbow of colour'. These carefree factories shifted the narrative around industrial buildings.[16] The Egyptian style became a symbol for new industries that had survived the Depression and were successfully expanding in a new age consumerism, led by the motor and electronic industries. In these buildings the Egyptian elements, such as the columns or porticoes, worked to articulate the long horizontal frontages. They were 'advertising buildings', in Reilly's words, whose conscious Egyptian styling and colours signalled the ambitions of modern manufacturing.

▽ FIG. 13.18: Foshay Tower in Minneapolis, Minnesota, USA, 1929. Designed by Léon Eugène Arnal, for the architects Magney & Tusler. Postcard from 1935.

In the US the Egyptian style was adapted to the modern American form of the skyscraper. Iconic Art Deco skyscrapers, such as the Chrysler Building, incorporated Egyptian motifs alongside a range of other elements and became symbolic of the power of the corporate American car industry. However, one of the most interesting towers of the period paid homage to the obelisk form. The Foshay Tower, built in Minnesota in 1929, was a thirty-two-floor and 136-metre-tall obelisk with a pyramid cap, its windows beautifully graduated as the soaring building tapered upwards (Fig 13.18). Once again, the starkness, purity and bold, simple forms of Egyptian architecture were translated into an unequivocally modern and forward-looking building. Indeed, many modernist architects, from Erich Mendelsohn to Le Corbusier, were influenced by the formal minimalism of Egyptian architecture, with monuments such as the mortuary temple of Hatshepsut proving particularly influential.

However, the most visible and influential promoter of mass-market Egyptian style was the film industry, and the theatres designed to house it. Egyptian-themed films, such as Karl Freund's *The Mummy* of 1932 with Boris Karloff and Cecil B. DeMille's *Cleopatra* of 1934, brought the tropes of ancient Egypt to enormous worldwide audiences, as Hollywood film outstripped everything except for the Bible and the Qur'an with its extraordinary reach.[17] A massive new wave of cinema-building took place to accommodate these vast new audiences. J. R. Learhart, giving the Royal Institute of British Architects lecture on 'Modern Cinema Design' in 1930, acknowledged that 'the modern cinema in all its complexity of planning and equipment has been aptly described as the architecture of pleasure ... Its appeal as being essentially directed to the great majority of average people who find in their picture theatres stimulation and pleasure ... in the atmosphere of warmth and comfort of colour and decoration – exotic in many cases.'[18] He went on to observe that 'in cinema design the outstanding current tendency is to internationalize decorative forms', listing Egypt as one style amongst a 'Rake's Progress' of appropriation. For modern audiences, Egypt denoted the fashionable and the fun, but carried with it a sense of history and grandeur in the wider architecture of pleasure – a feature exploited by many commercial architects.

London-born George Coles was one of the most famous and prolific cinema architects of the interwar years, designing nearly ninety theatres during the period. Forming a partnership with Percy Henry Adams in 1912, their company produced designs for Oscar Deutsch's Odeon chain, but it was for Carlton Cinemas that they delivered their most striking Egypto-Deco designs. The façades of the Carlton cinemas in Upton Park (1928) and Islington (1930) were some of the most dramatic and highly decorated buildings of the period. A distinctive feature of them was that they were clad with polychrome Hathernware tiles, an encaustic, moulded architectural tile produced in a range of colours and designs. These were used to dramatic effect to create the decorative schemes: a giant winged scarab dominates the façade at Upton Park, while friezes of colourful lotus flowers and giant papyrus columns feature in Islington (Fig.13.19). Sadly, the Egyptian-style decoration did not carry through to the interiors of the Carlton cinemas. However, one of the largest British cinemas in the Egyptian style was the Astoria at Streatham, built by Griggs and Son and designed by Edward A. Stone, which opened in 1930. Its Eygptian scheme ran through the entire building, and its interiors were designed by Henri & Laverdet. The foyer had a semi-vaulted ceiling and an elaborate plaster open frieze, supported by square piers with lotus capitals. Mural decorations depicting scenes from Egyptian history carried through the building and into the auditorium, while the ladies restroom featured a mural of an Egyptian female figure bathing in a lotus-filled pool (Fig.13.20). The brightly coloured Egyptianising decoration clearly evoked filmsets.

Egyptian-style architecture spread around the world, adopted in different contexts for different purposes; sometimes to denote a rejection of the colonial styles of Empire and in Egypt itself presenting a nationalist response to the new conditions of an independent nation. In all these contexts it denoted modernity and it was perhaps in the form and massing of ancient Egyptian architecture that its influence could be most clearly seen in new buildings around the world, rather than in the profusion of Egyptian decoration and motifs that the discovery of Tut's tomb had spawned across all media and made feel so contemporary. ⊙

△ FIG. 13.19: Carlton cinema, Upton Park, 1928. Cinema Theatre Association Archive

▷ FIG. 13.20: Astoria cinema, Streatham, 1930. The auditorium with its mural decoration. RIBA Collections.

黑人權力

14 PYRAMID POWER: COLD WAR 'EGYPTOMANIA' AND ITS AFTERLIVES

THEO WEISS

In the 1970s, amid ongoing Cold War tensions between East and West, 'Egyptomania' – a popular cultural and artistic phenomenon driven by a captivation with the icons and images of ancient Egypt – experienced an intense revival. Replaying many of the same fascinations that had marked the interest in this pharaonic legacy in the interwar period, this new wave was markedly global in its reach, diverse in its audiences and varied in its expressions. This fresh upsurge took in everyone from artists to politicians to celebrities and appeared in formats as wide-ranging as celluloid, canvas and vinyl, circulating in places as far apart as London, Cairo, Moscow and New York.

Of the many places in which this new fascination with the Egypt of the pharaohs emerged, three countries – Britain, Egypt and the United States – illustrate the internationalism of this renewed fervour and reveal its interconnected nature. Within this resurgence, 1972 marked a particularly significant moment. At this point museum exhibitions were highlighting Egyptian objects, and the visibility of Egyptian iconography in popular culture exploded. Beginning in that year, this essay explores how the visual cultures of these places on one side of the Iron Curtain were shaped by the fraught politics of the era and by a shared fascination with ancient Egyptian society that went far beyond the purely aesthetic, to speak directly to the concerns of the wider geopolitics of the Cold War era and the political realities that unfolded afterwards.

◁FIG. 14.1: Awol Erizku, *Nefertiti (Black Power)*, 2018. Sainsbury Centre, purchased with support from the Art Fund.

BRITAIN

In May 1972, during a packed mid-afternoon session at the House of Lords in Westminster, the subject of ancient Egypt and its significance to British society took centre-stage in an exchange between members. Following a debate on a recent request from NATO member states for the US to establish a new naval base in Greece, John Julius Cooper – Viscount Norwich – swung the discussion to more local matters. The viscount took to his feet to enquire whether 'in view of the quite extraordinary popularity' of an exhibition currently on show at the British Museum 'and the consequent difficulty of enjoying that exhibition at leisure', his fellow Lords might see fit to discuss with British Museum Trustees 'the possibility' of keeping this particular exhibition open until 2 a.m., 'by making government funds available'. As the viscount made clear, this particular issue was as urgent and vital as other, more obviously political matters, since it 'directly concerns everyone in this country' and was thus an issue in which 'the Government might legitimately intervene'.[1]

The exhibition in question was the British Museum's *Treasures of Tutankhamun*, which, at the time of Cooper's parliamentary appeal, had been open to the public for fewer than two months and was already on track to becoming the most-attended exhibition in British history (Fig. 14.2). Offering British visitors the most comprehensive display of items from Tutankhamun's tomb ever to be displayed outside Egypt, the exhibition showcased fifty objects (one for each year since Howard Carter and Lord Carnarvon's excavation of the site and, in late 1922, their entry into the tomb's innermost chambers). Across seven darkened galleries – each taking visitors deeper into the burial complex – viewers encountered artefacts including statues, canopic jars and furniture from the tomb and, in the show's final sections, the solid-gold mask of the young pharaoh. Although Carter's excavation was already well known to the British public, the blockbuster exhibition enabled UK audiences to examine every artefact for themselves and study their rich detailing up close. In doing so, it gave new energy to a familiar set of symbols that was further increased by pictures of those same symbols ceaselessly printed in national newspapers and magazines, in the mass-produced exhibition catalogue and in the numerous primetime television features that aired throughout the period. For the first time Tutankhamun was being presented to the British public so they could be part of the discovery and history that it revealed, rather than merely spectators of it.

Back in the House of Lords, concerned about an overnight museum becoming a haven for impropriety and indecorum (and conscious that such decisions sat ultimately with Museum Trustees), the Chamber concluded that instead of diverting government funds or overstretching police resources, the exhibition's run could be extended to give an even greater cross-section of the British public the opportunity to attend. Although this proposal was subsequently rejected, such extraordinary parliamentary interest in the event showed how the exhibition was inextricably entwined with diplomatic and geopolitical concerns, becoming a critical moment within the fraught political landscape of the Cold War by providing a powerful vehicle for reasserting Britain's power and prestige as the last vestiges of its global empire vanished.[2]

For Britain, Egypt had great significance, since it was there that it had maintained the Suez Canal, a vital piece of naval and trading infrastructure around which the final acts of the drama of imperial disintegration took place. Britain had effectively ruled Egypt since 1882, and in 1914 made Egypt a formal protectorate. But from the 1920s onwards Egyptian nationalism grew, culminating in full Egyptian independence in 1953. Despite this independence, Britain retained control of its major imperial asset, the Suez Canal, until 1956, when Egypt's president Gamal Abdel Nasser nationalised the waterway. This led to a British military attempt to re-enter Egypt and retake the canal – which failed so catastrophically that Britain's prime minister Anthony Eden was forced to resign and British-Egyptian relations were ruptured for decades to come.

Crucially, Britain's overconfidence also created an opportunity for Soviet influence in Egypt to grow. Under President Nasser, military support and various cultural and social projects were all underwritten with Soviet rubles. However, with Nasser's death in 1970 and the instalment of Anwar Sadat as president, Egyptian-Soviet relations began to sour. In this moment Britain saw an opportunity to rekindle and smooth relations with Egypt. Via UNESCO, the British state offered to support the rescue of ancient monuments that were soon to be swamped by Egypt's Aswan Dam. In exchange, Egypt would choose Britain as the first European nation to host an unparalleled exhibition of its cultural treasures – a gesture of goodwill and a commitment to closer friendship. For Britain, the transfer of Carter's finds from the Valley of Kings to the imperial metropole represented a rare triumph amid the ignominy of its empire's collapse, and the *Treasures of Tutankhamun* exhibition became an opportunity for late-imperial fanfare: the Royal Air Force was drafted in to transport priceless antiquities to Britain and the Queen was invited to host Egyptian dignitaries at its opening, all within the galleries of the nation's principal cultural establishment. Egypt's antiquities were once again made into the centrepiece of a very British spectacle.

Beyond such diplomatically charged displays, a fascination with ancient Egyptian visual culture fuelled a growing circle of independent artists throughout this period. Sometimes shunning the imperial wistfulness of their governments, and in other cases openly embracing it, artworks that referenced the

△ FIG. 14.2: Queues outside the British Museum in London for the *Treasures of Tutankhamun* exhibition, 30 March 1972.

ancient civilisation directly or drew heavily on a well-established reservoir of motifs – of pharaohs, pyramids and sphinxes – re-emerged in the latter half of the twentieth century, giving old material new meaning for a fresh generation of artists.

One artist animated by this long history of exchanges between Britain and Egypt, and by pharaonic Egyptian objects that he personally encountered in the British Museum, was the Bradford-born painter, printmaker and photographer David Hockey. It was during his years as a student at London's Royal College of Art that Hockney first signalled his interest in pharaonic iconography, Nilotic colourways and in the constant interplay between ancient and modern civilisations through his 1961 painting *A Grand Procession of Dignitaries in Semi-Egyptian Style* and, in the same year, *Egyptian Head Disappearing into Descending Clouds*. Both paintings were inspired by a poem by the Greek-Egyptian writer Constantine P. Cavafy, whose 1898 poem 'Waiting for the Barbarians' Hockney references in both the theatricality and half-hidden mystery of these images. In the following year, 1962, Hockney took this interest in a different, more satirical direction when he explored ancient Egypt's place in Western museums in his *Man in a Museum (or You're in the Wrong Movie)* (1962) (Fig. 14.3). Here Hockney played with the idea of living art and of the contradictions of the modern museum. In the painting, a roughly outlined human figure becomes dwarfed by a richly coloured, opulent pharaonic statue that seems to come alive only to turn its gaze offstage, away from its human onlookers.

At the age of 26 and having just graduated, Hockney undertook his own, personal tour of Egypt's ancient sites, first in 1963 (in the same year as Liz Taylor's *Cleopatra* was released) and again in 1978, by which time he was a well-established artist. On this first trip, sponsored by *The Sunday Times* (not coincidentally, the same publisher that sponsored Carter's excavations some forty years earlier), Hockney saw Egypt's great monuments at first hand – including the 'awe-inspiring' pyramids of Giza outside Cairo, which, he noted admiringly, 'were already two thousand years old and more when Cleopatra showed them to Julius Caesar'.[3] Following this visit, Hockney produced around forty works on paper and a single painting, *Great Pyramid at*

△ FIG. 14.3: David Hockney, *Man in a Museum (or You're in the Wrong Movie)*, 1962. British Council Collection.

Giza with Broken Head from Thebes. The paper works, drawn principally in wax and pencil, captured modern Egyptian life – its city bars and roadside billboards – but his painting offered a more exoticising vision of Egypt, with a towering pyramid and shattered sculpted heads buried in the sand. In later decades, as part of a series of 1970s commissions for stagesets for the opera *The Magic Flute*, Hockney returned to these romanticised Egypto-scapes, combining them with Masonic allusions and references to Egyptian-inspired, esoteric spirituality.

In the artworld of 1980s Britain, pharaonic Egypt played a starring role. During this period artists like the London-born painter Bridget Riley drew directly from a now well-established Egyptian aesthetic. Like Hockney, Riley continued a long tradition of artistic pilgrimages by visiting Egypt's monuments for herself. In the winter of 1979–80 she toured the Nile Valley and visited Cairo's museums. Upon her return, she produced a series of 'Egyptian Palette' prints – *Ka 2* (1980), *Ra 2* (1981) and *Achæan* (1981) – that merged her distinctive op-art style with a new, evocative colour palette drawn from her recollections of the landscapes, temples and tombs she had encountered.[4]

At the same time pharaonic iconography made a marked reappearance in British architecture and design – especially in the Postmodern movement. For Britain's Postmodern architects, a willing embrace of eclecticism created room for bold Egyptianising elements. In the swelling ranks of 'Po-Mo' buildings appearing across Britain, the columns of Luxor Temple and the monumental carvings at Thebes were integrated with new materials and engineering techniques to bring surprising flashes of the Nile's monumental visual culture to British streets. This could be seen in the bombastic façades of architect John Outram (who built Egyptian-inspired structures in London, Cambridge and Oxfordshire), but also in the monumental and often faintly satirical exteriors of Ian Pollard, especially his 1988 Kensington DIY warehouse, bedecked with lotiform columns and a large frieze depicting the Egyptian god Seth wielding a power drill (Fig. 14.4).[5] At London's Harrods department store, in a space designed by William Mitchell in consultation with British Museum Egyptologists, an Egyptian Room (replete with an 'Egyptian Escalator') inspired by the monuments of the XVIIIth-dynasty pharaoh Akhenaten was installed in 1992 – festooned in temple sculptures that included a Hathoric solar disc reminiscent of a lampshade and cartouches referencing items available in-store.

By the mid 1990s cross-cultural interactions between ancient Egyptian and contemporary Western aesthetics had themselves become a suitable topic for exhibition. In 1994 curator and Egyptologist James Putnam mounted the show *Time Machine – Ancient Egypt and Contemporary Art* at the British Museum to explore this phenomenon. The exhibition assembled artists whose work drew directly on pharaonic heritage, including the British artist Marc Quinn and the stone sculptor Stephen Cox, who was just beginning to develop the practice for which he would become famous: carving non-

▷ FIG. 14.4: Ian Pollard's now-demolished Egyptian inspired warehouse (with reliefs by Richard Kindersley) in Kensington, London, 1988.

figurative forms from rock quarried from 5,000-year-old mines in Egypt's eastern mountains (Fig. 14.5). In later decades Cox has continued his engagement with these millennia-old quarries and with the rich materials they provide by creating works that speak not only to each stone's unique qualities but to the storied landscapes from which they emerge. In recent years, Cox has undertaken many journeys to Egypt's remote quarries to produce single pieces that combine his fascination with this specific ancient civilisation with techniques derived from the stone-carving traditions of ancient Italy and India. In the mid-1990s, Cox produced among his most striking Egyptian-inspired works, *Lens of Khafre* (1995). Made from Kephren Diorite polished to a smooth, circular drum and on its reverse left unworked, the work's title references both the storied quarry in the far south of Egypt from which Cox sourced the stone but also the monument with which the quarry is most closely associated: the monumental seated figure of Khafre, who oversaw the construction of Egypt's second largest pyramid.

In many cases, both popular and artistic visions of Egypt consistently represented ancient Egypt as a proto-European civilisation and, in the same gesture, as one of the earliest notches on a historical timeline that transitioned from ancient Egypt to Classical Antiquity to Western modernity. But it was this common understanding of Egypt – as either an explicit or implicit progenitor of a modern-day White European society – that a growing number of British artists (many of them second-generation African and Caribbean art graduates) began to critique from the 1990s onwards. Among this growing circle of detractors was the Manchester-born painter Chris Ofili, whose Nigerian heritage and interest in the many overlooked characters of ancient African myth inspired his 1992 painting *Cleopatra* (see page 8). Drawing together the punkish style of Jean-Michel Basquiat and the distorted figuration of Georg Baselitz, Ofili's portrait purposefully subverted Western expectations of the beauty and civility associated with the late Egyptian, Ptolemaic queen (as consolidated through her recurrent portrayals as a slender, decorous beauty in popular Euro-American cinema since the 1910s). In Ofili's painting, Cleopatra is presented not as a European courtesan, but as a rough-hewn, captivating African queen (Fig. 0.1).

In 1996 another artist, the British-Ghanaian film-maker John Akomfrah delivered an equally critical take on Western historiography and its conceptualisation of Egypt as a proto-European rather than primarily African civilisation in his video work *The Last Angel of History*. Part didactic exercise, part archival dig, Akomfrah's

△ FIG. 14.5: Stephen Cox, *Lens of Khafre*, 1995.

film proposed a theory of black cultural displacement by referencing past and present black musicians and their connections to ancient history and to cosmic philosophy. In re-narrating history through a black British lens, the film built upon a pre-existing but chiefly African American historiographical tradition that understood ancient Egypt as an unequivocally African civilisation, from which modern black culture had emerged and from which European cultures had long drawn artistic and intellectual inspiration without credit or recognition. Politically speaking, Akomfrah's film brought a form of critical historicism that was largely absent from 1990s Britain, a society whose social values and historical outlook had been shaped by decades of sociocultural conservativism under Margaret Thatcher. Released shortly before the election of Labour leader Tony Blair in 1997, Akomfrah's film thus marked the beginning of a newly analytic art world in which reappraisals of historical narratives and critiques of classicism (including Egypt) would play a major role.

EGYPT

The year of the *Treasures of Tutankhamun* exhibition in London, 1972, was a critical one in Egypt, both politically and culturally. Egyptian president Anwar Sadat (newly installed, following President Gamal Abdel Nasser's death) turned the nation west and away from Soviet influence. From early on, Sadat's relation with Egypt's past contrasted to that of Nasser, who, though a committed internationalist and self-styled moderniser, closely engaged with pre-Islamic Egyptian history to bolster his political standing (Fig. 14.6). During his presidency Nasser carefully relocated many pharaonic monuments, such as in 1955, when he arranged the transfer of a monumental Ramses II statue to Cairo, where it became a powerful backdrop to his political campaigns. Israel's incursions into Egypt that same year saw Egypt emerge as a key player in the Cold War and caused Nasser to find new allies in the Soviet Union, especially for support in constructing the Aswan Dam, a major infrastructural project that had lost backing from Britain and others. Controversially, Nasser's dam project required the deluging of many ancient sites along the Nile, most notably the temples at Philae, and displacement of modern Sudanese communities. With the assistance of European engineers and the support of UNESCO, these monuments were subsequently disassembled and transferred elsewhere. By the 1970s the future of Egypt's heritage had therefore become a topic of popular

△ FIG. 14.6: Egyptian stamp showing President Nasser, the Sphinx and pyramids, *c.*1971.

conversation (evident in films such as the 1969 drama *The Night of Counting the Years*, in which a community struggles over whether to profit financially or culturally from a newly discovered tomb) and, with the rise of Sadat, the nation's past was fast becoming a global and geopolitical rather than purely national tool.

While the future course of state-sanctioned interest in pharaonic Egypt remained unclear within Egypt during the final decades of the twentieth century, the icons and images of the nation's ancient past incited new, independent Egyptian artists to explore how their country's idiosyncratic heritage could inspire their own practice. Within this group was Adam Henein, a sculptor and painter born in Cairo to a family from the ancient city of Asyut, on the Nile's west bank. Henein's sculptural forms and later etchings blended the typical iconographic features and characteristic materials (granite, papyrus and local metals) of his nation's visual history with highly abstracted modern forms. Both a draughtsman and an avant-gardist, Henein was frequently outspoken about his enthralment to pharaonic imagery, regularly recalling how a childhood visit to Cairo's Museum of Egyptian Antiquities spurred his interest in the artistry of his cultural ancestors and led to the creation of his first work in clay: a model figure of the XVIIIth-dynasty ruler Akhenaten. In many later works, this nod to pharaonic Egypt was also evident.[6] In *Man with Fish*, a bronze work from 1965 (at which time the artist lived between Luxor and Aswan), Henein evokes in outline the essence and spirit of local fishermen carrying their catch from nearby rivers (Fig. 14.7). With its rounded head and upright noble posture, the figure deliberately recalls the hieratic bearings of funerary reliefs while abstracting those forms. During the 1970s, as Henein moved to Paris and his work became increasingly abstract, his sculpture continued to convey the stillness and solemnity of pharaonic sculpture. When he returned to Cairo nearly a quarter of a century later, Henein was appointed by Egypt's then cultural minister to lead the restoration of the Great Sphinx of Giza – a project that began in 1981 and would take nearly a decade to complete.

The rich symbols of pharaonic Egyptian art offered some Egyptian artists a way to cement a collective cultural identity, especially against the dominant cultural forms of the major Cold War powers. This strong urge to cohere a modern visual identity from the remnants of the past is particularly apparent in the work of printmaker and designer Chant Avedissian, whose stencilled collages and costume designs bear the imprint of an alternate form of engagement with Egypt's ancient past.[7] Born in 1951 to Armenian parents but raised in Cairo, Avedissian studied printmaking in Montreal and France before returning to Egypt in 1981. At the end of that decade, as the Gulf War erupted from latent Cold War hostilities, he produced a series of works that drew explicitly on his homeland's long history and sought to illustrate a lucid Egyptian identity from a broad selection of historical and popular figures and images. This search for a new 'Egyptian aesthetic' that avoided cultural borders and boundaries and blended old and new can be seen in Avedissian's 1972 and 1982 sketchbooks (where he reproduced wall scenes from ancient temples and tombs), in his *Icons of the Nile* (a series of 120 individually stencilled and painted plates) and in his single-panel *Cities of Egypt/Greetings from Masr*. In each, Avedissian blended arcane motifs with the hyper-modernity of the age to create a mosaic of popular cultural references (singers, actors and politicians) and classical Egyptian allusions (sphinxes, pyramids and ibises). Later, in the 1980s, Avedissian embraced the pharaonic aesthetic more directly within his vibrant costume designs, in which he explored Pharaonic art in conversation with Bedouin and Central Asian designs (see Chapter 15).[8]

◁ FIG. 14.7: Adam Henein, *Man with Fish*, 1965. Private Collection.

▷ FIG. 14.8: Sara Sallam, *Plate 3*, digital photographic collage from the series *The Fourth Pyramid Belongs to Her*, Egypt, 2017. Tintera Gallery.

In the closing decades of the twentieth century several Egyptian artists took this captivation with ancient civilisation in new directions. Working against a backdrop of growing government interest in the touristic and geopolitical value of the nation's heritage and amid the continuous presence of figures such as 'mummies' and 'tomb robbers' in popular Egyptian cinema, young artists began to examine closely this enduring interest in the ancient culture. They began, in diverse and discrete ways, to critically explore how modern Egypt had been imagined both from within the country and from afar through the narrow historical lens of its ancient past.

Photographer and video-artist Maha Maamoun is one of the most prominent of these artists.[9] Born in the same year as the British Museum's *Treasures of Tutankhamun* opened, Maamoun considers in her work how today's Egyptians relate and respond to the heritage that surrounds them. In her 2009 film *Domestic Tourism II*, Maamoun explores how the pyramid – which she describes as a 'timeless' monument – is in fact enveloped within the starkly modern, urbanised narrative of Cairo's physical and social transformation (see Chapter 10).[10] Across sixty minutes of video-collage, Maamoun splices together clips of the pyramids at Giza from Egyptian films and soap operas to illustrate how, even within popular cultural forms, iconic pharaonic monuments such as Giza's pyramids act as 'silent protagonists': living, breathing structures that continue to shape the lives of Egyptians even as the societies in their shadows undergo radical transformations.

Multidisciplinary artist Sara Sallam is similarly interested in how contemporary Egyptian society positions itself in relation to the pharaonic trajectory that surrounds it.[11] Her work across print, photography, film, archival documentation and salvaged poetry often handles her fellow Egyptians' relationship with their past as an ambivalent one by signifying that the heroic associations imposed by colonial rule between past and present might be subverted by a more localised, personal and even familial engagement with the ever-present past. In *The Fourth Pyramid Belongs to Her* (2016–18), Sallam makes this case most directly, by transposing her own mourning for her recently deceased grandmother onto her fellow Egyptians' complex relationship with the age of the pharaohs (Fig. 14.8).

Mixing into new form her own textual reflections on the loss of her grandmother with collections of images extracted from European colonial documents such as the Napoleonic-era *Description de l'Égypte*, numerous photographs salvaged from family albums, original photography of daily life and stills taken from modern cinema and television, Sallam positions her grandmother as a colossal yet approachable pharaonic icon, inviting the viewer into her collage in order to re-consider the multiple registers at which nostalgia operates. In another work, *A Tourist Handbook: Egypt Outside of Egypt* – a series of pocket-sized tourist guidebooks to various European cities, published in 2021 – Sallam takes this interest in the limits of 'Egyptomania' overseas by exploring how the Egyptian past has become a clear mark of imperial triumph in European cities, especially as Egypt's sculptures were systematically removed and exported to European capitals, which were, in turn, re-shaped by these purposely de-contextualised monuments.

UNITED STATES

During the Cold War, in the US, visions of ancient Egypt were also being deployed as part of growing, popular struggles for political representation. In 1972, while British audiences were pouring into the *Treasures of Tutankhamun* exhibition in London, and Egypt's president was pivoting his nation away from Soviet communism towards Western capitalism, the Chicago-born jazz musician and avant-garde poet Sun Ra was fashioning his own take on Egypt's pharaonic past. In his feature-length experimental film *Space Is the Place* (released in 1974), which opens with a striking scene of Ra walking through a rich forested landscape dressed as a modern-day pharaoh surrounded by flying machines, he brought a radically different perspective to ancient Egypt's enduring significance before American audiences (Fig. 14.9). For Ra, Egypt represented a high point in black cultural expression and pride, which stood in stark contrast to the reality in which he found himself.[12] Ra's interest in Egypt was intellectual and political, a means of imagining liberation and envisioning equality and, for him, Egypt's ancient art and monuments were not lifeless relics, but testaments to an unbounded spirit, and a vital component for a latent future of black liberation.

In 1971 Ra and his twenty-two-strong 'Arkestra' toured Egypt, playing concerts in Cairo alongside Salah Ragab's Cairo Jazz Band and visiting the country's most iconic monuments. This journey, as Ra later recounted, connected the historical trajectories they were creating from afar in the United States and would lay the ground for a new form of African American pilgrimage. The trip also affirmed to Ra that Egyptian culture did not merely

△ FIG. 14.9: Sun Ra on the set of *Space is the Place*, 1972.

▽ FIG. 14.10: Anwar Sadat and Richard Nixon in front of the pyramids at Giza, June 1974.

provide a visual backdrop, but could instead become a touchstone for a radical political philosophy that would later become known as 'Afrofuturism'.

For Ra, the pyramids at Giza provoked a spiritual awakening and exposed how the past glories of black culture no longer served present-day African American communities. Yet three years later, in 1974, another American, President Richard Nixon, saw these monuments in a very different light. Motioning to their glittering peaks while standing alongside Egypt's new president, Anwar Sadat, Nixon positioned these monuments and ancient Egypt as the backdrop to the forging of a markedly modern alliance and as a tool to expand the very same Euro-American society that Sun Ra was seeking to critique (Fig. 14.10). In return for such support and US investment, Egypt's president would permit a series of Tutankhamun exhibitions across the US, in cities such as New York, Chicago, Boston and St Louis (Fig. 14.11). As in Europe, these hugely popular exhibitions pushed Tutankhamun back into the public spotlight and incited a wave of popular interest in ancient Egypt, with major artists – including Andy Warhol and Robert Rauschenberg – looking to Egypt for inspiration. In 1978 this wave reached its height when the comedian Steve Martin performed a musical sketch revolving around the commodification of the

boy pharaoh on the primetime national television show *Saturday Night Live*.

Ra's Afrofuturist philosophy and the production of Egyptian-inspired art that followed it persisted into the post-millennial period. In this post-Cold War era the same meaningful continuities between contemporary black culture and Egyptian antiquity appeared with even greater frequency in fine art and across popular visual culture. Propelled by the writings of critical Egyptologists, by historians such as Cheikh Anta Diop and, later, by Martin Bernal's *Black Athena* (an Afrocentric account of Western civilisation), Afrofuturism became more fully established in the American art world during the 1980s. Artists such as Jean-Michel Basquiat drew on Egypt's biblical links and depicted its ancient gods in paintings such as *History of the Black People*, and in other works, such as *Untitled (Geese+)*, reproduced rows of figures from Egyptian tomb paintings. A few decades later the mixed-media artist and critic Lorraine O'Grady took this subject in a different direction in her project *Miscegenated Family Album* (1980 and 1994), juxtaposing images of her family with those of ancient Egyptian rulers to speak to overlooked ancestral lineages.[13] In the following decade this trend continued in the work of Fred Wilson, who likewise tackled the topic of Egyptian blackness in his installation *Grey Area* (1993) – a series of reproduction Nefertiti busts ranging from white to grey and black arrayed alongside one another to highlight how the issue of race remains unsettled within modern Egyptology (Fig. 14.12).

More recently the American installation artist and photographer Awol Erizku has drawn on his Ethiopian heritage to examine the everyday spaces of African American life in which Egypt features, and to probe how its age-old motifs act as symbols of modern cultural resistance, even as they become increasingly commodified and globalised. In two photographic works from 2019, *Black Fire (Mouzone Brothas)* and *Malcolm x Freestyle (Pharaoh's Dance)*, Erizku addresses

▽ FIG. 14.11: The King Tut exhibit at the De Young Museum, 1979.

everyday 'Egyptomania' by assembling objects relating to contemporary American black culture in the style of a Dutch still-life. In tableaux, Erizku visualises a constant making and remaking of African American identities through ephemeral objects. Both sensational and pointedly satirical, the works juxtapose smoking candles, polished brass taps, gleaming pistols and stacked building bricks with replica antiques from both sub-Saharan and northern Africa, including a golden reproduction of a Tutankhamun mask. In the artist's 2018 neon installation *Nefertiti (Black Power)*, Nefertiti's iconic profile is cast in glowing neon as if it is a Hong Kong shop sign, appearing alongside a translation of 'Black Power' (Fig. 14.1). Through this striking juxtaposition, Erizku makes familiar connections between black liberation movements and pharaonic culture, but also seems to suggest that in becoming ever more globalised, such motifs might be in danger of becoming sterilised symbols of a black liberation that, though long anticipated, has yet to materialise.

Preoccupation with pharaonic Egypt during the Cold War and in the years afterwards has therefore been as much political as aesthetic. In Britain, ancient Egypt provided a tool for imperial nostalgia and for exerting authority in the shadow of its former empire. For Egypt, a rapidly transforming nation, its ancient past provided diplomatic leverage and a cultural touchstone that could unite its citizens. In the United States visions of this ancient civilisation were wielded by those struggling for civil rights. Across all of these places pharaonic Egypt was a vital symbolic resource in the late twentieth century, which propelled the geopolitical dynamics that marked the last decades of the Cold War. In the twenty-first century ancient Egypt's allure endures and its aesthetic and political value continues to be realised in new, often unexpected ways. ⊙

△ FIG. 14.12: Fred Wilson, *Grey Area*, 1993.

△ FIG. 15.1: Chant Avedissian, Sederi vest, 1988. Victoria and Albert Museum. Given by Art d'Égypte, Barjeel Foundation, Nadia Wassef and Hind Wassef, and those who wish to remain anonymous.

15 LOOKING TO THE EAST

CHANT AVEDISSIAN (1951–2018)

Apart from an equal dialogue, there are other ways to encounter another culture; one can try to learn from the other culture, or one can try to mould the other culture. For the past 200 years the French, then the British and later the Soviet colonial policymakers employed this second approach to encountering the other; 'Civilizing the Arabs' was the foreground of their expansionist economic interests. Learning from the other was high on the agenda of the Egyptians. But contrary to imperial mechanisms, the Egyptians' approach to learning from the other had limits, as Egyptians already had an older culture, with a different language and alphabet spread throughout a geographically vaster span. Above all, they also had a knowledge of their own country and its culture, unlike their colonial invaders. The Egyptians were already part of the culture of encounter and had been for centuries. From Saragossa to Samarkand, teachers and masters were known to each other, and masters and students alike could travel all that distance from west to east and back again, in search of knowledge shared by people of the same language and craft. [My work] is inspired by the work of myriad people from different places, which I discovered during journeys that always took me back to the same elementary forms, colours and shapes.

Using the three basic shapes of the rectangle, square and triangle, one is able to construct panels out of wood, paper, textile or any other material. It was in western Rajasthan, and particularly in Jaisalmer, that I first came in contact with the world of appliqué textile, which inspired me to make textile panels (Fig. 15.1). Travelling by train through the Thar desert, one arrives at this ancient city, through which merchants passed as they crossed Iran from Africa along the caravan route to India and China. The square is divided into rectangles and triangles. These squares placed together form the panels. Several assembled panels form the tent; it's a movable space, easily disassembled, folded and transported.

Textile tents are used for special occasions. In Egypt they are mainly used for weddings, funerals, official meetings or festivals. The textile panels are assembled by appliqué technique, using floral and geometric patterns that are found in wood or marble on and in buildings all over the country. Master drawings are transferred to the base, which is usually a thick cotton textile; these patterns are multiplied all over the base and reversed, as in a mirror. Colour is added by cutting textiles of different colours according to the rhythm of the base pattern. These pieces are then folded at the edges and sewn on to the base by hand. Modern printed versions are in use today, with designs inspired from traditional tent patterns. The material that I used to build my textile hangings is *dammour*, a popular and inexpensive Egyptian cotton. This was deliberately chosen primarily to overcome the concept that the more expensive, permanent and rare the materials of an 'artwork' are, the better it is. I hand-dyed the *dammour* and, after cutting it into geometric forms inspired from pharaonic patterns, Bedouin carpets, Central Asian brick walls or Syrian mother-of-pearl inlaid boxes, I sewed the pieces together by machine.

There is not much difference over a huge expanse of geography in the basic cuts of a traditional costume. The measurements comply to the length and width of the woven textile. This is usually divided to form the front, the back and the sleeves. Much as in Silk Road architecture, similarity is a constant feature of these costumes. The *haik* of the Atlas resembles the *melaya* of the Nile, which also resemble the sari of India (Fig. 15.2). The principle is one piece of unstitched textile. Similarly, caftans are found from Morocco to Mongolia. They are variations on a theme, and all of almost the same cut. The world of traditional Egyptian costumes – the diversity and the richness of weavers and their textiles, tailors and their cuts, embroiderers and their symbols – is a world whose beauty and richness can still be discovered. Through costumes, one embraces all aspects of a given geographical area. Costumes, houses, daily utensils, pottery and jewellery all reveal the way of life of a particular society. While working on these costumes I discovered the intelligence of economy in cutting a textile with minimal wasted material throughout the Arab world and later further east in Central Asia.

Despite the labelling of cultural heritage under different styles and dates, there are similarities between wall decorations in India and Upper Egypt, and wood textile blocks from Uzbekistan could as easily be found in Aleppo. The different periods in history, according to specialised scholars, are mixed and present in daily life. In Egypt, from Aswan in the south to Alexandria in the north, in real life the styles have no time, no date, no epoch; they are all present, sometimes imperceptibly mixed. ⊙

This text is based on extracts printed from Chant Avedissian, *Patterns, Costumes & Stencils* (London, 2009).

△ **FIG. 15.2:** Chant Avedissian, Costume prints, 1990. Photographic prints on aluminium. Victoria and Albert Museum. Given by Art d'Égypte.

16 PROCESSING (ANCIENT) EGYPT: SPECTACLES OF THE PAST

WILLIAM CARRUTHERS

On 25 November 2021 (the same day as US Thanksgiving, which was surely not a coincidence) the Upper Egyptian city of Luxor hosted an event celebrating the opening of the so-called *Tariq al-Kibash*, or 'Avenue of the Sphinxes'. The route is a long and, in large part, recently excavated processional way located between the two temple complexes of Luxor and Karnak, flanked by the sphinxes that give it its name (Fig. 16.2). The event commemorating its opening – a globally streamed spectacle of sound, light and performance – witnessed, amongst other things, a re-enactment of the ancient *Opet* festival, in which statues of local deities were paraded along the road in a celebration of fertility linked to the Nile's annual flood.[1] Egypt's president, Abdel Fattah el-Sisi, also walked along part of the 2.7-kilometre-long route, whose excavation, as many media outlets noted, had first begun in the late 1940s.[2] In this telling, the opening of the road (*tariq*'s literal meaning) was symbolic of a government that had finally managed to join the archaeological dots in the process of creating 'the new republic' (*al-jumhuriyya al-jadida*) that the country's leader had been busy promoting, in addition to tracing the links between this latest iteration of the Egyptian state and its ancient glories.[3]

This version of the route's story, however, elides the force that has gone into its making. The most recent – and by far the most expansive – work on the avenue had started in 2005 under the charge of the (in)famous archaeologist Zahi Hawass, then-Secretary General of Egypt's Supreme Council for Antiquities. Previously limited in extent (the open part of the route stretched perhaps a couple of hundred metres from the front of Luxor temple), excavating the rest of the avenue involved the wholesale demolition of residential properties in order to reach its often-fragmentary sphinxes.[4] This process of social disaggregation continued until Egypt's 2011 revolution temporarily halted the work, and also caused some degree of condemnation: explicitly, in the case of UNESCO, and rather more *sotto voce* in the case of many Egyptologists.[5] Residents who lost their homes during the project, which the Egyptian government restarted in 2017, reportedly received financial compensation and

◁FIG. 16.1: 'Mural of the Wailing Women' or 'Na'ehat' by artist Alaa Awad, originally painted on the ancient tomb of Ramose, Governor of Thebes during the XVIIIth Dynasty.

◁ FIG. 16.2: The Avenue of Sphinxes at the Luxor Temple, Egypt.

resettlement, although it is unclear exactly how much or where.[6] Unsurprisingly, then, the Luxor avenue's lavish opening celebration drew condemnation in some quarters for its destructive history, even as many lined up to praise the event and others clearly took pride in its undertaking.[7]

Who are such events and interventions for? What is the purpose of the historical and contemporary elisions that these actions represent, and why do they engender the varied responses that they do? Across the twentieth century and into the twenty-first, the changing governments of an itself-changing Egyptian state have time and again enacted interventions that mobilise the trappings of an idealised 'ancient Egyptian' past in pursuit of contemporary and future gain, even as the state and its officials have often treated the country's population rather less munificently. Egypt is of course not exceptional in this practice: writing from London, it is difficult to ignore the physical forms of 'invented tradition' sitting at the legislative heart of British life, the role of (often processional) ceremony in reproducing them, and the social hierarchies that such traditions represent.[8] In the last couple of centuries, however, Britain has sat rather differently from the rest of the world than Egypt has: not least due to the former's occupation of the latter, which began in 1882 and endured, in various forms, until the 1950s. Egypt – never a stable entity – has sat at the centre of global and regional political interventions that have tied the spectacle of its (ancient) past not only to the imperatives of often rapacious geopolitical strategy, but also to the domestic strategies that are indelibly linked to such currents.

The question, then, is how such spectacles and the ancient Egypt(s) they enact themselves trace the contours of these geopolitical waves. In this essay I will trace the specific – and sometimes uneasy – relationships with ancient pasts that such interventions reveal. Doing so, I will concentrate on events that took place after the July 1952 Free Officers' coup that presaged the (1956–70) presidency of Gamal Abdel Nasser. That coup constituted the current, republican and military-dominated iteration of Egypt – itself an entity that has taken several different territorial forms – and thus places recent events in Luxor in their most relevant geopolitical context. Such interventions, however, are themselves tied to earlier actions that help to place later ones in a more nuanced light.

FROM 'TYRANNICAL' ROYAL MUMMIES TO A RAMESSIDE RENAISSANCE

In 1931, Isma'il Sidqi Pasha, Egypt's prime minister, ordered the transfer of the twenty-four pharaonic-era royal mummies then held at Cairo's Egyptian Museum to a new location, disrupting their decades-long residence on what is today's Tahrir Square. The bodies would be moved to the neo-pharaonic tomb built a kilometre to the south for Sa'd Zaghlul, the leader of the 1919 revolution that had hastened Britain's declaration of Egypt's (nominal) independence (Fig. 16.3). Made unilaterally in 1922, that declaration meant that Britain retained troops in the country and a significant ability to interfere in Egypt's domestic affairs. It also created an Egyptian constitutional monarchy, and Sidqi's monarchist tendencies saw him move the mummies to Zaghlul's mausoleum 'as a means of arguing that the popular leader had been as much of a tyrant as the [apparently despotic] kings that preceded him'. As Hussein Omar discusses, learning of the plan, 'Zaghlul's widow, Safiya, was horrified and refused to allow her husband to lie next to the embalmed bodies'. When Sidqi resigned from his position in 1933, officials thus relented and moved the ancient rulers back to the Egyptian Museum.[9] Pharaohs might not always stand for tyranny, however hard politicians tried to make them.

Perhaps it was unsurprising then that, during the 1950s, official attempts to make use of ancient Egyptian spectacle suggested that pharaonic rulers might reflect less despotic connotations. Times, it seemed, were changing. The Free Officers' coup led to the abdication of Egypt's King Faruq and, later, British withdrawal from the country. And in the following years, under the growing influence of Nasser, the officers' actions, which initially enjoyed a set of rather 'unfocused goals', would also become billed as revolutionary.[10] More prosaically, as Joel Gordon has noted, this group of mid-ranking military men became 'caught up in the excitement of a flurry of major archaeological finds during the first years of their rule'. Consequently, the pharaoh Ramses II (r. *c.*1279–1212 BC) became 'a symbol of national power', and the display and manipulation of the ruler's image helped to make that point.[11] This Ramesside florescence had ironic roots in the British occupation of Egypt. Yet it was also linked to contemporary proclamations about the state of the country and its pan-Arab influence. In contrast to the ideas about pharaonic despotism ingrained in Sidqi Pasha's earlier actions, now it seemed that Ramses – whose body was amongst those held at the Egyptian Museum – might stand for popular authenticity, stability and the (actual or perceived) renaissance of Egyptian regional power.

▽ FIG. 16.3: The neo-pharaonic tomb of Sa'd Zaghlul, Cairo.

In March 1955, the Free Officer and minister of municipal and rural affairs, 'Abd al-Latif al-Baghdādī, ordered the transfer of a colossal statue of Ramses from Mit Rahina (the location of ancient Memphis, just south of Cairo) into the Egyptian capital's centre.[12] Repurposing a plan originally set forward – but never carried out – by the British consul-general Lord Kitchener in 1914,[13] the statue was driven across the city and re-erected in the square outside Cairo's major rail gateway at Bab al-Hadid, or what now became Ramses Station, replacing Mahmoud Mokhtar's 'iconic nationalist monument' *Nahdat Misr* (*Egypt's Renaissance*, see Chapter 12), which had stood outside the station since 1928 (Fig. 16.4).[14] As Joel Gordon notes, 'despite its dramatic combining of pharaonic, rural and gendered national symbols', Mokhtar's statue, now standing in the square in front of Cairo University, 'had by the late 1940s lost much of its emotional luster'.[15] Ramses now seemed to be a better bet for a position outside the major transport portal to the city, which was flooded daily with thousands of travellers arriving from Upper Egypt and the Nile Delta making – or attempting to make – their lives in Cairo.[16]

Following the figure's restoration, press articles thus negated the plan's colonial genealogy, attaching it instead to the legitimacy of the Egyptian masses. Journalists highlighted the authenticity of the workmen involved in the project at a time when Nasser – in the months after the resignation of fellow Free Officer Muhammad Naguib as Egypt's first president – had started to consolidate his power as the country's leader. One writer stated that 'it should be recalled that most of the workmen are from the Sa'id [Upper Egypt]. They take pride in the work ... because they consider themselves the grandchildren of Ramses II.'[17] Worked on by artisans who could be linked to the Upper Egyptian setting of ancient glories, Ramses became one of the most distinct symbols of the burgeoning revolutionary project.

Not only would school textbooks praise Ramses II as a 'good king'.[18] Those readings would relate the re-erection of his statue as a moment in which the

◁ FIG. 16.4: The Ramses II statue from Mit Rahina, Egypt, just after its installation outside Cairo station in the 1950s. American University in Cairo Special Collections.

▽ FIG. 16.5: Reassembling the Abu Simbel temples during UNESCO's Nubian campaign.

revolutionary – and later vocally pan-Arab – Egyptian government 'honoured' this 'courageous warrior'.[19] Ramses' ancient imperial pursuits saw him undertake multiple military campaigns in the area that became contemporary Syria, a historical echo that tied usefully to the amalgamation of the two countries in the short-lived (1958–61) United Arab Republic.[20] It was little wonder, then, that the pharaoh became a revolutionary symbol whose life was taught in Egyptian textbooks: here was a ruler who seemed to embody all of contemporary Egypt's ideals, even as his long-lived – and firmly Orientalist – characterisation by Egyptologists as a grandiose and bombastic ruler continued to sit stubbornly in the background.[21]

DEVELOPING AND INDEBTING RAMSES

Those negative pharaonic connotations would ultimately be hard to dispel, despite another series of events in which Ramses was used to promote the revolution's popular legitimacy. The same textbooks that glorified the pharaoh highlighted another revolutionary intervention in which Ramses II sat centrally. Although again the outcome of earlier planning, the construction of the Aswan High Dam became a centrepiece of Nasser's modernising presidency, and also one of the early Cold War's most notorious controversies: the structure was built with Soviet finance and expertise after Britain, the United States and the World Bank pulled backing from the project in 1955.[22] As the dam's floodwaters rose, so they began to submerge the region of Nubia, which was located to the dam's south and was split in half by the newly established Egyptian-Sudanese border (the Anglo-Egyptian Sudan having ceased to exist in 1956 after the Sudanese population voted to secede from post-coup Egypt).[23] Consequently, the many ancient temples in Nubia – several of which had been built under Ramses II – faced submersion, as did the homes of the Nubian population, who were ultimately forced to migrate.[24]

From 1960 until 1980, Egypt and Sudan worked with UNESCO to run an international campaign dedicated both to archaeological excavation in the region and to the preservation of those structures.

One of the most famous acts of the International Campaign to Save the Monuments of Nubia involved the cutting up and reassembly at a higher level of the two temples at Abu Simbel dedicated, respectively, to Ramses and his 'Great Royal Wife' Nefertari (Fig. 16.5). The same school textbooks that celebrated the re-erection of the pharaoh's statue now narrated the preservation work at Abu Simbel equally positively, glossing over the fact that much of this work – often overseen by European experts, but impossible without local labour – was paid for with Egyptian pounds held by the American Embassy in Cairo. Those pounds came from the sale of surplus wheat to Egypt as part of the US Public Law 480 ('Food for Peace') programme, which was predicated on the 1954 Agricultural Trade Development and Assistance Act. Public Law 480 enabled foreign countries to buy imported US food in their own currencies, leaving American embassies worldwide with substantial reserves of local cash; the work at Abu Simbel constituted a convenient way to spend much of the Egyptian portion.[25]

The wider place of such monumental intervention has never been stable, however. For one, Egyptologists argued over the merits of saving Abu Simbel, said to be 'a monument to a despot, and not a particularly good one'.[26] Yet beyond such Orientalist quibbles, in the decades after the Nubian campaign, the Cold War *quid pro quo* that materialised at the site altered in a way that reflected changes in global political economy and, more specifically, economic changes set in train under the presidency of Nasser's successor. Anwar al-Sadat took charge of Egypt in 1970 after Nasser's death. And after the October 1973 Arab-Israeli War and Egypt's re-establishment of a foothold east of the Suez Canal, the new president began a process termed *infitāh* (lit. 'opening', but more commonly the 'open door'): a move towards private investment from both Gulf and Western sources and away from the socialist policies and import substitution put in place under Nasser.[27] Now it was debt – and the increasing promotion of such financing through international development – that would reshape the display of the ancient Egyptian past, including that of Ramses II.

Thus, in April 2021, when Egypt's Ministry of Tourism and Antiquities (founded in 2019) moved the bodies of the pharaonic-era rulers previously displayed in Tahrir Square's Egyptian Museum several kilometres to the south to the new National Museum of Egyptian Civilization (or NMEC), the event embodied this context, albeit in a way that illustrates what happens when such financing is diverted elsewhere and the rubrics of development are called into question (Fig. 16.6). Initiated as a concept through the 1982 launch of UNESCO's International Campaign for Egyptian Museums, NMEC's existence has long been constituted by the trickle of funding that the project's trust fund – and UNESCO's consistently depleted coffers – have provided, even as the presidency of Husni Mubarak, which started in 1981, saw increased effort directed towards the opening of museums across Egypt.[28] The 1982 campaign (conceived as a follow-up to the work in Nubia) gave priority to another project: the Nubia Museum in Aswan, which opened in 1997 (Fig. 16.7). NMEC's cornerstone was thus only laid in 2004; further losing impetus in the period after Egypt's 2011 revolution, a temporary exhibit opened at the museum in 2017.[29] Thus, when the April 2021 *Mawkib al-Mumiyyat al-Malikiyya*, or 'Parade of the

▷ FIG. 16.6: The National Museum of Egyptian Civilization, Cairo.

◁ FIG. 16.7: The Nubia Museum, Aswan.

Royal Mummies' (rendered in English as the 'Pharaohs' Golden Parade'), heralded the opening of NMEC's permanent collection, the event attempted to elide the institution's chequered history with a performance of dance and music – and a spectacle of sound and light – that presaged the later Luxor performance. Yet even as many Egyptians themselves proffered unabashedly enthusiastic comment about it, arguments about the parade raged on social media for days.[30] The country's government might well have made use of a vision of the ancient past to promote a particular idea of Egypt, yet it was not at all clear that that vision – and the politics of global development within which it was enmeshed – was one that had done Egypt many favours.

Instead, another Mubarak-era project is servicing Egyptian loans. It is one in which Ramses, again, plays a central role. In 2006, the Egyptian government moved the pharaoh's statue back from Ramses Station to a location adjacent to the Great Pyramid on the Giza plateau. Retracing most of his earlier route in reverse, Ramses – in a move no less spectacular and media-friendly than more recent events in the country – now became a symbol of another Egyptian government's ambitions. The statue's new location was the site of the still-to-be-completed Grand Egyptian Museum: an institution conceived as a partner to NMEC, whose construction has been funded since 2008 by soft loans funnelled through JICA, the Japan International Cooperation Agency.[31] Moving Ramses to Giza constituted not only a symbol of the Mubarak regime's intentions, but also a signal to international debtors that Egypt was a state that would, now and in the future, repay investment. At the time of writing, the current Egyptian leadership, interested in promoting a picture of state – and thus financial – stability (*al-istiqrār*), is pushing hard for the Grand Egyptian Museum's completion.[32] Pictures of the Ramses statue often sit at the centre of this work, alongside images of the conservation labs and the Egyptian specialists charged with caring for the thousands of objects that form the institution's collection (Fig. 16.8). The visual symbolism is not hard to comprehend, even as criticisms surrounding such projects have taken on a new force.

▽ FIG. 16.8: Statue of Ramses II in the entrance hall of the Grand Egyptian Museum.

RESHAPING THE CITY

Put bluntly, the political economy of such development work has at times made the description of such pharaonic symbols in tyrannical terms significantly easier. This, perhaps, is how the latest series of (ancient) Egyptian spectacles should be understood: not only as a more forceful continuation of earlier heritage interventions, but also as events whose force – and blunt pharaonic symbolism – garner significant political criticism even as they attempt to deflect that possibility. Now, despite such criticisms, these interventions seek to expunge all that came between the 2011 end of the Mubarak presidency and the start of the Sisi presidential era in 2014, materially eliding any memory of the popular political uprising that caused the former president's overthrow (not to mention the short-lived presidency of the Muslim Brotherhood's Mohamed Morsi from 2012 to 2013).

Central to this state-backed political expulsion has been the removal of people from the spectacles at hand, despite the popular support that recent processions sometimes seem to have garnered. As Hussein Omar and others have noted, during the Pharaohs' Golden Parade, the route of the procession had been cleared of spectators: the event was, after all, specifically manufactured for viewing on TV or over streaming services.[33] In 2021's Luxor event, spectators also seemed notable by their absence. Yet that absence is about more than ensuring that the perceived political danger of the Egyptian crowd might be negated. Instead, it is about ensuring that memories of that and other such crowds – and of the Egypts they have inhabited – might be forgotten, reshaped, or erased.

This point does not simply relate to Egypt's 2011 revolution and the events that would follow it. Rather, it is about the role of Egyptian urban spaces as vectors of popular manifestation, in addition to how those spaces connect (or not) to visions of Egypt's ancient past. Even as, in 1955, the statue of Ramses II was moved and unveiled next to Cairo's Bab al-Hadid, it was not the only event under the Free Officers that engendered the reshaping of part of the city. Under new leadership, Cairo itself began to be remade. As Gehan Selim has discussed, under Nasser and his cohort 'the target was to turn Cairo's buildings, streets and public spaces into symbolic representations of the regime's revolutionary discourse to ensure its success in changing the Egyptians' everyday lives'.[34] Tahrir Square – so central to events five decades later – was an integral part of that action. Built under Egypt's Khedive Isma'il in 1867 as part of a wider plan to institute a 'European'-style quarter on marshland located between the Nile and the west of the then-city of Cairo, the square was originally named Midan al-Isma'iliyya (or Isma'iliyya Square) after the development – and the ruler – that initiated it.[35] It was only in the 1950s, under the Free Officers, that the square gained its current name, in addition to a reshaped form: one that kept some pharaonic symbolism intact, but also worked to void that symbolism of some of its colonial baggage.

Using the space made free by the 1951 demolition of the barracks that had long stood on the square's western edge (and which had most recently served as quarters for British soldiers), the Free Officers saw fit to reshape the location that now became *Midan al-Tahrir*, or 'Liberation' Square. On the square's north side, the Egyptian Museum, inaugurated in 1902, stood as a reminder of pharaonic glories (and, having been designed by a Frenchman, of overtly European-style architecture), not least in the display of the objects from the tomb of Tutankhamun, whose retention in the country had been a matter of urgency for post-1922 Egyptian governments.[36] In the years after 1952, however, the western side of the square became something of a centrepiece for the revolution that Nasser and the Free Officers created. Three buildings constituted this image, all designed by Egyptian architect Mahmoud Riad: the Nile Hilton, opened in 1958 (initially the 'Nile Hotel', with design modifications for Hilton carried out by the American architect Welton Becket); the Arab League, opened in 1964; and the Arab Socialist Union, which had originally been designed as a building for the Cairo Municipality, but upon its foundation in 1962 had become the headquarters of Egypt's only political party.[37]

As the city always had done, Cairo's remodelled order would itself witness popular gatherings.[38] When Nasser died in 1970, an estimated five to six million mourners descended upon the city – including Tahrir Square – to witness his funeral procession.[39] Three years later similarly large crowds attended the funeral procession of singer Umm Kulthum, herself a fixture of revolutionary imagery who was known across the region as *Kawkab al-Sharq*, or the 'Star of the East'.[40] Yet other mass outcries have been more critical of Egypt's status quo. In January 1977, Cairo, alongside other Egyptian cities, provided the venue for the 'bread intifada' (or *intifadat al-khubz*) directed against policies implemented under the presidency of Anwar al-Sadat. For two days, Egyptians protested at the – ultimately cancelled – removal of subsidies on basic foodstuffs that had been enforced by the World Bank and the International Monetary Fund in exchange for loans that would help decrease the country's debt burden and prop up Sadat's liberalising economy.[41] And in October 1981, Sadat himself would be assassinated during a Cairo military parade commemorating the 1973 Arab-Israeli War. As Nezar AlSayyad has noted, 'one of the last things Sadat would see during his final moments was the Monument to the Unknown Soldier': a memorial built to commemorate victims of that conflict, located opposite the grandstand where the president had been sitting (Fig. 16.9).[42] Ironically, the tomb 'replicated a shape that had become emblematic of Egypt as a nation: the pyramid'.[43] And Sadat's assassin, the Islamist army officer Khalid al-Islambuli, would shout, 'I have killed pharaoh!'[44] Under Sadat, a renewed representational push to the pharaonic coupled with the growing inequities of a liberalising economy – and the wider regional 'Islamic revival' – to hasten the president's end.[45] Pharaohs, it seemed, might not always represent the masses.

Fast-forward to 2011 and pharaonic imagery would again play a role in Egyptian life, albeit very differently. As protests in Cairo begat the downfall of Mubarak and a period of political uncertainty, the streets surrounding Tahrir Square became covered in graffiti supporting the uprising (Fig. 16.1). Unsurprisingly, perhaps, some of that graffiti drew on pharaonic motifs, subverting official uses of the ancient Egyptian past and suggesting how they might be used to express rather different meanings from the ones that places like the Monument to the Unknown Soldier enshrine.[46] Under the presidency of Abdel Fattah el-Sisi, however, symbolism has seen a return to official form. Even before the Pharaohs' Golden Parade, Tahrir Square had been subject to reformulation on pharaonic lines, as if to make sure that no memory of recent political events – and their creative subversion of ancient Egyptian imagery – might be recalled.

Causing controversy within and outside Egypt, officials from the Ministry of Tourism and Antiquities organised the move to the square of four ram-headed sphinxes of *c.*1200 BC from behind the first pylon of Karnak temple, alongside the repositioning in the same location of an obelisk from the Delta-site of Tanis (contemporary San al-Hagar), capital of Egypt's XXIst dynasty (Fig. 16.10). As the Egyptologist Tom Hardwick has noted, the 'symbolism [of such moves] could not be plainer'.[47] In 2013, Tahrir Square had been one among several Cairo locations witness to mass protests against the presidency of Mohamed Morsi, leading not only to the contested 'revocouption' that heralded Sisi's rise to power, but also to the massacre of pro-Morsi demonstrators elsewhere in the city.[48] Playing a central role during the Pharaohs' Golden Parade, the pharaonicised Tahrir Square now heralded the representational cementing not only of regime stability, but also of the military establishment that – other than in the brief case of Morsi – has provided every president of the Egyptian republic.

Cairo itself, meanwhile, has been subject to large-scale remodelling in the past few years, a process that has often involved military contractors. At the time of writing, road-building in parts of the UNESCO World Heritage-listed area of Historic Cairo – encompassing not only the core of the pre-nineteenth-century city, but also its necropolises (the famous 'City of the Dead') – continues to lead to the demolition of scores of family

▽ FIG. 16.9: The Monument to the Unknown Soldier, Nasr City, Cairo.

△ FIG. 16.10: The re-shaped Tahrir Square, Cairo, 2020.

tombs. Likewise, this remodelling work (deemed essential to an expanded Cairo's development) has placed the homes of the many 'informal' residents of the cemeteries in jeopardy. Despite a lack of public criticism from UNESCO, there has been significant protest directed against these actions within Egypt.[49] Yet these demolitions continue, as do those of historical structures in the rest of the country and the gargantuan construction projects to which these development plans are connected.[50]

CONCLUSION: CREATING THE PAST

The symbolism of such demolitions, however, is selected, linked to the value placed on different types of past by the Egyptian government. Still, in the official imagination, the pharaonic always seems to be preferential. In early November 2021, a few weeks before the opening of Luxor's Avenue of the Sphinxes, Egypt's Ministry of Interior released a video promoting its new prison complex – officially a 'Correctional and Rehabilitation Center' – at Wadi al-Natrun on the edge of the country's Western Delta. Soundtracked with a song performed by Medhat Saleh and Mai Farouk called 'A Chance for Life', the video was lampooned and criticised in equal parts for its startling removal from the documented reality of the grim situation in Egypt's jails.[51] Before visualising their journey from criminality to personal and institutional reform, the video featured scenes of inmates – all of whom had apparently agreed to take part – arriving on a bus at the front of the complex, whose entrance gate (not unlike other examples of official architecture in the country) takes the form of an idealised ancient Egyptian temple.[52] Once they had passed through that portal and been processed into the pristine new institution, the message of the video seemed to be that, regardless of reports about the abject treatment of inmates in other Egyptian prisons, the officials of this ancient land would attend with appropriate benevolence to the wayward citizenry now incarcerated there. The gate, with all its implied civilisational currency, acted as the symbol of a process whose reality was questionable at best, and for an audience of international and local observers who found their credulity stretched beyond limits.

This sort of critical response, however, has never entirely obtained in relation to Egypt's other pharaonic spectacles. During the twentieth century and beyond, such events have not only repeatedly taken place, but have also found some form of appreciative audience: often internationally, but also domestically. Likewise, the pharaonic past has at times been turned against the Egyptian state, mobilised by the country's people in efforts to assert forms of popular legitimacy. In this sense – and despite the contemporary state's repeated promotion of the pharaonic above all else – it is not at all clear that 'Egypt's effective past is materially that of its Islamic heritage and the more recent European inlay'.[53] Rather, the 'effective past' changes according to whose demands that past needs to meet. Processing (ancient) Egypt, Egypt itself perhaps comes into focus. ⊙

ACKNOWLEDGEMENTS

ANNA FERRARI & BENJAMIN HINSON

Visions of Ancient Egypt started as an exhibition research project at the Victoria and Albert Museum (V&A), and the Sainsbury Centre is grateful for the V&A's early support and generous loans. The exhibition has developed in new ways at the Sainsbury Centre, especially with the opportunity to include highlights from the Sainsbury Centre collection, including Francis Bacon, Alberto Giacometti and significant ancient Egyptian works, allowing for a greater focus on the impact of ancient Egypt on British modern and Modernist art. The Centre has provided a different but rich context for this project, which has led to an exciting integration of all the arts.

Over the years, many people have generously offered their support and knowledge to make this exhibition happen. We are immensely grateful to them all.

At the V&A, Anna Jackson and Tim Stanley have been staunch supporters throughout the project.

In particular, we are indebted to Mai Eldib for sharing her extensive knowledge and for her invaluable help in sourcing works by Egyptian artists. These are key to the exhibition and are due to Mai's unfailing support.

We are deeply grateful to all institutional and private lenders. Their generosity has made this exhibition possible. We thank: The Christie Archive Trust; Birmingham Museums Trust; Ivor Braka; British Council Collection; The British Library; British Museum; Mark and Cleo Butterfield; The Courtauld, London; Eleanor Dobson; Egypt Exploration Society; Fitzwilliam Museum, University of Cambridge; UK Government Art Collection; Griffith Institute, University of Oxford; Guildhall Art Gallery, City of London; Harris Museum, Art Gallery & Library, Preston; Henry Moore Foundation; Kenwood House, English Heritage; Laing Art Gallery, Tyne & Wear Archives & Museums; Lee Miller Archives; National Museums Liverpool, World Museum; National Museum Wales; P&O Heritage Collection; Paul Reeves; Royal Collections, the Netherlands; Royal College of Art; National Maritime Museum, Greenwich; Brighton & Hove Museums; Russell-Cotes Art Gallery & Museum; Shapero Rare Books, London; Sir John Soane's Museum; Tate; Touchstones Rochdale Art Gallery, Link4Life; Towneley Hall Art Gallery & Museum; Van Cleef & Arpels Collection; Victoria and Albert Museum; V&A Wedgwood Collection; Rupert Wace; Wartski, London; Wellcome Collection, London; Michael and Mariko Whiteway; Wyvern Collection; York Museums Trust (York Art Gallery); and the private lenders who wish to remain anonymous.

Our deepest thanks also go to the contemporary artists who have so generously agreed to lend their works: Nora Al-Badri and Nikolai Nelles, Stephen Cox, Awol Erizku, Khaled Hafez, Esmeralda Kosmatopoulos, Maha Maamoun and Sara Sallam; and to galleries who have supported the exhibition: Ben Brown Fine Arts London, Gallery Desmet, Gypsum Gallery, Nome Gallery Berlin and Tintera.

To the authors who have contributed rich and lively essays to this book, we are very grateful. In particular we would like to acknowledge Omniya Abdel Barr, who accompanied us on a research trip to Cairo in the early stages of the project and made numerous invaluable introductions.

Such a project could not have come together without the help of many scholars, curators and collectors who enthusiastically shared their ideas and provided invaluable help in shaping this book and exhibition. We thank: Sabah Abdel Razik Saddik, Emad Abou Ghazi, Kate Bailey, Robert Blyth, Stephanie Boonstra, Francisco Bosch-Puche, Antonia Boström, Isabella Campagnol, Laura Carderera, Ashley Cooke, Louise Cooling, Cathy Costain, Susie Cox, Jasmine Day, Rowan De Saulles,

△ Khaled Hafez, *Flying Beatle*, 2016. Courtesy the artist.

Amina Diab, Elizabeth Fleming, Moira Gallagher Ferguson, David Gange, Alexandra Gerstein, Jal Hamad, Aleya Hamza, Monica Hanna, Tom Hardwick, Jean-Marcel Humbert, Grace Hummel, Andrew Humphreys, Joe Keogh, Linda Lloyd Jones, Alexandra Loske, Adam Lowe, Daniel Lowe, MCAD photos, Kieran McCarthy, Liam McNamara, Stephanie Moser, Laurence Mouillefarine, Emilie Ortolan, Neil Parkinson, Thierry Pautot, Martin Pel, Bruce Peter, Aurélie Petiot, Clare Phillips, Clive Polden, Sophie Pretorius, Mathew Prichard, Katherine Purcell, Ilona Regulski, Mustafa Sakr, Annamarie Sandecki, Frances Sands, Logan Sisley, Neal Spencer, Louise Stewart, Valérie Thomas, Mercedes Volait, Duncan Walker, Catherine Warsi and Joanna Whalley.

Our thanks to Andrés Ros Soto for his exhibition design, George Sexton Associates for the lighting, Andrew Johnson for his graphics and for this book's design, Brenda Stones for the index and Mandy Greenfield for her careful editing of this book. At the Sainsbury Centre we thank Ghislaine Wood, Tania Moore, Vanessa Tothill, Theo Weiss, Joanna Roberts, Laura Reeves, Natalie Baerselman Le Gros and Roger Bishop for making the exhibition happen.

Ultimately, such projects would not be possible without generous supporters. We are immensely grateful to Viking for supporting the exhibition, and to Sotheby's for stepping in to help with loans from Egypt. We are thankful for the continued support of the Exhibition Circle patrons and the Corporate Club, including Loveday & Partners for their support of the exhibition.

Finally, we thank our partners, Rebecca Bennett Collins and Thomas Holroyd, and our families for their patience and support. ⊙

AUTHOR BIOGRAPHIES

OMNIYA ABDEL BARR is an architect specialising in Islamic art and architecture. She holds a PhD on Islamic history from Provence University, Aix-Marseille (2015) and an MSc in Conservation from the KUL, Leuven (2004). She is the Barakat Trust Fellow at the Victoria and Albert Museum and the Head of Development at the Egyptian Heritage Rescue Foundation.

DANA ARNOLD, is Professor of Architecture at the Manchester School of Architecture. She has written extensively on eighteenth- and early nineteenth-century British architecture and culture. She serves on the Advisory Board of the Arts and Humanities Research Council and was a member of the assessment panel for Art and Design in the 2021 Research Excellence Framework.

CHANT AVEDISSIAN (1951–2019) was an Egyptian-Armenian artist. His diverse works ranged from textiles to stencil patterns, exploring the glories of Egypt's past (both pharaonic and recent) within a broader context of artistic commonalities linking the cultures of the Middle East and North Africa. Across multiple media, Avedissian explored themes of nationhood, tradition and culture. Today his work is globally renowned.

WILLIAM CARRUTHERS is a Leverhulme Early Career Fellow in the Department of Art History and World Art Studies at UEA. He is the author of *Flooded Pasts: UNESCO, Nubia, and the Recolonization of Archaeology* (2022) and the editor of *Histories of Egyptology: Interdisciplinary Measures* (2014). He holds a PhD in the history and philosophy of science from the University of Cambridge.

ELEANOR DOBSON is Associate Professor in Nineteenth-Century Literature at the University of Birmingham. She is the author of *Victorian Alchemy: Science, Magic and Ancient Egypt* (2022) and *Writing the Sphinx: Literature, Culture and Egyptology* (2020).

ANNA FERRARI is Curator of Art and Visual Culture at the Science Museum and co-curator of *Visions of Ancient Egypt*. Her research focuses on modern and contemporary art, with a particular interest in French Modernism. She has worked on several exhibitions at the Victoria and Albert Museum, including *Ocean Liners* (2018), and has curated exhibitions for Barbican Art Gallery and the Royal Academy of Arts.

BENJAMIN HINSON is an Egyptologist and curator in the Middle East Section of the Victoria and Albert Museum, and co-curator of *Visions of Ancient Egypt*. His research projects focus on the collecting history of Egyptian objects within museums and on the revival of pharaonic imagery within twentieth-century Egyptian crafts.

MAHA MAAMOUN is an Egyptian artist, curator and publisher. She is a founding board member of the Contemporary Image Collective (CiC) – an independent non-profit space for art and culture founded in Cairo in 2004 – and co-founder of Kayfa ta, an alternative publishing platform (2012). She is currently a member of the curatorial team of Forum Expanded (Berlinale) and the Akademie der Kunst der Welt (Cologne).

ELIZABETH PRETTEJOHN is Professor and Head of Department, History of Art, at the University of York. She has written widely on the art of the Pre-Raphaelites, the Aesthetic Movement and the classical tradition in modern art. She is an active guest curator and has co-curated exhibitions on Lawrence Alma-Tadema, John William Waterhouse, Dante Gabriel Rossetti and *Imagining Rome* (on Victorian representations of ancient Rome).

NADIA RADWAN is Assistant Professor of World Art History at the University of Bern, Switzerland. Her research focuses on Middle Eastern modern and contemporary art and architecture, non-Western Modernisms, Arab feminisms, nostalgia and Orientalism, and the global museum. Her book *Les Modernes d'Égypte* was published in 2017 and she is currently finishing her second book on the politics of global abstraction.

ELLA RAVILIOUS is Curator of Architecture and Design in the Art, Architecture, Photography and Design Department at the Victoria and Albert Museum She is also studying for an AHRC-funded PhD on the history of the V&A's photography collection at the Photographic History Research Centre at De Montfort University, Leicester.

SARA SALLAM is an Egyptian artist based in the Netherlands. She works with photography, film and writing, often re-appropriating archival material and self-publishing books. She has exhibited internationally, and her work features in private collections in Australia, Belgium and Switzerland. Her research-based practice explores narration, fiction and temporal juxtapositions as ways to decolonise her ancient Egyptian heritage.

THEO WEISS is Assistant Curator at the Sainsbury Centre and assistant curator of *Visions of Ancient Egypt*. As a cultural historian and anthropologist, he is interested in how visual and material culture circulates within different societies and shapes social and political movements. He has worked with a number of international cultural institutions and writes regularly about material culture, museums and heritage.

GHISLAINE WOOD is Deputy Director of the Sainsbury Centre, UEA. As a design historian, she has curated many international exhibitions, including the Sainsbury Centre's *Art Deco by the Sea* (2019) and the Victoria and Albert Museum's *Ocean Liners: Speed and Style* (2017), *British Design 1948–2012*, *Surreal Things: Surrealism and Design* (2007) and *Art Deco 1910–1939* (2003). She has published widely in the field and is consultant curator for *Visions of Ancient Egypt*.

SELECT BIBLIOGRAPHY

Abou El Futouh, T. (et al.), *Past of the Coming Days: Performance & Film Programme: Sharjah Biennial 9* (Sharjah, 2009).

Abou Ghazi, B., and G. Boctor, *Mouktar ou le Réveil de l'Égypte* (Cairo, 1949).

Abou Ghazi, E., 'Le Canal vu par les Egyptiens', *L'Épopée du Canal de Suez* (Paris, 2018).

Abu-Lughod, I., *The Arab Rediscovery of Europe: A Study in Cultural Encounters* (London, 1963, republished 2011).

al-Jabarti, 'Abd al-Ra mān, *Napoleon in Egypt: Al-Jabarti's Chronicle of the French Occupation, 1798*, Introduction by Robert L. Tignor, trans. S. Moreh (Princeton, NJ, 2004).

Anon., 'In Egypt, a Motorcade of Mummies Says More About the Modern Nation than the Ancient Past', *Apollo* (7 April 2021), www.apollo-magazine.com/royal-mummies-parade-egypt/.

Ater, R., 'Making History: Meta Warrick Fuller's Ethiopia', *American Art* 17(3), (Autumn 2003), pp.12–31.

Ater, R., *Remaking Race and History: The Sculpture of Meta Warrick Fuller* (Berkeley, CA, 2011).

Avedissian, C., *Patterns, Costumes & Stencils* (London, 2009).

Ayad, L., 'The "Negress" of Alexandria: African Womanhood in Modern Egyptian Art', *African Arts* 51(4), (2021), pp.20–37.

Barassi, S., 'A Master in the Making', in *Becoming Henry Moore*, ed. Hannah Higham (London, 2017), pp.10–77.

Bardaouil, S., and T. Fellrath, *Tea with Nefertiti: The Making of the Artwork by the Artist, the Museum and the Public* (Doha, 2012).

Bardaouil, S., and T. Fellrath (eds), *Art et Liberté: Rupture, War and Surrealism in Egypt (1938–1948)*, (Paris, 2016).

Behdad, A., and L. Gartlan (eds), *Photography's Orientalism: New Essays on Colonial Representation* (Los Angeles, CA, 2013).

Benton, C., T. Benton and G. Wood (eds), *Art Deco 1910–1939* (London, 2003).

Bernal, M., *Black Athena: The Afroasiatic roots of Classical Civilization*, 2 vols (New Brunswick, NJ, 1987–91).

Bhabha, H. K., *The Location of Culture* (London, 1994).

Boas, G., *The Hieroglyphics of Horapollo* (2nd edition; New York, 1993).

Bricault, L., M. J. Versluys and P. Meyboom, *Nile into Tiber: Egypt in the Roman World* (Leiden, 2007).

Brier, B., *Egyptomania: Our Three Thousand Year Obsession with the Land of the Pharaohs* (London, 2013).

Bull, C. H., *The Tradition of Hermes-Trismegistus: The Egyptian Priestly Figure as a Teacher of Hellenized Wisdom* (Leiden, 2018).

Carrott, R., *The Egyptian Revival: Its Sources, Monuments and Meaning, 1808–1858* (Berkeley, CA, 1978).

Carruthers, W., *Histories of Egyptology: Interdisciplinary Measures* (London, 2014).

Carruthers, W., *Flooded Pasts: UNESCO, Nubia, and the Recolonization of Archaeology* (Ithaca, NY, 2022).

Caylus, A., *Comte de, Recueil d'antiquités égyptiennes, étrusques, grecques, romaines, et gauloises* (Paris, 1752–57).

Çelik, Z., *Displaying the Orient: Architecture of Islam at Nineteenth-Century World's Fairs* (Berkeley, CA, 1992).

Chaille, F. (ed.), *The Cartier Collection: Jewelry* (Paris, 2018).

Challis, D., and G. Romain, 'Ronald Moody: Sculpture and interwar Britain' (n.d.), www.ucl.ac.uk/equiano-centre/educational-resources/fusion-worlds/artists/ronald-moody-sculpture-and-interwar-britain.

Childs, A. L., and S. H. Libby (eds), *Blacks and Blackness in European Art of the Long Nineteenth Century* (Farnham, 2014).

Colla, E., '"Non, non! Si, si!": Commemorating the French Occupation of Egypt (1798–1801)', *MLN* 118(4), French Issue (September 2003), pp.1043–69.

Colla, E., *Conflicted Antiquities: Egyptology, Egyptomania, Egyptian Modernity* (Durham, NC, and London, 2007).

Collins, P., and L. McNamara, *Discovering Tutankhamun* (Oxford, 2014).

Conner, P., *The Inspiration of Egypt. Its Influence on British Artists, Travellers and Designers, 1700–1900* (Brighton, 1983).

Curl, J. S., *The Egyptian Revival: Ancient Egypt as the Inspiration for Design Motifs in the West* (London, 1982).

Curran, B. A., *The Egyptian Renaissance: The Afterlife of Egypt in Early Modern Italy* (Chicago, 2007).

Dagen, P., *Le Peintre, le poète, le sauvage: Les Voies du primitivisme dans l'art français* (Paris, 1998).

el-Daly, O., *Egyptology: The Missing Millennium. Ancient Egypt in Medieval Arabic Writings* (London, 2005).

Day, J., *The Mummy's Curse: Mummymania in the English-Speaking World* (London, 2006).

Denon, D. V., *Voyage dans la Basse et la Haute Égypte pendant les campagnes du Général Bonaparte*, 2 vols (Paris, 1802).

Description de l'Égypte, ou Recueil des observations et des recherches qui ont été faites en Égypte pendant l'expédition de l'armée française (1809–29).

Didier Hess, V., and H. Rashwan (eds), *Mahmoud Saïd: Catalogue raisonné*, 2 vols (Milan, 2015).

Dobson, E., *Writing the Sphinx: Literature, Culture and Egyptology* (Edinburgh, 2020).

Doyle, N., 'The Earliest Known Uses of "L'Égyptomania / Egyptomania" in French and English', *Journal of Ancient Egyptian Interconnections* 8 (2016), pp.122–5.

Dresser, C., *The Art of Decorative Design* (London, 1862).

Dresser, C., *Principles of Decorative Design* (London, 1873).

Drimmer, S., 'The Hieroglyphs of Kingship: Italy's Egypt in Early Tudor England and the Manuscript as Monument', *Memoirs of the American Academy in Rome* 59/60 (2014–15), pp.255–83.

Du Bois, W. E. B., *The Negro* (first published 1915; London, 1916).

Du Camp, M., *Égypte, Nubie, Syrie: Paysages et Monuments* (Paris, 1852).

Earle, S. (ed.), *Aaron Douglas: African American Modernist* (New Haven, CT, 2007).

Elliott, C., *Egypt in England* (Swindon, 2012).

Elshahed, M., *Cairo Since 1900: An Architectural Guide* (Cairo, 2020).

Enan, L., 'Si tu le sais, alors c'est une catastrophe: la commémoration, pourquoi, pour qui?', *Egypte/Monde Arabe* 1 (1999), pp.13–23.

Esanu, O. (ed.), *Art, Awakening and Modernity in the Middle East: The Arab Nude* (London, 2018), pp.71–85.

Esposito, D., 'Inspired by Antiquity: Sir Edward Poynter and the British Museum', *British Museum Magazine* 42 (Spring 2002), pp.23–5.

Esposito, D., 'From Ancient Egypt to Victorian London: The Impact of Ancient Egyptian Furniture on British Art and Design 1850–1900', *The Journal of the Decorative Arts Society 1850 to the Present* 27 (2003), pp.80–93.

Fechheimer, H., *La Sculpture égyptienne*, trans. C. Marchand (Paris, 1920).

Finnegan, R., *English Explorers in the East (1738–1745): The Travels of Thomas Shaw, Charles Perry and Richard Pococke* (Leiden, 2019).

Fischer von Erlach, J. B., *Entwurff einer Historischen Architectur* (Vienna, 1721).

Flam, J., and M. Deutch (eds), *Primitivism and Twentieth Century Art: A Documentary History* (Berkeley, CA, 2003).

Gange, D., *Dialogues with the Dead: Egyptology in British Culture and Religion* (Oxford, 2013).

Gange, D., 'Religion and Science in Late Nineteenth-Century British Egyptology', *History Journal* 49(4), (2016), pp.1083–1103.

Garnier, B., 'Rodin l'Égyptien', in M. Volait and E. Perrin (eds), *Dialogues artistiques avec les passés de l'Égypte: Une perspective transnationale et transmédiale* (Paris, 2017), http://books.openedition.org/inha/7185.

Gendzier, I. L., 'James Sanua and Egyptian Nationalism', *Middle East Journal* 15(1), (Winter 1961), pp.16–28.

Gere, C., and J. Rudoe, 'Jewellery at the 1862 Exhibition', *The Journal of the Decorative Arts Society 1850 to the Present* 38 (2014), pp.82–105.

Gere, C., and M. Whiteway, *Nineteenth-Century Design: From Pugin to Mackintosh* (London, 1993).

Giacometti, A., *Écrits* presented by M. Leiris and J. Dupin, and prepared by M. L. Palmer and F. Chaussende (Paris, 1990).

Giehlow, K., *The Humanist Interpretation of Hieroglyphs in the Allegorical Studies of the Renaissance*, trans. R. Raybould (Leiden, 2015).

Golia, M., *Photography and Egypt* (Cairo, 2010).

Hafez, K., *Il était une fois à Éden* (Cairo, 2019).

Hardwick, T., 'Why Is the Egyptian Government Moving Ancient Monuments Around the Country?', *Apollo* (29 February 2020), www.apollo-magazine.com/egyptian-government-moving-ancient-monuments/.

Harrison, M., *Francis Bacon: Catalogue raisonné* (London, 2016).

Harrison, M. (ed.), *Inside Francis Bacon* (London, 2020).

Haworth-Booth, M., *The Art of Lee Miller* (London, 2007).

Hockney, D., and N. Stangos (eds), *That's the Way I See it: David Hockney* (London, 1993).

Hoock, H., 'The British State and the Anglo-French Wars over Antiquities, 1798–1858', *The Historical Journal* 50(1), (2007), pp.49–72.

Hope, T., *Household Furniture and Interior Decoration* (London, 1807).

Humbert, J.-M., *L'Egyptomanie dans l'art occidental* (Paris, 1989).

Humbert, J.-M., M. Pantazzi and C. Ziegler, *Égyptomanie: L'Égypte dans l'art occidental 1730–1930* (Paris, 1994).

Humbert, J.-M., and C. Price (eds), *Imhotep Today: Egyptianising Architecture*. Encounters With Ancient Egypt Series (London, 2003).

Iversen, E., *Obelisks in Exile, Vol. I: The Obelisks of Rome* (Copenhagen, 1968).

Jeffreys, D., *Views of Ancient Egypt Since Napoleon Bonaparte: Imperialism, Colonialism and Modern Appropriations*. Encounters With Ancient Egypt Series (London, 2003).

Jones, O., *The Grammar of Ornament* (London, 1856).

Karnouk, L., *Modern Egyptian Art 1910 –2003* (Cairo, 2005).

Khazindar, M., and P. Gribaudo, *Adam Henein* (London, 2005).

Kircher, A., *Sphinx Mystagoga, sive Diatribe hieroglyphica* (Amsterdam, 1676).

Kirschke, A. H., *Aaron Douglas: Art, Race, and the Harlem Renaissance* (Jackson, MS, 1995).

Lefkowitz, M. R., and G. Maclean Rogers, *Black Athena Revisited* (London, 1996).

Livingstone, M., *David Hockney: Egyptian Journeys* (Cairo, 2002).

Meinertas, L., 'A Napoleonic Medal Cabinet', *Luxury* 4(2–3), (2017), pp.171–6.

Meyboom, P. G. P., *The Nile Mosaic of Palestrina: Early Evidence of Egyptian Religion in Italy* (Leiden, 1995).

Mitchell, T., *Colonising Egypt* (Berkeley, CA, 1988, republished 1991).

Montfaucon, B. de, *L'Antiquité expliquée et représentée en figures* (Paris, 1719–24).

Moody, C., 'Ronald Moody: A Man True to his Vision', *Third Text* 8/9 (1989), pp.5–24.

Moody, R., Interview with Macdonald Hastings from the BBC transcript of 'Anything to Declare?' 43 (1–4 December 1950), Tate Archives, Papers of Ronald Moody, TGA 956/3/5/3.

Moser, S., *Wondrous Curiosities: Ancient Egypt at the British Museum* (Chicago, 2006).

Moser, S., *Designing Antiquity: Owen Jones, Ancient Egypt and the Crystal Palace* (New Haven, CT, and London, 2012).

Moser, S., *Painting Antiquity: Ancient Egypt in the Art of Lawrence Alma-Tadema, Edward Poynter and Edwin Long* (New York, 2020).

Nadelhoffer, H., *Cartier: Jewellers Extraordinary* (New York, 1984).

Naughton, G., *David Roberts: Travels in the Holy Land* (London, 2013).

Norden, F., *Voyage d'Egypte et de Nubie* (Copenhagen, 1755).

Osman, D. N., 'Occupiers' Title to Cultural Property: Nineteenth-century Removal of Egyptian Artifacts', *Columbia Journal of Transnational Law* 36 (1999), pp.969–1002.

Pautot, T., R. Perrin and M. Etienne, *Alberto Giacometti et l'Égypte antique* (Paris, 2021).

Piranesi, G. B., *Diverse maniere d'adornare i cammini ed ogni altra parte degli edifizi desunte dall'architettura Egizia, Etrusca, e Greca, con un Ragionamento Apologetico in defesa dell'Architettura Egizia, e Toscana* (Rome, 1769).

Pococke, R., *A Description of the East and some other countries* (London, 1743).

Prettejohn, E., and P. Trippi (eds), *Lawrence Alma-Tadema: At Home in Antiquity* (Munich, 2016).

Pugin, A. W. N., *An Apology for the Revival of Christian Architecture in England* (London, 1843).

Putnam, J., and W. V. Davies (eds), *Time Machine: Ancient Egypt and Contemporary Art* (London, 1994).

Quirke, S., *Hidden Hands: Egyptian Workforces in Petrie Excavation Archives 1880–1924* (London, 2010).

Radwan, N., *Les Modernes d'Égypte: Une renaissance nationale des beaux-arts et des arts appliqués* (Bern, 2017).

Reid, D. M., *Whose Pharaohs? Archaeology, Museums, and Egyptian National Identity from Napoleon to World War I* (Cairo, 2002).

Reid, D. M., *Contesting Antiquity in Egypt: Archaeologies, Museums, & the Struggle for Identities from World War I to Nasser* (Cairo, 2015).

Riggs, C., 'Colonial Visions: Egyptian Antiquities and Contested Histories in the Cairo Museum', *Museum Worlds: Advances in Research* 1 (2013), pp.65–84.

Riggs, C., *Egypt*. Lost Civilizations (London, 2017).

Riggs, C., *Photographing Tutankhamun: Archaeology, Ancient Egypt, and the Archive* (London, 2018).

Roullet, A., *The Egyptian and Egyptianizing Monuments of Rome* (Leiden, 1972).

Said, E., *Orientalism* (London, 1978).

Sandys, G., *Relation of a Journey begun an. Dom. 1610* (London, 1615).

Seggerman, A. D., 'Modern Art in Egypt and Constellational Modernism: A New Approach to Global Modern Art' (2019), https://mavcor.yale.edu/mavcor-journal/collections/modernism-on-the-nile.

Shaw, T., *Travels in Barbery and the Levant* (London, 1743).

Skipwith, J. (ed.), *Rhapsodies in Black: Art of the Harlem Renaissance* (London, 1997).

Spier, J., T. Potts and S. E. Cole (eds), *Beyond the Nile: Egypt and the Classical World* (Los Angeles, CA, 2018).

Stevenson, A., *Scattered Finds: Archaeology, Egyptology and Museums* (London, 2019).

Swetnam-Burland, M., *Egypt in Italy: Visions of Egypt in Roman Imperial Culture* (Cambridge, 2015).

Sylvester, D., *The Brutality of Fact: Interviews with Francis Bacon* (London, 2016).

Taylor, J. H., and H. Dorey, *Sir John Soane's Greatest Treasure: The Sarcophagus of Seti I* (London, 2017).

Trafton, S., *Egypt Land: Race and Nineteenth-Century American Egyptomania* (Durham, NC, and London, 2004).

Tromans, N. (ed.), *The Lure of the East: British Orientalist Painting* (London, 2008).

Ucko, P., and T. Champion (eds), *The Wisdom of Egypt: Changing Visions through the Ages*. Encounters With Ancient Egypt Series (London, 2016).

Versluys, M. J., *Aegyptiaca Romana: Nilotic Scenes and the Roman Views of Egypt* (Leiden, 2002).

Versluys, M. J., *Beyond Egyptomania: Objects, Styles and Agency* (Berlin, 2020).

Vever, H., *French Jewelry of the Nineteenth Century* (*La Bijouterie française au XIXème siècle*), trans. K. Purcell (first published 1906–8; London, 2001).

Volait, M., 'Architectures de la décennie pharaonique en Égypte (1922–1932)', in J.-C. Vatin (ed.), *Images d'Égypte: De la fresque à la bande dessinée* (Cairo, 1992), pp.163–86.

Volait, M., and E. Perrin (eds), *Dialogues artistiques avec les passés de l'Égypte: Une perspective transnationale et transmédiale* (Paris, 2017), http://books.openedition.org/inha/7185.

Walker, S., and P. Higgs, *Cleopatra of Egypt: From History to Myth* (London, 2001).

Watkin, D., and P. Hewat-Jaboor (eds), *Thomas Hope: Regency Designer* (New Haven, CT, and London, 2008).

Winckelmann, J., *Geschichte der Kunst des Alterthums* (Dresden, 1764).

Winegar, J., *Farouk Hosny/Adam Henein: Contemporary Egyptian Artists and Heirs to an Ancient Tradition* (New York, 1999).

Winegar, J., *Creative Reckonings: The Politics of Art and Culture in Contemporary Egypt* (Stanford, CA, 2006).

PHOTOGRAPHIC CREDITS

© Photo by Emad Abdelhady. Courtesy May Moein Zeid & Adel Youssry Khedr: Fig. 12.2

© Al-Ahram Foundation Collection, Cairo: Fig. 12.1

© Archives ArtTalks. Courtesy Fatenn Mostafa: Fig. 12.8

© Archives Emad Abou Ghazi: Figs. 12.1, 12.3, 12.4, 12.5, 12.7

© Artepics / Alamy Stock Photo: Figs. 5.5, 5.10

© The Arthur Conan Doyle Encyclopedia: Fig. 9.6

© The Artist: Figs. 0.7, 4.1, 4.3, 10.1, 10.2, 14.8

© Courtesy the Artist and Adrian Sassoon. Photo by Stephen Cox: Fig. 14.4

© The Artist. Courtesy Ben Brown Fine Arts, London: Cover, Fig. 14.1

© The Artist and Tintera Gallery: Figs. 4.2, 14.8

© Axis Images / Alamy Stock Photo: Fig. 1.11

© Bibliothèque nationale de France: Fig. 8.3

© Birmingham Museum and Art Gallery. Photo by Birmingham Museums Trust, licensed under CC0: Fig. 7.2

© British Library / Bridgeman Images: Fig. 1.12

© British Library Board. All Rights Reserved / Bridgeman Images: Fig. 1.13

© The Trustees of the British Museum: Figs. 1.6, 6.1, 7.3, 11.6

© Cartier: Fig. 13.1

© The Christie Archive Trust: Figs. 13.2, 13.8

© Cleopatra's Boudoir: Fig. 13.12

Ⓟ Photo from Cooper Hewitt / Simthsonian Design Museum. Smithsonian: Fig. 2.14

Creative Commons: Fig. 16.8

© Dahesh Museum of Art, New York / Bridgeman Images: Fig. 5.11

Photo by Eleanor Dobson: Figs. 9.1, 9.2

[EES.BAL.NEG.10] © Courtesy of The Egypt Exploration Society: Fig. 6.3

© Estate of Francis Bacon. All rights reserved, DACS. Photo Sainsbury Centre: Fig. 11.12

© Photo by Evening Standard / Hulton Archive via Getty Images: Fig. 14.2

© Fine Art Images / Heritage Images / Alamy Stock Photo: Fig. 5.8

© Fiskars. Photo courtesy Stoke-on-Trent City Archives: Fig. 7.1

© Photo by Gary Fong / San Francisco Chronicle via Getty Images: Fig. 14.11

© Gallery Desmet: Fig. 1.5

© Griffith Institute, University of Oxford: Figs. 3.10, 3.11, 5.3

© Dina Hafez: Fig. 3.12

© Harris Museum & Art Gallery, Preston: Fig. 5.2

© Reproduced by permission of The Henry Moore Foundation: Figs. 11.5, 11.7

© Historic England Archive / Bridgeman Images: Fig. 0.4

© David Hockney. The British Council. Photo credit: The British Council: Fig. 14.3

Photo by Denisa Ilie, courtesy Sainsbury Centre: Figs. 1.7, 2.5, 8.2, 8.4, 8.7, 8.8, 11.11, 13.7, 13.9, 13.13

© iStock by Getty Images: Fig. 16.2

© The J. Paul Getty Museum: Fig. 3.9

© John Rylands Library: Fig. 1.10

© Koninklijke Verzamelingen, Den Haag: Fig. 1.4

© The Jacob and Gwendolyn Knight Lawrence Foundation, Seattle / Artists Rights Society (ARS), New York and DACS, London 2022: Fig. 11.4

© Laing Art Gallery / Bridgeman Images: Fig. 0.3

© Liverpool World Museums: Fig. 1.2

© Ian Macpherson London / Alamy: Fig. 13.15

© Borislav Marinic / Alamy Stock Photo: Fig: 14.6

© Meta Vaux Warrick Fuller. Photo courtesy Smithsonian: Fig. 11.3

Ⓟ Photo from The Metropolitan Museum of Art: Fig. 3.2

© Mohamed Naghi Museum, Cairo. Courtesy Fatenn Mostafa: Fig. 12.11

© National Maritime Museum, Greenwich, London: Fig. 2.4

© Newport Museum and Art Gallery / Bridgeman Images: Fig. 5.6

Photo from The New York Public Library: Figs 0.8, 0.9, 2.7, 2.8

© North American Star System Production: Fig. 14.9

© Powerhouse Museum Collection. Purchased with funds donated by Patrons of the Powerhouse, 1984. Photo by Marinco Kojdanovski: Fig. 2.13

© P&O Heritage Collection www.poheritage.com: Fig. 8.5, p.179

Photo © RMN-Grand Palais (Musée du Louvre) / Michel Urtado: Fig. 6.4

Image courtesy Paul Reeves: Figs. 7.4, 7.5

© Rare Books and Special Collections Library, The American University in Cairo: Fig. 16.4

© RIBA Collections: Figs. 13.14, 13.16, 13.19

Photo by Rijksmuseum, Amsterdam, licensed under CC0: Figs. 5.1, 5.12

Courtesy the Royal College of Art Collection and Victoria Miro © The Artist: Fig. 0.1

© Royal Collection Trust: Fig. 3.8

Photo courtesy Paul Ruddock: Fig. 1.8

© Photograph reproduced with the kind permission of the Russell-Cotes Art Gallery & Museum, Bournemouth: Fig. 0.2

Photo Sabrina Amrani Gallery: Fig. 15.1

Sainsbury Centre: p.2

© The Science and Society Picture Library / Getty Images: Fig. 3.3

© Shapero Rare Books, London. Photo by Natasha Marshall: Fig. 13.10

© Sir John Soane's Museum, London: Figs. 2.1, 2.2

© Sir John Soane's Museum, London. Photo by Ardon Bar-Hama: Fig. 1.9, 2.15

© Sotheby's: Figs. 12.6, 12.8, 14.7

© Sotheby's / akg-images: Fig. 5.7

© Succession Alberto Giacometti / DACS 2022: Figs. 11.2, 11.10

© Succession Alberto Giacometti / DACS 2022. Photo Sainsbury Centre: Figs.11.1

© Tate: Figs. 5.9, 11.9, 12.9

© Touchstones Rochdale Art Gallery, Link4Life: Fig. 5.4

© Towneley Hall Art Gallery & Museum, Burnley / Bridgeman Images: Fig. 5.13

© 20th Century Fox / Kobal / Shutterstock: Fig. 0.5

© Image: Crown Copyright: UK Government Art Collection: Fig. 11.8

Photo by Roland Unger: Fig. 16.6

© V&A Wedgwood Collection: Fig. 2.6

© Van Cleef & Arpels: Fig. 13.11

© Ivan Vdovin / Alamy Stock Photo: Fig. 1.1

© Victoria and Albert Museum, London: Figs. 2.9, 2.10, 2.11, 2.12, 3.1, 3.4, 3.5, 3.7, 7.6, 7.7, 9.7

© Estate of the Artist / Victoria and Albert Museum, London: Figs. 13.6, 15.2

© Visual Haggard: Figs. 9.3, 9.5

Photo courtesy Rupert Wace: Figs. 13.3, 13.4, 13.5

Photo © Warner Bros / Kobal / Shutterstock: Fig. 0.6

© Wartski, London: Figs. 8.1, 8.5

Ⓟ Photo from Wellcome Collection: Figs. 2.3, 3.6, 6.2

© Claudia Wiens / Alamy Stock Photo: Fig. 16.1

Photo from Wikimedia Commons: Figs. 1.3, 5.14, 14.10, 16.3, 16.5, 16.6, 16.7, 16.9, 16.10

© Fred Wilson. Photo by Ellen Labenski, courtesy Pace Gallery: Fig. 14.12

© Courtesy S. J. Wolfe: Fig. 9.4

© Photo: Herbert Wright: Fig.14.4

NOTES

INTRODUCTION

1 Ulrich Haarmann, 'Medieval Muslim Perceptions of Pharaonic Egypt', in Antonio Loprieno, *Ancient Egyptian Literature: History and Forms* (Leiden, 1996), p.607.
2 Donald M. Reid, *Whose Pharaohs? Archaeology, Museums, and Egyptian National Identity from Napoleon to World War I* (Berkeley, CA, 2002), pp.9, 11; Elliott Colla, *Conflicted Antiquities: Egyptology, Egyptomania, Egyptian Modernity* (Durham, NC, and London, 2007), p.13. The frequent use of terms like 'rape' in these book titles, as in Peter France, *The Rape of Egypt: How the Europeans Stripped Egypt of its Heritage* (London, 1991), suggests Egypt as victim rather than active agent.
3 Reid, 2002, and *Contesting Antiquity in Egypt: Archaeologies, Museums & the Struggle for Identities from World War I to Nasser* (Cairo, 2015); Okasha el-Daly, *Egyptology: The Missing Millennium. Ancient Egypt in Medieval Arabic Writings* (London, 2005); Colla, 2007.
4 John Soane, 'Lecture 1', in David Watkin, *Sir John Soane: The Royal Academy Lectures* (Cambridge, 2000), p.37.
5 Noreen Doyle, 'The Earliest Known Uses of "L'Égyptomania / Egyptomania" in French and English', *Journal of Ancient Egyptian Interconnections* 8 (2016), pp.122–5.
6 Anonymous, 'Review of *Mémoires de la Comtesse de Lichtenau*, &c., (Paris, 1809)', *The Monthly Review: or, Literary Journal* (1810), p.470.
7 Donald M. Reid, 'Indigenous Egyptology: The Decolonization of a Profession?', *Journal of the American Oriental Society* 105(2), (1985), pp.233–46, and Reid, 2002; Colla, 2007; William Carruthers, *Histories of Egyptology: Interdisciplinary measures* (New York, 2014).
8 David O'Connor and Andrew Reid, *Ancient Egypt in Africa*. Encounters with Ancient Egypt (London, 2003); Karen Exell, *Egypt in Its African Context: Proceedings of the conference held at the Manchester Museum, University of Manchester, October 2–4, 2009* (Oxford, 2011). See primarily the controversies generated by Martin Bernal, *Black Athena: The Afroasiatic roots of Classical civilization*, 2 vols (New Brunswick, NJ, 1987–91); Mary R. Lefkowitz and Guy Maclean Rogers, *Black Athena revisited* (London, 1996).
9 Helen Whitehouse, 'Egyptomanias', *American Journal of Archaeology* 101(1), (1997), p.161; Brian Curran, 'Review: Egyptomania: Egypt in Western Art, 1730–1930 by Jean-Marcel Humbert, Michael Pantazzi and Christiane Ziegler', *The Art Bulletin* 78(4), (1996), pp.741–2.
10 Patrick Conner, *The Inspiration of Egypt: Its Influence on British Artists, Travellers and Designers, 1700–1900* (Brighton, 1983); Gereon Sievernich and Hendrik Budde, *Europa und der Orient, 800–1900* (Berlin, 1989); Jennifer Hardin, *The Lure of Egypt: Land of the Pharaohs revisited* (St Petersburg, 1996).
11 Bernard de Montfaucon, *L'Antiquité expliquée et représentée en figures* (Paris, 1719–24); Johann Bernhard Fischer von Erlach, *Entwurff einer Historischen Architectur* (Vienna, 1721); Anne Claude, Comte de Caylus, *Recueil d'antiquités égyptiennes, étrusques, grecques, romaines, et gauloises* (Paris, 1752–7).
12 Alexandra von Lieven, 'Urteile über die Kunst der Ägypter – Platon und Winckelmann', in Adolf H. Borbein and Ernst Osterkamp, *Kunst und Freiheit, Eine Leitthese Winckelmanns und ihre Folgen* (Mainz, 2020), pp.203–18.
13 Augustus W. N. Pugin, *An Apology for the Revival of Christian Architecture in England* (London, 1843).
14 Caroline van Eck, '"Nachleben", mnemohistory and the agency of things Egyptian', in Miguel J. Versluys, *Beyond Egyptomania: Objects, Styles and Agency* (Berlin, 2020), pp.11–12, contra Nikolaus Pevsner and Susanne Lang, 'The Egyptian revival', in Nikolaus Pevsner, *Studies in Art, Architecture and Design* (New York, 1968), pp.213–35; Richard Carrott, *The Egyptian Revival: Its Sources, Monuments and Meaning, 1808–1858* (Berkeley, CA, 1978); James S. Curl, *The Egyptian Revival: Ancient Egypt as the Inspiration for Design Motifs in the West* (London, 1982).
15 John Loring, 'Egyptomania: The Nile Style', *The Connoisseur* CC 804 (February 1979), pp.114–21. See also Curl, whose original 1982 *The Egyptian Revival* was reprinted in 1994 as *Egyptomania* in the wake of the blockbuster exhibition of the same name that year.
16 Bob Brier, *Egyptomania: Our Three Thousand Year Obsession with the Land of the Pharaohs* (London, 2013).
17 Miguel J. Versluys, 'Haunted by Egypt: A long-term perspective on history, mnemohistory and material culture', in Versluys, 2020, p.17; Jean-Marcel Humbert, 'Plaidoyer pour l'égyptomanie, ou comment s'approprier une Égypte Fantasmée', ibid., pp.39–52.
18 Conner, 1983.
19 Stephanie Moser, 'Reconstructing Ancient Worlds: Reception Studies, Archaeological Representation and the Interpretation of Ancient Egypt', *Journal of Archaeological Method and Theory* 22(4), (2015), pp.1263–1308. Works that combine the two fields include Jean-Marcel Humbert and Clifford Price, *Imhotep Today: Egyptianising Architecture* (London, 2003); David Jeffreys, *Views of Ancient Egypt Since Napoleon Bonaparte: Imperialism, Colonialism and Modern Appropriations* (London, 2003).
20 Lucy Hughes-Hallett, *Cleopatra: Histories, Dreams and Distortions* (1990); Mary Hamer, *Signs of Cleopatra: History, Politics, Representation* (London, 1993); Michel Chauveau, *Cleopatra: Beyond the Myth* (Ithaca, NY, 2002).
21 Christopher Pelling, 'Anything truth can do, we can do better: The Cleopatra legend', in Susan Walker and Peter Higgs, *Cleopatra of Egypt: From History to Myth* (London, 2001), pp.292–301.
22 John of Nikiou, *Chronicle* LXVII.9; trans. Robert H. Charles, *The Chronicle of John, Bishop of Nikiu* (London, 1916).
23 Ammianus Marcellinus, *Res Gestae* XXVIII 4.9.
24 Abu al-Hassan al-Mas'udi, Muruj, *Muruj al-Dhahab wa Ma'adin al-Jawhar* 1, (Beirut, 1988), p.304; for this quote see el-Daly, 2005, p.133. The trope of Cleopatra as scientist may have been through conflation with a different figure named Cleopatra, active in Alexandria during the third century BC, who was apparently a famed alchemist.
25 Five of the twenty-three volumes of the *Description* were devoted to Egyptian antiquities.
26 Elliott Colla, '"Non, non! Si, si!": Commemorating the French Occupation of Egypt (1798–1801)', *MLN* 118(4), French Issue (September 2003), pp.1043–69, on p.1056.
27 Dominique Vivant Denon, *Voyage dans la Basse et la Haute Égypte pendant les campagnes du Général Bonaparte* (first ed. 1802; London, 1817), pp.251 and 252, where Denon describes the plight of Egyptians who he claims suffered at the hands of both the French and the Mameluks. Laila Enan, 'Si tu le sais, alors c'est une catastrophe: la commémoration, pourquoi, pour qui?', *Egypte/Monde Arabe* 1 (1999), pp.13–23.
28 Jean-Baptiste Joseph Fourier, 'Préface historique', in Edme-François Jomard et al., *Description de l'Égypte ou Recueil des observations et des recherches qui ont été faites en Égypte pendant l'expédition de l'armée française*, vol. 1 (second ed. Paris 1821), p.i.
29 Edward W. Said, *Orientalism* (first pub. 1978; London, 2003), p.83.
30 Said, 2003, p.84.
31 Colla, 2003, p.1052.
32 Enan, 1999.

CHAPTER 1: A MILLENNIUM AND A HALF OF EGYPT

1 Diodorus Siculus, *Bibliotheca Historica*, Book XVIII.4, 5.
2 Jane Draycott, 'The Symbol of Cleopatra Selene: Reading Crocodiles on Coins in the Late Republic and Early Principate', *Acta Classica* 55 (2012), pp.43–56.
3 Molly Swetnam-Burland, '"Aegyptus Redacta": The Egyptian Obelisk in the Augustan Campus Martius', *Art Bulletin* 92(3), (2010), pp.135–53; and *Egypt in Italy: Visions of Egypt in Roman Imperial Culture* (Cambridge, 2015), pp.65–104.
4 A useful compendium of all Rome's monuments remains Anne Roullet, *The Egyptian and Egyptianising Monuments of Rome* (Leiden, 1972).
5 Laurent Bricault and Jean Leclant, *Atlas de la diffusion des Cultes isiaques: IVe s. av. J.-C.–IVe s. ap. J.C.* (Paris, 2001).
6 This essay attempts not to distinguish cults as 'Egyptian' or 'Greco-Roman'. On the problems with this separation, see Valentino Gasparini and Richard L. Gordon, 'Egyptianism. Appropriating "Egypt" in the "Isiac" cults of the Greco-Roman World', *Acta Antiqua Academiae Scientiarum Hungaricae* 58 (2018), pp.571–606.
7 Klaas A. D. Smelik and Emily A. Hemelrijk, '"Who Knows Not What Monsters Demented Egypt Worships?": Opinions on Egyptian Animal Worship in Antiquity as Part of the Ancient Conception of Egypt', *Aufsteig und Niedergang der römischen Welt* II, 17(4), (1984), pp.1852–2000.
8 Ludwig Koenen, 'Egyptian Influence in Tibullus', *Illinois Classical Studies* I (1976), pp.127–59.
9 Molly Swetnam-Burland, 'Egyptian Objects, Roman Contexts: A Taste for Aegyptiaca in Italy', in Laurent Bricault, Miguel J. Versluys and Paul Meyboom, *Nile into Tiber: Egypt in the Roman World* (Leiden, 2007), pp.120–3.
10 Robert A. Wild, *Water in the Cultic Worship of Isis and Sarapis* (Leiden, 1981), pp.101–26.
11 Jean-Claude Grenier, 'La Decoration statuaire du "Serapeum" du "Canope" de la Villa Adriana: Essai de reconstruction et d'interprétation', *Mélanges de l'École française de Rome* 101–2 (1989), pp.925–1019; and Zaccaria Mari and Sergio Sgalambro, 'The Antinoeion of Hadrian's Villa: Interpretation and Architectural Reconstruction', *American Journal of Archaeology* 111 (2007), pp.83–104.
12 See Miguel J. Versluys, 'Aegyptiaca Romana, the Widening Debate', in Bricault, Versluys and Meyboom, 2007, pp.1–14.
13 Miguel J. Versluys, *Aegyptiaca Romana: Nilotic Scenes and the Roman Views of Egypt* (Leiden, 2002); I. Bragantini, 'The Cult of Isis and Ancient Egyptomania in Campania', in David L. Balch and Annette Weissenrieder, *Contested Spaces: Houses and Temples in Roman Antiquity and the New Testament* (Tübingen, 2012), pp.21–33; Caitlin Barrett, 'Recontextualizing Nilotic Scenes: Interactive Landscapes in the Garden of the Casa dell'Efebo, Pompeii', *American Journal of Archaeology* 121(2), (2017), pp.293–332.
14 Swetnam-Burland, 2015, pp.150–4, who also discusses the various purposes attributed to the mosaic.
15 Eva M. Mol, 'The Perception of Egypt in Networks of Being and Becoming: A Thing Theory Approach to Egyptianising Objects in Roman Domestic Contexts', *Theoretical Roman Archaeology Conference Proceedings 2012* (Oxford, 2013), p.127; Swetnam-Burland, 2015, p.28.

16 Bragantini, 2012, p.27; Barrett, 2017, pp.295–6.
17 Robert S. Bianchi, 'Two Silver Skyphoi with Nilotic Scenes Revisited', *Égypte Nilotique et Méditerranéene* 14 (2021), pp.115–33.
18 Mol, 2013; and 'Romanising Oriental Cults? A Cognitive Approach to Alterity and Religious Experience in the Roman Cults of Isis', in Aleksandra Nikolowska and Sander Müskens, *Romanising Oriental Gods? Religious Transformations in the Balkan Provinces in the Roman Period, New Finds and Novel Perspectives* (Skopje, 2015), pp.89–111; Swetnam-Burland, 2007, pp.113–18; Gasparini and Gordon, 2018.
19 Further Roman pyramids once existed but are now lost, such as the Meta Romuli once located between the Vatican and the mausoleum of Hadrian, historically believed to have been the tomb of Romulus.
20 Swetnam-Burland, 2015, pp.89–90.
21 Ilrene Iacopi, *The House of Augustus: Wall Paintings* (Milan, 2008), pp.29–33.
22 Eric M. Orlin, 'Octavian and Egyptian Cults: Redrawing the Boundaries of Romanness', *The American Journal of Philology* 129(2), (2008), pp.232–53.
23 Dimitri Laboury and Marie Leclane, 'Lost in Translation? On "Aegyptiaca" in the Middle Ages', in Miguel J. Versluys, *Beyond Egyptomania: Objects, Styles and Agency* (Berlin, 2020), pp.115–32.
24 Claudia La Malfa, 'Reassessing the Renaissance of the Palestrina Nile Mosaic,' *Journal of the Warburg and Courtauld Institutes* 66 (2003), pp.267–72.
25 The key work on the Renaissance uses of ancient Egypt remains Brian A. Curran, *The Egyptian Renaissance: The Afterlife of Egypt in Early Modern Italy* (Chicago, 2007).
26 N. Randolph Parks, 'On the Meaning of Pinturicchio's Sala dei Santi', *Art History* 2 (1979), pp.291–317; Curran, 2007, Chapter 6.
27 For the authors of the *Corpus Hermeticum*, see Christian H. Bull, *The Tradition of Hermes-Trismegistus: The Egyptian Priestly Figure as a Teacher of Hellenized Wisdom* (Leiden, 2018), Chapter 1. On the dating and possible identity of Horapollo, see Claude-Françoise Brunon, 'Signe, Figure, Langage: Les "Hieroglyphica" d'Horapollon', in Yves Giraud, *L'Emblème de la Renaissance* (Paris, 1981), pp.29–48; George Boas, *The Hieroglyphics of Horapollo* (second ed.; New York, 1993), pp.3–29.
28 Berthold Hub, 'Filarete and the East: The Renaissance of a Prisca Architectura', *Journal of the Society of Architectural Historians* 70(1), (2011), pp.18–37.
29 Phyllis W. Lehmann, *Cyriacus of Ancona's Egyptian Visit and its Reflections in Gentile Bellini and Hieronymous Bosch* (Locust Valley, PA, 1978).
30 Karl Giehlow, *The Humanist Interpretation of Hieroglyphs in the Allegorical Studies of the Renaissance* (trans. Robin Raybould; Leiden, 2015); Ludwig Volkmann, *Hieroglyph, Emblem and Renaissance Pictography* (trans. R. Raybould; Leiden, 2018).
31 Godelieve Denhaene (ed.), *Lambert Lombard: Peintre de la Renaissance, Liège 1505/06–1566. Essais interdisciplinaires et Catalogue de l'exposition* (Brussels, 2006), pp.87–97; Yassana Croizat-Glazer, 'The Role of Ancient Egypt in Masquerades at the Court of François Ier', *Renaissance Quarterly* 66(4), (2013), pp.1206–49.
32 Sonja Drimmer, 'The Hieroglyphs of Kingship: Italy's Egypt in Early Tudor England and the Manuscript as Monument', *Memoirs of the American Academy in Rome* 59/60 (2014/15), pp.255–83.
33 Elliott Colla, *Conflicted Antiquities: Egyptology, Egyptomania, Egyptian Modernity* (Durham, 2007), p.74.
34 Okasha el-Daly, *Egyptology: The Missing Millennium. Ancient Egypt in Medieval Arabic Writings* (London, 2005), p.17.
35 For medieval Arabic writers on Egypt, see Ulrich Haarmann, 'In Quest of the Spectacular: Noble and Learned Visitors to the Pyramids around 1200 A.D.', in Wael Hallaq and Donald Little, *Islamic studies presented to Charles J. Adams* (Leiden, 1991), pp.57–67; and Martyn Smith, 'Pyramids in the Medieval Islamic Landscape: Perceptions and Narratives', *Journal of the American Research Center in Egypt* 42 (2007), pp.1–14.
36 Colla, 2007, pp.78–9.
37 el-Daly, 2005, pp.48, 89.
38 Smith, 2007, p.3.
39 Ibid., p.5.
40 Alexander Fodor, 'The Origins of the Arabic Legends of the Pyramids', *Acta Orientalia Hungarica* 23 (1983), pp.335–63; Smith, 2007, pp.9–12.
41 el-Daly, 2005, Appendix 2.
42 Doris Behrens-Abouseif, 'Between Quarry and Magic: The Selective Approach to Spolia in the Islamic Monuments of Egypt', in A. Payne, *Dalmatia and the Mediterranean. Portable Archaeology and the Poetics of Influence* (Leiden, 2014), pp.402–25.
43 el-Daly, 2005, p.81.
44 Martin Plessner, 'Hermes Trismegistus and Arab Science,' *Studia Islamica* 2 (1954), pp.45–59.
45 el-Daly, 2005, pp.57–73, in particular the list of early Arabic 'translations' on pp.66–7.
46 Erik Hornung, *The Secret Lore of Egypt: Its Impact on the West* (trans. David Lorton; Cornell, 2001), p.38; el-Daly, 2005, p.112.
47 Italo Ronca, 'Senior de Chemia: A Reassessment of the Medieval Latin Translation of Ibn Umayl's Al-ma al-Waraqi wa l-ard al-najimiyya', *Bulletin de Philosophie Médiévale* 37 (1995), pp.9–31.
48 el-Daly, 2005, pp.31–44.
49 For such seals, see Hans Goedicke, 'The Seal of the Necropolis', *Studien zur Altagyptischen Kultur* 20 (1993), pp.67–79.
50 Charles Burnett, Keiji Yamamoto and Michio Yano, 'Al-Kindi on Finding Buried Treasure', *Arabic Science and Philosophy* 7 (1997), pp.57–90.
51 el-Daly, 2005, p.72, Fig. 24.

CHAPTER 2: AMBIGUOUS EXCHANGES

1 Helen Dorey, 'Sir John Soane's Acquisition of the Sarcophagus of Seti I', *Georgian Group Journal* 1 (1991), pp.26–35; John H. Taylor and Helen Dorey, *Sir John Soane's Greatest Treasure: The Sarcophagus of Seti I* (London, 2017); and Gillian Darley, *John Soane, The Accidental Romantic* (New Haven, CT, and London, 1999), esp. pp.273–4.
2 See Tim Knox, *Sir John Soane's Museum, London* (London, 2009).
3 *The Morning Post* (22 April 1824).
4 This act of what would be considered vandalism today probably follows the trend of travellers to Egypt leaving inscriptions at sites they visited. These included commemorative military inscriptions, Grand Tourists celebrating highlights of their journeys, and excavators marking a site where history was unearthed.
5 Giovanni Battista Belzoni, *Narrative of the Operations and Recent Discoveries within the Pyramids, Temples, Tombs, and Excavations in Egypt and Nubia* (London, 1820) and the accompanying Giovanni Battista Belzoni, *Plates Illustrative of the Researches ad Operations of G. Belzoni in Egypt and Nubia* (London, 1821).
6 The party on Saturday 26 March was noted as having the most eminent guests, including the Duke of Sussex, Lord and Lady Liverpool, the Chancellor of the Exchequer, as well artists such as Sir Thomas Lawrence, and the Romantic poet Samuel Taylor Coleridge. See Dorey, 1991, p.32.
7 For instance, to achieve the desired lighting effects, Soane hired 108 lamps, chandeliers and candelabra. Ibid., p.30.
8 Belzoni had a financial interest in the sale of the sarcophagus, but only if the sum achieved was more than £2,000. As a consequence, he earned nothing from his discovery.
9 The plans for the Egyptian Hall were drawn up by architect Peter Frederick Robinson. His design was partly inspired by the success of the Egyptian Room in Thomas Hope's house in Duchess Street, which was open to the public and had been well illustrated in Hope's *Household Furniture and Interior Decoration* (London, 1807). The hall cost £16,000 to build.
10 R. Ackermann, *The Repository of Arts*, etc., vol. iii (June 1810); ibid., second series, vol. xi (1 June 1821), pp.375–6. The first day attracted 1,900 admissions, at 2s. 6d. each.
11 G. Belzoni, *Description of the Egyptian tomb, discovered by G. Belzoni* (London, 1821). After his exhibition closed, Belzoni left for an expedition to Africa, where he died in 1823 before the installation of Seti's sarcophagus at Soane's house.
12 On this point see, for example, Paul Greenhalgh, *Ephemeral Vistas: The Expositions Universelles, Great Exhibitions and World's Fairs, 1851–1939* (Manchester, 1990); John E. Findling, *Chicago's Great World's Fairs* (Manchester, c.1994); and Erik Mattie, *World's Fairs* (Princeton, NJ, 1998).
13 Ackermann, 1821, second series, vol. xiii (1 February 1822), pp.108–10.
14 Critique of the colonial ambitions of the West and its feeling of cultural superiority over the East was first articulated by Edward Said in his *Orientalism* (London, 1978). Said's views have been developed and challenged. There is a vast literature on this topic; see, for instance, Homi K. Bhabha, *The Location of Culture* (London, 1994). Bhabha's notion of hybridity re-evaluates the assumption of colonial identity. This view has subsequently been questioned by, for example, Amar Acheraiou, *Questioning Hybridity, Postcolonialism and Globalization* (London, 2011).
15 Juan Cole, *Napoleon's Egypt: Invading the Middle East* (London, 2007).
16 On this point see, for example, T. G. H. James, 'Napoleon and Egyptology: Britain's Debt to French Enterprise', in R. G. W. Anderson (ed.), *Enlightening the British: Knowledge, Discovery and the Museum in the Eighteenth Century* (London, 2003). More broadly, the display of Egyptian antiquities in the British Museum is covered in Stephanie Moser, *Wondrous Curiosities: Ancient Egypt at the British Museum* (Chicago, 2006).
17 As noted, for example, by Leslie Poles Hartley in *The Go-Between* (London, 1953) and by David Lowenthal in *The Past is a Foreign Country* (Cambridge, 1985; 2nd revised and expanded edn 2015).
18 On this point, see Abigail Harrison Moore, 'Voyage: Dominique-Vivant Denon and the Transference of Images of Egypt', *Art History* 25(4), (September 2002), pp.531–49.
19 There were several subsequent editions in many languages, some of which have the slightly different title *Voyages dans la basse et la haute Égypte pendant les campagnes de Bonaparte*.
20 Dominique Vivant Denon, *Voyage dans la Basse et la Haute Égypte pendant les campagnes du Général Bonaparte*, 2 vols (Paris, 1802), Preface, p.ii.
21 I discuss the visual language of architectural drawings at length in Dana Arnold, *Architecture and Ekphrasis: Space, Time and the Embodied Description of the Past* (Manchester, 2020).
22 Denon, 1802, p.171.
23 Africanness recognises the diversity of African identity after the (post-) colonial moment and its debasing racialising ideology. See Charles Ngwena, *What is Africanness? Contesting nativism in race, culture and sexualities* (Pretoria, 2018).
24 On this point see, for instance, Darcy Grimaldo Grigsby, 'Eroded Stone, Petrified Flesh and the Sphinx of Race', *Parallax* 13(2), (2007) pp.21–40; and Robert Bernasconi, 'Black Skin, White Skulls: The Nineteenth-Century Debate over the Racial Identity of the Ancient Egyptians', *Parallax* 13(2), (2007), pp.6–20.
25 On this point see, for example, Jeremy W. Pope, 'Ägypten und Aufhebung: G. W. F. Hegel, W. E. B. Du Bois, and the African Orient', *The New Centennial Review* 6(3), (Winter 2006), pp.149–92.
26 James Stuart and Nicholas Revett, *The Antiquities of Athens: Measured and Delineated by James Stuart, FRS and FSA, and Nicholas Revett, Painters and Architects*, vol. 1 (London, 1762); vol. 2 (London, 1787).

27 Denon, 1802, p.240.
28 It is now in the State Museum of Ceramics, Kuscovo, Russia.
29 Charles Truman, *The Sèvres Egyptian service, 1810–12* (London, 1982).
30 Models of ancient architecture were popular amongst architects and connoisseurs in this period. For example, Soane had an extensive collection. See Helen Dorey, 'Sir John Soane's Model Room', *Perspecta* 41, 'Grand Tour' (2008), pp.46, 26, 92–3, 170–71.
31 The original preparatory drawings are held at the British Museum, BM P&D 1836,0109.57.
32 It is possible that Denon was directly involved in the design of this cabinet. It is of extremely high quality and bears a striking resemblance to a medal cabinet, also by Percier and Biennais, that is known to have come from Denon's own collection (Metropolitan Museum of Art, inv. no. 26.168.77). See Anthony Griffiths, 'The End of Napoleon's Histoire Métallique', *Medal* 18 (Spring 1991), and Leela Meinertas, 'A Napoleonic Medal Cabinet', *Luxury* 4(2–3), (2017), pp.171–6.
33 For a full discussion of Hope, see David Watkin, *Thomas Hope and the Neoclassical Ideal* (London, 1968). The Duchess Street house was demolished in 1851, its contents being taken to Hope's country house, The Deepdene, where they remained accessible to the public.
34 See ibid.
35 Thomas Hope, *Household Furniture and Interior Decoration* (London, 1807), plate viii.
36 Said, 1978.
37 Rudolph Wittkower, 'Piranesi and Eighteenth Century Egyptomania', *Studies in the Italian: Baroque* (London, 1975), pp.260–73.
38 A bilingual edition in German with a new English translation was published as *Reflections on the Imitation of Greek Works in Painting and Sculpture* (London, 1986).
39 Giovanni Battista Piranesi, *Diverse maniere d'adornare i cammini ed ogni altra parte degli edifizi desunte dall'architettura Egizia, Etrusca, e Greca, con un Ragionamento Apologetico in defesa dell'Architettura Egizia, e Toscana* (1769).
40 Ibid., p.4
41 Ibid., p.10
42 For a full discussion of the cultural context of *Diverse maniere*, see Susan M. Dixon, 'Giovanni Battista Piranesi's Diverse maniere d' adornare i cammini and Chimneypiece Design as a Vehicle for Polemic', *Studies in the Decorative Arts* 1(1), (Autumn 1993), pp.76–98.
43 Piranesi, 1769, p.2
44 Adolph Paul Oppé (ed.), 'The Memoirs of Thomas Jones', *Walpole Society Annual* 32 (1946–8), p.54.
45 For a full discussion of Soane's thinking and transcription of his lectures (twelve in total), see David Watkin, *Sir John Soane: Enlightenment Thought and the Royal Academy Lectures* (Cambridge, 1996).
46 Ibid., transcript of 'Lecture 1', pp.291–302.
47 Some of the notes are dated 24 April 1807. Soane Case 168; Archives 1/2/25, 1/43, 1/139, 1/184/1. See also Watkin, 1996, pp.176–8. Towards the end of his life in 1835, Soane also acquired the full set of volumes of *Description de l'Égypte*.
48 SM Archives 1/139, 'Hints etc. Lect.1'.
49 Watkin, 1996, transcript of 'Lecture 1', pp.291–302.
50 SM 1/43 and Denon, 1802, p.113.
51 SM 27/3/3.
52 SM 27/3/6.
53 Watkin, 1996, transcript of 'Lecture 1', pp.291–302.
54 Ibid.
55 There is a vast literature on this topic. See, for instance, Eilean Hooper-Greenhill, *Museums and the Shaping of Knowledge* (London and New York, 1992).

CHAPTER 3: EGYPT THROUGH NINETEENTH-CENTURY PHOTOGRAPHY

1 Edward Said, *Orientalism* (London, 1978, 1985), p.84. Said's hugely influential book, first published in 1978, changed the terms of the debate around scholarship into the history of the region by Western academics, debunking the romanticisation and 'othering' of Arab nations and culture.
2 Christina Riggs, *Photographing Tutankhamun: Archaeology, Ancient Egypt, and the Archive* (London, 2020).
3 Christina Riggs, 'We know it intimately', *London Review of Books* 42(20), (22 October 2020), p.34.
4 Ricardo A. Caminos, 'The Talbotype Applied to Hieroglyphics', *Journal of Egyptian Archaeology* 52, (1966), pp.65–70.
5 Ibid.
6 Maxime Du Camp, *Égypte, Nubie, Syrie: Paysages et Monuments* (Paris, 1852).
7 Elizabeth Anne McCauley, 'The Photographic Adventure of Maxime du Camp', in *Perspectives on Photography*, eds Dave Oliphant and Thomas Zigal (Austin, TX, 1982), p.26.
8 Julia Ballerini, 'The invisibility of Hadji-Ishmael: Maxime Du Camp's 1850 photographs of Egypt', *The Classic* 5, (13 March 2021), https://theclassicphotomag.com/the-in-visibility-of-hadji-ishmaelmaxime-du-camps-1850-photographs-of-egypt/.
9 Larry Schaaf, 'Charles Piazzi Smyth's 1865 Conquest of the Great Pyramid', *History of Photography* 3(4), (October 1979), pp.342–3.
10 Ali Behdad, *Camera Orientalis* (Chicago and London, 2016), p.33.
11 Stephanie Moser, *Designing Antiquity: Owen Jones, Ancient Egypt and the Crystal Palace* (London, 2012), p.17.
12 Behdad, 2016, p.258.
13 Linda Nochlin, 'The Imaginary Orient', in *The Politics of Vision: Essays on Nineteenth Century Art and Society* (New York, 1989), p.127.
14 Behdad, 2016, p.25.
15 Maria Golia, *Photography and Egypt* (Cairo, 2010), pp.26–7.
16 Sylvie Aubenas and Mercedes Volait, *Gustave Le Gray, 1820–1884* (Los Angeles, 2002), pp.175–208
17 Golia, 2010, p.57.
18 Lucie Ryzova, 'Mourning the Archive: Middle Eastern Photographic Heritage between Neoliberalism and Digital Reproduction', *Comparative Studies in Society and History* 56(4), (October 2014), pp.1027–61
19 Omniya Abdel Barr, from a telephone conversation with Tareq Shamma, February 2022.

CHAPTER 5: VISIONS OF ANCIENT EGYPT IN NINETEENTH-CENTURY PAINTING

1 For the complicated history of the painting's exhibitions and restorations, see Vern G. Swanson, *The Biography and Catalogue Raisonné of the Paintings of Sir Lawrence Alma-Tadema* (London, 1990), pp.131–2.
2 The fullest account is in Stephanie Moser, *Painting Antiquity: Ancient Egypt in the Art of Lawrence Alma-Tadema, Edward Poynter and Edwin Long* (Oxford, 2020), pp.73–96. I am indebted to Moser's research throughout this essay.
3 Georg Ebers, *Lorenz Alma Tadema: His Life and Works*, trans. Mary J. Safford (New York, 1886), pp.38–9.
4 Ibid., pp.35–6 (quotation marks in the original).
5 See, for example, Nicholas Tromans (ed.), *The Lure of the East: British Orientalist Painting* (London, 2008); Emily M. Weeks, *Cultures Crossed: John Frederick Lewis and the Art of Orientalism* (London and New Haven, CT, 2014).
6 Letter from David Roberts to D. R. Hay, 28 May 1842, quoted in Helen Guiterman and Briony Llewellyn, *David Roberts* (London, 1986), p.80.
7 Moser, 2020, pp.107–8 (Poynter), 77–83 (Alma-Tadema).
8 Stephanie Moser, *Designing Antiquity: Owen Jones, Ancient Egypt and the Crystal Palace* (New Haven, CT, and London, 2012), pp.157–83.
9 Georgiana Burne-Jones, *Memorials of Edward Burne-Jones* (London, 1904), vol. I, p.289.
10 Donato Esposito, 'Inspired by Antiquity: Sir Edward Poynter and the British Museum', *British Museum Magazine* 42 (Spring 2002), pp.23–5.
11 Moser, 2020, p.144.
12 Ibid., pp.100, 152.
13 Ebers, 1886, p.36.
14 Moser, 2020, pp.185–8.
15 See Michael Musgrave, *The Musical Life of the Crystal Palace* (Cambridge, 1995) pp.37 and 243, n.40. Thanks to Tim Barringer for this information.
16 *Work* was also the title of Ford Madox Brown's major painting of 1852–65 (Manchester Art Gallery), although it is unclear whether there is any relationship. For further details, see Allen Staley, *The New Painting of the 1860s: Between the Pre-Raphaelites and the Aesthetic Movement* (New Haven, CT, and London, 2011), pp.215–18.
17 Poynter's quotation came from Exodus 1:8, 14; Handel's libretto used Exodus 1:8, 11, 13 and 2:23.
18 Sculpture of a lion, British Museum (EA1).
19 'Pictures of the Year', *Saturday Review*, 13 July 1867, p.53.
20 Ebers, 1886, pp.66–7.
21 Ivo Blom, 'The Second Life of Alma-Tadema', in *Lawrence Alma-Tadema: At Home in Antiquity*, eds Elizabeth Prettejohn and Peter Trippi (Munich, 2016), pp.193–6.
22 For a full account of Long's Egyptian paintings, see Moser, 2020, pp.218–82.
23 Quoted from *The Magazine of Art*, ibid., p.237.

CHAPTER 6: VISIONS OF ANCIENT EGYPT IN THE MUSEUM

1 Sally Macdonald, 'Lost in Time and Space: Ancient Egypt in Museums', in Sally Macdonald and Michael Rice, *Consuming Ancient Egypt* (London, 2003), pp.87–99; Stephanie Moser, *Wondrous Curiosities: Ancient Egypt at the British Museum* (Chicago, 2006), 'Archaeological Representation: The Consumption and Creation of the Past', in Barry Cunliffe, Chris Godsen and Rosemary Joyce, *The Oxford Handbook of Archaeology* (Oxford, 2008), pp.1048–77, and 'The Devil is in the Detail: Museum Displays and the Creation of Knowledge', *Museum Anthropology* 33(1), (2010), pp.22–32; Christina Riggs, 'Ancient Egypt in the Museum: Concepts and Constructions', in Alan Lloyd, *A Companion to Ancient Egypt, Volume II* (Chichester, 2010), pp.1129–53; Gemma Tully, 'Re-presenting Ancient Egypt: Reengaging Communities through Collaborative Methodologies for Museum Display', *Archaeological Review from Cambridge* 26(2), (2011), pp.137–52.
2 Riggs, 2010, p.1144.
3 Moser, 2006, p.1132; Moser, 2008, p.1056; Riggs, 2010, pp.1132–3.
4 Moser, 2006, p.43; Elliott Colla, *Conflicted Antiquities: Egyptology, Egyptomania, Egyptian Modernity* (Durham and London, 2007), p.9.
5 Alexander Gordon, *Twenty-Five Plates of all the Egyptian Mummies, and other Egyptian Antiquities in England* (London, 1737–9).
6 George Sandys, *Relation of a Journey* (London, 1615), p.133, and *Musaeum Tradescantianum* (London, 1656), p.42; Richard Pococke, *A Description of the East and some other countries, Vol. 1* (London, 1743), pl.76 opp. p.284.
7 Helen Whitehouse, 'Egyptology and Forgery in the Seventeenth Century: The Case of the Bodleian Shabti', *Journal of the History of Collections* 1(2), (1989), pp.187–95.
8 Thomas Shaw, *Travels in Barbery and the Levant* (London, 1743), p.422.
9 On Tradescant's cabinet, see Sandys, 1656. The objects associated with Shaw now in the Ashmolean have been traced by Helen Whitehouse, 'An Early Dynastic Dish from Thomas Shaw's Travels', *Journal of Egyptian Archaeology* 88 (2002), pp.237–42.
10 Arthur MacGregor, 'Egyptian Antiquities', in Arthur MacGregor, *Sir Hans Sloane: Collector, Scientist, Antiquary Founding Father of the British Museum* (London, 1994), pp.174–89; Moser, 2006, pp.93–124.
11 Holger Hoock, 'The British State and the Anglo-French Wars over Antiquities, 1798–1858', *The Historical Journal* 50(1), (2007), pp.49–72.

12 Donald M. Reid, *Whose Pharaohs? Archaeology, Museums, and Egyptian National Identity from Napoleon to World War I* (Berkeley, CA, 2002), pp.37–46; Riggs, 2010, pp.1134–7.
13 Colla, 2007, p.27. A biography of one of the most famous instances of this colonial collecting, the 'Memnon Head', is given on pp.24–66.
14 This period is most associated with Franco-British rivalry, but in the first half of the nineteenth century major public museums also opened in, for example, Turin (1824), Munich (1830) and the Vatican (1839).
15 Colla, 2007, p.60.
16 Todd Porterfield, *The Allure of Empire: Art in the Service of French Imperialism, 1798–1836* (Princeton, NJ, 1998).
17 Carol Duncan, *Civilizing Rituals: Inside Public Art Museums* (London, 1995), pp.26–7.
18 Moser, 2006, pp.86–9.
19 Riggs, 2010, p.1135. On Egyptian art and the building of the Townley Gallery, see Ian Jenkins, *Archaeologists and Aesthetes in the Sculpture Galleries of the British Museum, 1800–1939* (London, 1992), pp.102–10.
20 Riggs, 2010, p.1137. Shelley's 'Ozymandias', inspired by the 'Memnon Head' installed at the British Museum in 1819, epitomises this impression.
21 *The Gentleman's Magazine* 80 (July–December 1810), p.209 (cited in Jenkins, 1992, p.107).
22 Moser, 2006, Chapters 3–5.
23 Colla, 2007, p.104. This narrative was forcefully taken up by the American consul in Egypt, George Gliddon, in *An Appeal to the Antiquaries of Europe on the Destruction of the Monuments of Egypt* (London, 1841).
24 Reid, 2002, pp.54–8. Some blame can be laid at Muhammad Ali himself, whose attitudes towards antiquities were complicated; Reid, 2002, p.54, characterises his view of antiquities as 'bargaining chips to be exchanged for European diplomatic and technical support'.
25 Colla, 2007, pp.116–20.
26 Reid, 2002, pp.106, 107 Fig. 20.
27 Donald M. Reid, 'French Egyptology and the Architecture of Orientalism: Deciphering the Facade of Cairo's Egyptian Museum', in Leon Carl Brown and Matthew S. Gordon, *Franco-Arab Encounters: Studies in Memory of David C. Gordon* (Beirut, 1996), pp.35–69.
28 Reid, 2002, pp.7–8; Mohamed Elshahed, 'The Old and New Egyptian Museums: Between Imperialists, Nationalists and Tourists', in William Carruthers, *Histories of Egyptology: Interdisciplinary measures* (London, 2014), p.261.
29 Wendy Doyon, 'The Poetics of Egyptian Museum Practice', *British Museum Studies in Ancient Egypt and Sudan* 10 (2008), pp.1–37, explores the colonial context surrounding Egypt's museums up to the present day.
30 This theme has been studied extensively by Alice Stevenson, 'Artefacts of Excavation: The British Collection and Distribution of Egyptian Finds to Museums, 1880–1915', *Journal of the History of Collections* 26(1), (2014), pp.89–102, *Scattered Finds: Archaeology, Egyptology and Museums* (London, 2019) and 'Circulation as Negotiation and Loss: Egyptian Antiquities from British Excavations, 1880–present', in Felix Driver, Mark Nesbitt and Caroline Cornish, *Mobile Museums: Collections in Circulation* (London, 2021), pp.261–82; Alice Stevenson, Emma Libonati and Alice Williams, '"A Selection of Minor Antiquities": A Multi-sited View on Collections from Excavations in Egypt', *World Archaeology* 48(2), (2016), pp.282–95.
31 Thomas G. H. James, *Excavating in Egypt: The Egypt Exploration Society* (London, 1982).
32 David Gange, 'Religion and Science in Late Nineteenth-Century British Egyptology', *History Journal* 49(4), (2016), pp.1083–1103.
33 Dalia N. Osman, 'Occupiers' Title to Cultural Property: Nineteenth-century Removal of Egyptian Artifacts', *Columbia Journal of Transnational Law* 36 (1999), pp.969–1002.
34 Amara Thornton, 'Exhibition Season: Annual Exhibitions in London, 1880s–1930s', *Bulletin of the History of Archaeology* 25(2), (2015), pp.1–18.
35 Stevenson, 2014.
36 Ibid., p.91.
37 David K. van Keuren, 'Museums and Ideology: Augustus Pitt-Rivers, Anthropology and Social Change in Later Victorian Britain', *Victorian Studies* 28(1), (1984), pp.171–89.
38 Stevenson, 2014, p.953; Stevenson et al., 2016, p.285. Stevenson, 2021, p.269, updates this to 180 institutions.
39 Riggs, 2010, pp.1132 and 1138.
40 Timothy Mitchell, *Colonising Egypt* (Berkeley, CA, 1988), pp.5–7; Sharon Macdonald, 'Exhibitions of Power and Powers of Exhibition', in Sharon Macdonald, *The Politics of Display: Museums, Science, Culture* (London, 1998), pp.10–11; Colla, 2007, p.137.
41 Tony Bennett, *The Birth of the Museum: History, Theory, Politics* (New York, 1995), pp.59–88.
42 Stephanie Moser, *Designing Antiquity: Owen Jones, Ancient Egypt and the Crystal Palace* (New Haven, CT, 2012); Cecilia Hurley, 'Pharaohs, Papyri and Hookahs: Displaying and Staging Egyptian Antiquities in Nineteenth Century European Exhibitions', in Miguel J. Versluys, *Beyond Egyptomania: Objects, Styles and Agency* (Berlin, 2020), pp.185–210.
43 Stephen Quirke, *Hidden Hands: Egyptian Workforces in Petrie Excavation Archives 1880–1924* (London, 2010); Joanne Rowland, 'Documenting the Qufti Archaeological Workforce', *Egyptian Archaeology* 44 (2014), pp.10–12; Wendy Doyon, 'On Archaeological Labor in Modern Egypt', in Carruthers, 2014, pp.141–56; Christina Riggs, *Photographing Tutankhamun: Archaeology, Ancient Egypt, and the Archive* (London, 2018).
44 Stephanie Moser, *Painting Antiquity: Ancient Egypt in the Art of Lawrence Alma-Tadema, Edward Poynter and Edwin Long* (New York, 2020).

CHAPTER 7: REFORMISTS, AESTHETICS AND PRE-RAPHAELITES

1 Judith Bronkhurst, *William Holman Hunt: A Catalogue Raisonné*, vol. 2 (New Haven, CT, 2006), pp.23–4, no. D.40.
2 William Holman Hunt, *Pre-Raphaelitism and the Pre-Raphaelite Brotherhood* (London, 1905), pp.134–6.
3 Charlotte Gere and Michael Whiteway, *Nineteenth-Century Design: From Pugin to Mackintosh* (London, 1993), p.91, fig. 95.
4 Holman Hunt, 1905, p.204.
5 Stephanie Moser, *Painting Antiquity: Ancient Egypt in the Art of Lawrence Alma-Tadema, Edward Poynter and Edwin Long* (Oxford, 2020), p.273, fig. 5.38; pp.335–7, 359.
6 On the significant importance of this stool on nineteenth-century art and design, see ibid., pp.78–9, fig. 2.15, and repeatedly throughout.
7 Patrick Conner, *The Inspiration of Egypt* (Brighton, 1983), p.105, nos 221–2; Jean-Marcel Humbert, Christiane Ziegler and Michael Pantazzi, *Égyptomania: L'Égypte dans l'art occidental 1730–1930* (Paris, 1994), pp.465–6, no. 311.
8 Christopher Dresser, *Principles of Decorative Design* (London, 1873), p.121.
9 Ibid., pp.4–8.
10 Owen Jones, *The Grammar of Ornament* (London, 1868), p.24.
11 Widar Halén, 'Christopher Dresser and the "Modern English" Style: His Later Designs for Wallpapers and Hangings', *The Journal of the Decorative Arts Society 1850 to the Present* 14 (1990), p.14.
12 Christopher Dresser, *Studies in Design for House Decorators, Designers, and Manufacturers* (London, 1874–6), p.8.
13 Michael Whiteway, *Christopher Dresser 1834–1904* (Milan, 2001), pp.70–71, nos 34–5; Judy Rudoe, 'Dresser and His Sources of Inspiration', in Michael Whiteway, *Shock of the Old: Christopher Dresser's Design Revolution* (New York, 2004), pp.86–7, figs 102–3, p.104, fig. 136.
14 Examples are illustrated in Widar Halén, *Christopher Dresser* (Oxford, 1990), fig. 99; Whiteway, 2001, p.58, no. 17, pp.64–5, nos 29–30.
15 Dresser, 1873, fig. 27, p.55.
16 Christopher Dresser, *Japan: Its Architecture, Art, and Art Manufactures* (London, 1882).
17 Kevin H. F. O'Wilde, '"The House Beautiful": A Reconstruction of Oscar Wilde's American Lecture', *Victorian Studies* 17(4), (1974), pp.395–418.
18 'Foul snake and speckled adder with their young ones crawl from stone to stone; for ruined is the house and prone the great rose-marble monolith!' (line 110); 'the god is scattered here and there: deep hidden in the windy sand; I saw his giant granite hand still clenched in impotent despair' (line 116).
19 Susan Weber Soros, *E. W. Godwin: Aesthetic Movement Architect and Designer* (Yale, 1999a), p.250, and *The Secular Furniture of E. W. Godwin* (New Haven, CT, 1999b), pp.64–5.
20 Edward William Godwin, *Art Furniture designed by Edward W. Godwin, F.S.A. and manufactured by William Watt* (London, 1877), p.viii.
21 Soros, 1999b, p.143, no. 207.
22 Godwin, 1877, pl. 15. A flower stand and piano stool with identical braces are also shown in pl. 12, in a scene of drawing-room furniture, alongside Anglo-Japanese and 'Queen Anne Style' pieces.
23 On Godwin's imitators, see Soros, 1999b, pp.72–3.
24 Moser, 2020, p.355.
25 Gere and Whiteway, in Whiteway, 2004, p.26.
26 Bronkhust, 2006, pp.23–4. Holman Hunt recalled this himself in his later memoirs (Holman Hunt, 1905, p.337).

CHAPTER 8: JEWELLERS, GOLDSMITHS AND THE EGYPTIAN TASTE c.1867

1 Henri Vever, *French Jewelry of the Nineteenth Century*, trans. Katherine Purcell (London, 2001), pp.744 and 748. Vever's *La Bijouterie française au XIXème siècle* was first published in 1906–8.
2 For an example of earlier nineteenth-century Egyptianising jewellery, see parts of an 1830 enamelled necklace at the Musée des Arts décoratifs, Paris, inv. 24349, reproduced in Jean-Marcel Humbert, Christiane Ziegler and Michael Pantazzi, *Égyptomania: L'Égypte dans l'art occidental 1730–1930* (Paris, 1994), cat. 218, which featured schematic Egyptian figures depicted in black and white enamel on gold.
3 Despite operating in Egypt, the Suez Canal Company was controlled by foreigners (52 per cent of shares were French-owned while the Viceroy of Egypt bought 44 per cent). To finance modernisation and infrastructure projects, including the Suez Canal, Egypt took out large loans and spiralled into debt. In 1875 the British government bought Egypt's shares in the Suez Canal Company and Khedive Isma'il, who was forced to declare bankruptcy, was eventually deposed by the British in 1879. For an Egyptian perspective on the Canal, see Emad Abou Ghazi, 'Le canal vu par les Egyptiens', *L'Epopée du Canal de Suez* (Paris, 2018), pp.46–51; Caroline Piquet, 'Le canal de Suez et les grandes puissances: enjeux stratégiques (de sa conception à 1956)', ibid., pp.38–45; Valeska Huber, *Channelling Mobilities: Migration and Globalisation in the Suez Canal Region and Beyond, 1869–1914* (Cambridge, 2013).
4 After its display in London, the jewellery was published in *Facsimiles of the Egyptian Relics Discovered in the tomb of Queen Aah-Hotep exhibited at the International Exhibition of 1862* (London, 1863).
5 On the representations of Egypt and ancient Egypt at world fairs, see Zeynep Çelik, *Displaying the Orient: Architecture of Islam at Nineteenth-Century World's Fairs* (Berkeley, CA, 1992), pp.111–19; Timothy Mitchell, *Colonising Egypt* (Berkeley, CA, 1988, 1991), Chapter 1; Stephanie Moser, *Designing Antiquity: Owen Jones, Ancient Egypt and the Crystal Palace* (London, 2012); Donald Malcolm Reid, *Whose Pharaohs?: Archaeology, Museums, and Egyptian*

National Identity from Napoleon to World War I (Berkeley, CA, 2002) pp.125–30.
6 Charlotte Gere and Judy Rudoe, 'Jewellery at the 1862 Exhibition', *The Journal of the Decorative Arts Society 1850 to the Present* 38 (2014), pp.82–105.
7 Susan Weber Soros and Stefanie Walker (eds), *Castellani and Italian Archaeological Jewelry* (London, 2004).
8 Gere and Rudoe, 2014, p.88.
9 The complete set was sold at auction in 1930. For a reproduction, see Geoffrey Munn, *Castellani and Giuliano* (London, 1984), pl. 125. See also a similar brooch at the Musée des Arts décoratifs, Paris, inv. 9827.
10 These objects were a highlight of Baugrand's display and are illustrated and described at length in Jules Mesnard, *Les Merveilles de l'Exposition universelle de 1867, Arts-industrie: bronzes, meubles, orfèvrerie, porcelaines, faïences, cristaux, bijoux, dentelles, soieries, tissus de toutes sortes, papiers peints, tapisseries, tapis, glaces, etc.*, vol. 2 (Paris, 1867), pp.182–8.
11 Illustrated in Vever, 2001, p.740.
12 Émilie Bérard, 'La Maison Mellerio, Joaillier du Second Empire', *Spectaculaire Second Empire* (Paris, 2016), pp.128–33, on p.132.
13 Other notable Egyptianising jewellery by Mellerio included a *parure d'inspiration égyptienne* (*c.*1870), which incorporated ancient Egyptian amulets and a pair of bracelets in the form of snakes.
14 Vever, 2001, p.760.
15 Daniel Marchesseau, 'Trésors d'Argent', *Trésors d'Argent: Les Froment-Meurice orfèvres romantiques parisiens* (Paris, 2003), p.21.
16 Marie-Madeleine Massé, 'Émile Froment-Meurice', ibid., p.182.
17 Originally it may have been patinated so that the parts in low-relief were black, which would have made the design more visible. Conversation between the author and metal conservator Joanna Whalley.
18 L. Dussieux, *Les Artistes français à l'étranger* (Paris, 1876), p.393.
19 An internal P&O memo about the garniture from 1957 records that 'During the construction of the railway from Alexandria to Suez via Cairo, the Company extended financial backing to the Pacha in the form of loans up to about a quarter of a million pounds.' 'Memorandum for the management: Egyptian Clock and Vases in the small board-room', 20 June 1957, P&O Archives. The author would like to thank Susie Cox, Senior Curator at DP World Heritage, for sharing the archives. Osama M. Ettouney, 'Railways along the Nile: The Early Years, 1851–1879', *Railroad History* 202 (Spring–Summer 2010), pp.60–69.
20 Transcript of a letter from Mohamed Sherif Pasha, 20 August 1865, P&O Archives.
21 Isma'il commissioned Giuseppe Verdi to compose the opera *Aïda*, whose premiere was originally intended to celebrate the inauguration of the Suez Canal.
22 Musée des Arts décoratifs, Paris, inv. D21.
23 The author would like to thank Dr Benjamin Hinson for his description of the iconography.
24 Humbert et al., 1994, cat. 329, p.483.

CHAPTER 9: NINETEENTH-CENTURY MUMMY FICTION

1 Sara Sallam, *You Died Again On Screen* (2018–20), sarasallam.com/you-died-again-on-screen.
2 [Jane Webb], *The Mummy!: A Tale of the Twenty-Second Century*, 3 vols (London, 1827), vol. 1, pp.231–2.
3 Edgar A. Poe, 'Some Words with a Mummy', *American Review: A Whig Journal* 1(4), (1845), pp.363–70 (p.365).
4 Albert Smith, 'Mr Grubbe's Night with Memnon', *Illuminated Magazine* (May 1843), pp.31–5 (p.34).
5 Ibid., p.35.
6 Théophile Gautier, *The Romance of a Mummy*, trans. F. C. de Sumichrast (New York, 1901), p.301.
7 Ibid., p.302.
8 Eleanor Dobson, 'Sleeping Beauties: Mummies and the Fairy-Tale Genre at the Fin de Siècle', *Journal of International Women's Studies* 18(3), (2017), pp.19–34.
9 Jasmine Day, 'The Rape of the Mummy: Women, Horror Fiction and the Westernisation of the Curse', in *Mummies and Science, World mummies research: Proceedings of the VI World Congress on Mummy Studies*, ed. Pablo Altoche Peña, Conrado Rodríguez Martín and Ángeles Ramírez Rodríguez (Santa Cruz de Tenerife, 2008), pp.617–21.
10 The precedents to Alcott's text were unearthed by S. J. Wolfe, Robert Singerman and Jasmine Day. See Jasmine Day, *The Mummy's Curse: Mummymania in the English-Speaking World* (London, 2006), pp.46–7; and S. J. Wolfe, *Mummies in Nineteenth Century America: Ancient Egyptians as Artefacts* (Jefferson, NC, 2009).
11 Louisa May Alcott, 'Lost in a Pyramid', *The New World* 1(1), (16 January 1869), p.8.
12 H. Rider Haggard, *Cleopatra* (London, 1889), p.177.
13 Marie Corelli, *Ziska: The Problem of a Wicked Soul* (Bristol, 1897), p.343.
14 Eleanor Dobson, *Writing the Sphinx: Literature, Culture and Egyptology* (Edinburgh, 2020), pp.65–87.

CHAPTER 11: MODERNISM AND ANCIENT EGYPT: HARLEM, PARIS AND LONDON

1 The author would like to thank Thierry Pautot from the Fondation Giacometti, Sophie Pretorius from the Estate of Francis Bacon and Logan Sisley from the Hugh Lane Gallery for their advice and help in the research of this essay.
2 Hedwig Fechheimer, *La Sculpture égyptienne*, trans. Charlotte Marchand (Paris, 1920), p.1, and see p.4.
3 Ibid., p.4.
4 Marc Etienne, 'Giacometti et l'art de l'Égypte antique: les facettes d'un regard', in Thierry Pautot, Romain Perrin and Marc Etienne, *Alberto Giacometti et l'Égypte antique* (Paris, 2021), pp.30–51, on p.33.
5 For a discussion of the problematic historical concept of 'Primitivism' in twentieth-century art and the ethnocentric and prejudiced views it reflects, see Jack Flam with Miriam Deutch (eds), *Primitivism and Twentieth-Century Art: A Documentary History* (London, 2003).
6 Ibid., p.4.
7 Gauguin, *Oviri*, quoted in Philippe Dagen, *Le Peintre, le poète, le sauvage: Les Voies du primitivisme dans l'art français* (Paris, 1998). Gauguin drew from a wide range of sources, including a photograph of a Theban tomb in the British Museum for his 1892 painting *Ta matete (Le Marché)*, today in the Kunstmuseum Basel.
8 'Nous sommes les deux plus grands peintres de l'époque, toi dans le genre "égyptien", moi dans le genre moderne ...' Henri Rousseau, quoted in Fernande Olivier, *Picasso et ses amis* (Paris, 1933), p.113. All translations are the author's own, unless otherwise stated.
9 Anna Akhmatova, 'Amedeo Modigliani', *The New York Review of Books* (July 1975), pp.32–3, on p.32.
10 Guillaume Apollinaire, *Les Peintres cubistes: Méditations esthétiques*, 1913, quoted in Dagen, 1998, p.173.
11 Rupert R. Arrowsmith, *Modernism and the Museum: Asian, African, and Pacific Art and the London Avant-Garde* (Oxford, 2010), p.95.
12 Rodin himself was a passionate collector of ancient art, including Egyptian antiquities. Between 1893 and 1917 he acquired more than 800 Egyptian objects, which represented one-eighth of his entire collection. See Bénédicte Garnier, 'Rodin l'Égyptien', in Mercedes Volait and Emmanuelle Perrin (eds), *Dialogues artistiques avec les passés de l'Égypte: Une perspective transnationale et transmédiale* (Paris, 2017), www.books.openedition.org/inha/7191 (accessed 22 May 2022).
13 The fair was intended to celebrate the contribution of immigrants to American society and included African Americans as 'honorary immigrants', euphemistically avoiding the violent history of Africans' enslavement. Renée Ater, *Remaking Race and History: The Sculpture of Meta Warrick Fuller* (Berkeley, CA, 2011), p.102.
14 Renée Ater, 'Making History: Meta Warrick Fuller's Ethiopia', *American Art* 17(3), (Autumn 2003), pp.12–31, on p.17.
15 Today a racist slur, the term 'negro' was historically used to refer to African Americans.
16 W.E.B. Du Bois, *The Negro* (first published 1915; London, 1916), p.40.
17 Ater, 2003, p.20.
18 Lois Mailou Jones also drew on similar ideas when she painted *The Ascent of Ethiopia* in 1932, which links Ethiopia, ancient Egypt and African American culture.
19 Quoted in James Hamilton, *The British Museum, Storehouse of Civilizations* (London, 2018), p.153.
20 Moore's notebook from 1920, *History of Sculpture Notebook*, includes references to Assyrian, Chaldean, Egyptian but also Greco-Roman classical sculpture, as well as Greek, Byzantine, Gothic and Renaissance architecture. Sebastiano Barassi, 'A Master in the Making', ed. Hannah Higham, *Becoming Henry Moore* (London, 2017), pp.10–77, on p.24. See also Alice Stevenson, *Scattered Finds: Archaeology, Egyptology and Museums* (London, 2019), pp.154–5.
21 Henry Moore, *Henry Moore at the British Museum* (London, 1981), p.8.
22 One of his siblings was the doctor and civil-rights activist Harold Moody, who founded the League of Coloured Peoples in London in 1931.
23 Extract of Moody's interview with Macdonald Hastings from the BBC transcript of 'Anything to Declare?' no. 43 (1–4 December 1950), Tate Archives, Papers of Ronald Moody, TGA 956/3/5/3. On Moody and ancient Egypt, see Debbie Challis and Gemma Romain, 'Ronald Moody: Sculpture and interwar Britain', www.ucl.ac.uk/equiano-centre/educational-resources/fusion-worlds/artists/ronald-moody-sculpture-and-interwar-britain (accessed 22 May 2022).
24 Moody, BBC transcript of 'A Sculptor' (1 July 1951), TGA 956/3/6/1.
25 In 1933 Giacometti also looked to the Egyptian alabaster lamp when he designed *Lampe égyptienne*, a lotus-shaped plaster lamp, for the decorator Jean-Michel Frank.
26 The exhibition *Alberto Giacometti et l'Égypte antique* at the Giacometti Institute in Paris in 2021 examined Giacometti's lifelong interest in ancient Egypt. Pautot, Perrin and Etienne, 2021.
27 Mariana Jung, '100 Years of the Discovery of Nefertiti', in Friederike Seyfried (ed.), *In the Light of Amarna: 100 Years of the Nefertiti Discovery* (Berlin, 2012), pp.421–6, on p.423.
28 '. . . les œuvres du passé que je trouve les plus ressemblantes à la réalité sont celles qu'en général on juge les plus éloignées d'elle (– je veux dire les arts de style): la Chaldée, l'Egypte, Byzance, le Fayoum, des choses chinoises, des miniatures chrétiennes du haut moyen âge. Et pas du tout ce qu'on nomme réalisme, (hein? Ou plutôt, la peinture égyptienne est pour moi une peinture réaliste; pourtant c'est elle qu'on dit la plus stylisée.) N'importe qui d'entre nous ressemble beaucoup plus à une sculpture égyptienne qu'à tout autre sculpture jamais faite.' Giacometti in Pierre Schneider, 'Au Louvre avec Alberto Giacometti', *Preuves* 139 (September 1962), pp.23–30, on p.26.
29 David Sainsbury, in Ian Collins (ed.), *Masterpieces of the Sainsbury Centre* (Norwich, 2015), p.106. It remains unidentified in the Fondation Giacometti's collection. The Fondation holds a small number of Egyptian objects that belonged to the sculptor. Correspondence between the author and Thierry Pautot, 17 February 2022.
30 This was the first of eight portraits of Lisa that Bacon painted, four of which survive. Martin Harrison, *Francis Bacon: Catalogue raisonné* (London, 2016) p.452.
31 Ibid.
32 Eric Allden mentioned Brunton's visits to Bacon on 31 July 1929, 14 August, 20 August and 1 November 1929. Francesca Pipe, 'Bacon's first Patrons: Eric

Allden's diary', in Martin Harrison (ed.), *Inside Francis Bacon* (London, 2020), pp.13–61.

33 The entire contents of Bacon's studio were donated to the Hugh Lane Gallery in Dublin in 1998, including 7,000 items of archives, some of which are presented in Martin Harrison and Rebecca Daniels, *Francis Bacon: Incunabula* (London, 2008).

34 I would like to thank Logan Sisley for the list of books and leaves from the Hugh Lane Gallery.

35 David Sylvester, *The Brutality of Fact: Interviews with Francis Bacon* (London, 2016), p.132.

CHAPTER 12: MODERN VISIONS OF ANCIENT EGYPT

1 For a study of this generation of artists, see Nadia Radwan, *Les Modernes d'Égypte: Une Renaissance nationale des beaux-arts et des arts appliqués* (Bern, 2017).

2 The prince made a *waqf* (Islamic endowment of property) of more than 500,000 square metres of agricultural land and rented a villa in the neighborhood of Darb al-Jamamiz to establish the school.

3 On this topic, see Lara Ayad, 'The "Negress" of Alexandria: African Womanhood in Modern Egyptian Art', *African Arts* 51(4), (2021), pp.20–37.

4 Pan-Arabism: a movement that advocates the political, cultural and socioeconomic unity of Arabs across the different states that emerged after decolonisation.

5 Valérie Didier Hess, and Hussam Rashwan (eds), *Mahmoud Saïd: Catalogue raisonné*, 2 vols (Milan, 2015).

6 On the nude genre in Mahmoud Saïd's work and other Egyptian modern artists, see Nadia Radwan, 'Ideal Nudes and Iconic Bodies in the Works of the Egyptian Pioneers', in Octavian Esanu (ed.), *Art, Awakening and Modernity in the Middle East: The Arab Nude* (London, 2018), pp.71–85.

7 Abbas Mahmud al-Aqqad, 'Timthal Nahdat Misr (The statue of Nahdat Misr)', *al-Balagh al-usbu'i* (25 May 1928), p.13.

8 The monument was displaced in 1954, under Gamal Abdel Nasser, in front of Cairo University, where it stands today. It was replaced by the colossal statue of Ramses II brought from Mit Rahina (Memphis). The latter was transferred in 2006, by decision of the former Secretary General of the Supreme Council of Antiquities, Zahi Hawass, near the Pyramids of Giza.

9 The largest blocks, some of which weigh more than fifty-five tonnes, were shipped along the Nile in November 1922. *En souvenir de l'inauguration officielle de la statue Le Réveil de l'Égypte inaugurée de [le?] 20 mai 1928; Tadhkar al-ihtifal al-rasmi raf' al-sitar 'an timthal nahdat Misr* (bilingual), (Cairo [n. d.]).

10 Letter from Prince Yusuf Kamal to Mahmoud Mokhtar, quoted in Badr Abou Ghazi and Gabriel Boctor, *Mouktar ou le Réveil de l'Égypte* (Cairo, 1949), p.46. Translated from French by the author.

11 The Macchiaioli were a group of Italian painters active during the second half of the nineteenth century. Like the French Impressionists, they advocated outdoor painting and experiments with natural light and colours.

12 Quoted in Saad el-Khadem et al., *Mohamed Naghi (1888–1956): Un Impressionniste égyptien* (Cairo, 1988), p.18.

13 On this topic and about the transnational career of Mohamed Naghi, see Brenda Segone, 'Le voyage en Occident de Muḥammad Nāǧī (1888–1956): Esquisse d'un nationalisme', *Annales islamologiques* 54 (2020), www.journals.openedition.org/anisl/8753; doi.org/10.4000/anisl.8753.

14 Louis Marcerou, 'Une Renaissance de la Céramique arabe en Égypte', *L'Égyptienne*, hors-série (1926), p.49.

15 I have elsewhere addressed this topic: see Nadia Radwan, 'How a Ceramic Vase in the Art Salon Changed Artistic Discourse in Egypt', in Nadia von Maltzahn and Monique Bellan (eds), *The Art Salon in the Arab Region: The Politics of Taste Making* (Beirut, 2018), pp.113–31.

CHAPTER 13: EGYPTO-DECO OR HOW TUT SHAPED MODERN LIFE

1 The cover was designed by Robin Macartney, who worked with Agatha Christie's second husband, the archaeologist Max Mallowan.

2 The Egypt Exploration Fund was founded in 1882 by Amelia Edwards and Reginald Stuart Poole in order to explore, survey and excavate in Egypt. See 'Egypt Exploration Fund (EEF)', Artefacts of Excavation, www.egyptartefacts.griffith.ox.ac.uk/resources/egypt-exploration-fund-eef

3 Hugues Tavier, 'Carter's Palette', in *Tutankhamun: Discovering the Forgotten Pharaoh* (Liège, 2020), p.38.

4 Evidence for a tomb of Tutankhamun, in the form of his embalming cache, had previously been discovered during the excavations supported by the American Egyptophile Theodore M. Davis, who previously held the concession for the Valley of the Kings.

5 See Christina Riggs, *Tutankhamen: The Original Photographs* (London, 2017), and *Treasured: How Tutankhamen Shaped a Century* (London, 2021).

6 Quoted in T. G. H. James, *Howard Carter: The Path to Tutankhamun* (first ed. 1992; London, 2001), pp.480–85.

7 Guillaume Apollinaire, *Concerning the Art of the Blacks* (Paris, 1917). Quoted in Jack Flam with Miriam Deutch (eds), *Primitivism and Twentieth Century Art: A Documentary History* (Berkeley, CA, 2003), p.107.

8 Several examples of these coats are known, including one with coloured embroidery in the collections of the Museum of London.

9 Théophile Gautier had attended the official celebrations of the opening of the Suez Canal by Khedive Isma'il in 1869.

10 Quoted in Hans Nadelhoffer, *Cartier: Jewellers Extraordinary* (New York, 1984), p.152.

11 See Louis-René Vian, *Paquebots de légende, décors de rêve* (Paris, 1991), p.30.

12 The company was established in 1890 by James Frederick Wiltshaw, William Herbert Robinson and James Alcock Robinson, trading under the name of Wiltshaw and Robinson. The trademark 'Carlton Ware' was introduced in 1894. In 1911 Wiltshaw formed a new limited company called Wiltshaw and Robinson Limited.

13 Professor C. H. Reilly, 'Landmarks of the Year, A Retrospect of 1928', *Architects' Journal* (9 January 1929), p.51, and see *Architects' Journal* (21 November 1928), p.740; *The Building*, vol. 3 (London 1928), p.398.

14 *Architects' Journal* (23 October 1929), pp.594–5.

15 Joan S. Skinner, *Form and Fancy: Factories and Factory Buildings by Wallis, Gilbert & Partners 1916–1939* (Liverpool, 1997).

16 *Architects' Journal* 71 (28 May 1930), p.814.

17 In 1932 the League of Nations could report that only the Bible and the Qur'an had an indisputably larger circulation than the latest Hollywood films. See 'Art Deco and Hollywood Film', in Charlotte Benton, Tim Benton and Ghislaine Wood (eds), *Art Deco 1910–1939* (London, 2003), p.325.

18 J. R. Learhart, 'Modern Cinema Design', lecture at RIBA in the *Architects' Journal* (3 December 1930), p.841.

CHAPTER 14: PYRAMID POWER

1 House of Lords, Hansard, *Tutankhamun Exhibition* (HL Deb 01 May 1972 vol. 330 cc560-3560. 2.33 p.m.).

2 After opening in Britain, the *Treasures of Tutankhamun* exhibition toured for nearly a decade between 1972 and 1981, touring to the USSR, the United States, Canada and both East and West Germany.

3 Cited in David Hockney and Nikos Stangos (eds), *That's the Way I See it: David Hockney* (London, 1993), p.36.

4 Paul Moorhouse, *Bridget Riley* (London, 2003), p.22. In doing so, Riley joined the ranks of other prominent British artists who toured Egypt during the 1980s, including the painters and printmakers Howard Hodgkin and Patrick Procktor.

5 Jean-Marcel Humbert and Clifford Price (eds), *Imhotep Today: Egyptianizing Architecture* (London, 2003), pp.115–16. Egyptian design elements are also evident in other London buildings, such as Terry Farrell's MI5 building on the riverside at Vauxhall, and Renton, Howard, Wood & Levin's Canary Riverside Plaza Hotel (formerly the Four Seasons Hotel) at Canary Wharf. On Egypt's influence on Postmodernism in London, see Pablo Bronstein, *A Guide to Postmodern Architecture in London* (Cologne, 2008), and Charles Jencks, *Post-Modern Triumphs in London: Architectural Design Profile 91* (New York, 1991).

6 Deepa Pant, 'Enchanting Explorations', *Bazaar Magazine* (Kuwait, Oct. 2011). See also Michael Gibson, *Henein* (London, 1988).

7 Chant Avedissian and Rose Issa, *Cairo Stencils* (London, 2006). For a broader survey, see Mark D'Amata, 'Chant Avedissian: A Contemporary Artist of Egypt', *African Arts*, 35(2), (2002) pp. 78–81.

8 Chant Avedissian, *Patterns, Costumes and Stencils* (London, 2009).

9 Maha Maamoun, *La Loi de l'Existence* (Beirut, 2017); Francis McKee, Maha Maamoun, Ala Younis and Mai Abu ElDahab (eds), *How to know what's really happening* (Berlin, 2016); for further exploration of Maamoun's work, see Kasia Redzisz and Aleya Hamza, *Objects in mirror are closer than they appear* (London, 2013); Okwui Enwezor (ed.), *Contemporary African Photography from the Walther Collection: Events of the Self, Portraiture and Social Identity* (Göttingen, 2010).

10 Maha Maamoun interviewed by Shaina Anand, www.vdrome.org/maha-maamoun-domestic-tourism-ii/

11 www.sarasallam.com/. I am grateful to the artist for sending me her comments and thoughts on the works discussed here.

12 Paul Youngquist, *A Pure Solar World: Sun Ra and the Birth of Afrofuturism* (Austin, TX, 2016), pp.42–6. See also William Sites, *Sun Ra's Chicago: Afrofuturism and the City* (Chicago, 2020).

13 Catherine Morris and Aruna D'Souza (eds), *Lorraine O'Grady: Both/And* (New York, 2021). Also Lauren O'Grady and Aruna D'Souza, *Writing in Space, 1973–2019* (Durham, NC, 2020).

CHAPTER 16: PROCESSING (ANCIENT) EGYPT

1 For the event, see 'In Photos: Egypt Reopens Ancient Avenue of Sphinxes in Luxor', *Ahram Online* (25 November 2021), www.english.ahram.org.eg/NewsContent/9/40/443339/Antiquities/Ancient-Egypt/In-Photos-Egypt-reopens-ancient-Avenue-of-Sphinxes.aspx (accessed 3 February 2022).

2 For one example, see Navine El-Aref, 'Luxor: The Great Procession', *Ahram Online* (21 November 2021), www.english.ahram.org.eg/News/440812.aspx (accessed 3 February 2022).

3 On Sisi's 'new republic', see Muhammad Kamal, 'Sisi Can't Disguise Egypt's Dictatorship as a "New Republic"', *Dawn: Democracy for the Arab World Now* (5 July 2021), www.dawnmena.org/sisi-cant-disguise-egypts-dictatorship-as-a-new-republic/ (accessed 3 February 2022).

4 On Zahi Hawass and this earlier work, see Ian Parker, 'The Pharaoh: Is Zahi Hawass Bad for Egyptology?', *The New Yorker* (8 November 2009), www.newyorker.com/magazine/2009/11/16/the-pharaoh (accessed 3 February 2022).

5 Ibid. For UNESCO's report on Luxor, see UNESCO, 'World Heritage Committee Thirty-Second Session, Quebec City, Canada, 2–10 July 2008: Item 7B of the Provisional Agenda; State of Conservation of World Heritage Properties Inscribed on the World Heritage List', WHC-08/32.COM/7B (Paris, 22 May 2008), www.unesdoc.unesco.org/ark:/48223/pf0000246949?3=null&queryId=861b537c-7a70-4247-9f97-3c7be5codf06 (accessed 3 February 2022).

6 For reports of this compensation, see, e.g., Egypt Today Staff, 'Antiquities Min. Reviews Progress of Avenue of Sphinxes', *Egypt Today* (16 April 2018), www.egypttoday.com/Article/6/47995/Antiquities-min-reviews-progress-of-Avenue-of-Sphinxes (accessed 3 February 2022); and Amr Emam, 'Egypt Reviving Luxor's Grand Avenue of Sphinxes', *Al-Monitor* (2 October 2020), www.al-monitor.com/originals/2020/10/egypt-restore-luxor-grand-avenue-sphinxes-tourism.html (accessed 3 February 2022).

7 Two months before the Luxor event, the demolition of the nineteenth-century palace of Tawfiq Pasha Andraos, located just outside the Luxor temple site perimeter, drew considerable criticism, for which see Ibrahim Ayyad, 'Destruction of 120-Year-Old Palace Sparks Anger in Egypt', *Al-Monitor* (6 September 2021), www.al-monitor.com/originals/2021/09/destruction-120-year-old-palace-sparks-anger-egypt (accessed 3 February 2022).

8 On 'invented tradition', see, most famously, Eric Hobsbawm and Terence Ranger (eds), *The Invention of Tradition* (Cambridge, 1983).

9 Hussein A. H. Omar, 'Pharaohs on Parade', *London Review of Books* blog (6 April 2021), www.lrb.co.uk/blog/2021/april/pharaohs-on-parade (accessed 3 February 2022).

10 Joel Gordon, *Nasser's Blessed Movement: Egypt's Free Officers and the July Revolution* (New York, 1992), p.4.

11 Joel Gordon, 'Broken Heart of the City: Youssef Chahine's *Bab al-Hadid* (Cairo Station)', *Journal for Cultural Research* 16(2–3), (2012), p.229.

12 My discussion of this and other events highlighted in this piece draws on William Carruthers, 'Spectacles of the Past', *Jadaliyya* (12 May 2021), www.jadaliyya.com/Details/42719 (accessed 3 February 2022). That piece itself draws on William Carruthers, 'Heritage, Preservation, and Decolonization: Entanglements, Consequences, Action?', *Future Anterior: Journal of Historic Preservation History, Theory, and Criticism* 16(2), (2019), pp.ii–xxiv.

13 On that plan, see Donald Malcolm Reid, *Contesting Antiquity in Egypt: Archaeologies, Museums, & the Struggle for Identities from World War I to Nasser* (Cairo, 2015), p.362.

14 Gordon, 2012, p.228. On the process of moving the statue (and the modern history of the statue more generally), cf. Amr Bayoumi (dir.), *Ramses Rah Fayn?* [*Where Did Ramses Go?*], a 2019 documentary relating the statue's story.

15 Gordon, 2012, pp.228–9.

16 On the station itself, see ibid., pp.224–5.

17 'Ramsis al-Thani Yaqifu 'ala Qadamayhi!' ['Ramses II Stands on His Feet!'], *al-Musawwar* (12 August 1955).

18 Gerard Coudougnan, *Nos ancêtres les Pharaons: l'histoire pharaonique et copte dans les manuels scolaires égyptiens* (Cairo, 1988), p.97.

19 Ibid., Coudougnan's words.

20 On the United Arab Republic, see James P. Jankowski, *Nasser's Egypt, Arab Nationalism, and the United Arab Republic* (Boulder, CO, and London, 2002).

21 For a contemporary Egyptological account of Ramses in this vein, see John Wilson, *The Burden of Egypt: An Interpretation of Ancient Egyptian Culture* (Chicago, 1951), pp.247–53.

22 On the Aswan High Dam, see Ahmad Shokr, 'Hydropolitics, Economy, and the Aswan High Dam in Mid-Century Egypt', *The Arab Studies Journal* 17(1), (2009), pp.9–31.

23 On the early years of Sudanese independence, see Alden Young, *Transforming Sudan: Decolonization, Development, and State Formation* (Cambridge, 2017).

24 On that migration, see Nicholas S. Hopkins and Sohair R. Mehanna (eds), *Nubian Encounters: The Story of the Nubian Ethnological Survey, 1961–1964* (Cairo, 2010).

25 On Abu Simbel, see Lucia Allais, 'Integrities: The Salvage of Abu Simbel', *Grey Room* 50 (2013), pp.6–45. On the Nubian campaign and its colonial genealogies, see William Carruthers, *Flooded Pasts: UNESCO, Nubia, and the Recolonization of Archaeology* (Ithaca, NY, 2022).

26 Allais, 2013, p.33.

27 For one account of the *infitāh* and its genealogies, see Malak Zaalouk, *Power, Class, and Foreign Capital in Egypt: The Rise of the New Bourgeoisie* (London, 1989).

28 On those openings, see Zahi A. Hawass, 'A New Era for Museums in Egypt', *Museum International* 57(1–2), (2005), pp.7–23.

29 Interviewed that year, Mahrous Said, NMEC's then-director, stated that 'the challenge is to find funding. When we have the funds, we will finish our permanent exhibition within two to three years.' For the quote, see Hannah McGivern and Aimee Dawson, 'Egypt Revives Major Museum Projects, Six Years After Revolution', *The Art Newspaper* (4 April 2017), www.theartnewspaper.com/news/egypt-revives-major-museum-projects-six-years-after-revolution (accessed 3 February 2022).

30 On the Cairo parade, see Carruthers, 2021. For a positive take on the event, see Nada El Sawy, 'Egyptian Production Designer Mohamed Attia Says Mummies Parade a Career Highlight', *The National* (23 April 2021), www.thenationalnews.com/mena/egypt/egyptian-production-designer-mohamed-attia-says-mummies-parade-a-career-highlight-1.1209139 (accessed 3 February 2022).

31 On JICA and the Grand Egyptian Museum, see 'What Is the Grand Egyptian Museum?', JICA-GEM Joint Conservation Project website, www.jicagem.com/about/what-is-the-grand-egyptian-museum/ (accessed 3 February 2022). For a critical perspective on the institution, see Mohammed Elshahed, 'The Old and New Egyptian Museums: Between Imperialists, Nationalists, and Tourists', in William Carruthers (ed.), *Histories of Egyptology: Interdisciplinary Measures* (New York, NY, and Abingdon, 2015), pp.255–69.

32 At the time of writing, the opening of the Grand Egyptian Museum is scheduled for the second half of 2022, for which see Hatem Maher, 'Egypt to Mark Centenary of Tutankhamun Tomb Discovery by Inaugurating New, Lavish Museum', *ABC News*, 14 January 2022, www.abcnews.go.com/International/egypt-mark-centenary-tutankhamun-tomb-discovery-inaugurating-lavish/story?id=82247869 (accessed 3 February 2022).

33 Omar, 2021. Cf. Anon., 'In Egypt, a Motorcade of Mummies Says More About the Modern Nation than the Ancient Past', *Apollo*, 7 April 2021, www.apollo-magazine.com/royal-mummies-parade-egypt/ (accessed 3 February 2022).

34 Gehan Selim, 'Instituting Order: The Limitations of Nasser's Post-Colonial Planning Visions for Cairo in the Case of the Indigenous Quarter of Bulaq (1952–1970)', *Planning Perspectives* 29(1), (2014), p.67.

35 On the nineteenth-century expansion of Cairo, see, e.g., Nezar AlSayyad, *Cairo: Histories of a City* (Cambridge, MA, 2011). On Midan al-Isma'iliyya itself, see Khaled Adham, 'Tahrir Square through Two Transitions', *Society of Architectural Historians* blog (24 February 2011), www.sah.org/publications-and-research/sah-blog/sah-blog/2011/02/24/tahrir-square-through-two-transitions-by-khaled-adham (accessed 4 February 2022).

36 On the Egyptian Museum, see Ezio Godoli and Mercedes Volait (eds), *Concours pour le musée des Antiquités égyptiennes du Caire, 1895* (Paris, 2010). On Egypt's successful retention of the Tutankhamun objects, see, e.g., Elliott Colla, *Conflicted Antiquities: Egyptology, Egyptomania, Egyptian Modernity* (Durham, NC, 2007), and Christina Riggs, *Photographing Tutankhamun: Archaeology, Ancient Egypt, and the Archive* (London, 2019).

37 On these buildings, see Adham, 2011, and Mohamed Elshahed, *Cairo Since 1900: An Architectural Guide* (Cairo, 2020).

38 Over the years Cairo had witnessed many popular gatherings and protests. In January 1952 the Cairo Fire had crystallised many of the tensions inherent to such events, for which see Nancy Y. Reynolds, *A City Consumed: Urban Commerce, the Cairo Fire, and the Politics of Decolonization in Egypt* (Stanford, CA, 2012).

39 On Nasser, see, e.g., Anne Alexander, *Nasser* (London, 2005).

40 On Umm Kulthum, see Virginia Danielson, *The Voice of Egypt: Umm Kulthūm, Arabic Song, and Egyptian Society in the Twentieth Century* (Chicago, IL, 1997), and Raphael Cormack, *Midnight in Cairo: The Female Stars of Egypt's Roaring '20s* (London, 2021).

41 On the 'bread intifada', see David Seddon, 'The Politics of Adjustment: Egypt and the IMF, 1987–1990', *Review of African Political Economy* 47 (1990), p.95.

42 AlSayyad, 2011, p.255.

43 Ibid.

44 On Khalid al-Islambuli, see Arthur Goldschmidt, *Biographical Dictionary of Modern Egypt* (Boulder, CO, and London, 2000), p.90.

45 On the 'Islamic revival' and its relationship with 'heritage' (writ broadly), see, e.g., Nathalie Peutz, 'Heritage in (the) Ruins', *International Journal of Middle East Studies* 49(4), (2017), pp.721–8.

46 On Egypt's revolutionary graffiti, see Basma Hamdy and Don 'Stone' Karl, *Walls of Freedom: Street Art of the Egyptian Revolution* (Berlin, 2014).

47 Tom Hardwick, 'Why Is the Egyptian Government Moving Ancient Monuments Around the Country?', *Apollo*, 29 February 2020, www.apollo-magazine.com/egyptian-government-moving-ancient-monuments/ (accessed 4 February 2022).

48 On the uncertain (and often unhelpful) terminology of the events of 2013, see Yasmin Moll, 'The Wretched Revolution', *Middle East Research and Information Project* 273 (2014), www.merip.org/2014/12/the-wretched-revolution/ (accessed 4 February 2022). On the massacre of protesters in Cairo's Rabi a al-'Adawiyya Square (alongside other killings of the period), see 'All According to Plan: The Rab'a Massacre and Mass Killings of Protestors in Egypt', Human Rights Watch website, 12 August 2014, www.hrw.org/report/2014/08/12/all-according-plan/raba-massacre-and-mass-killings-protesters-egypt (accessed 4 February 2022).

49 For a summary of the situation, see, e.g., Heba Saleh, '"City of the Dead" Faces Being Bulldozed in Cairo's Highway Drive', *Financial Times*, 15 January 2022, www.ft.com/content/807b86f9-e3b1-448c-ad9e-428ec98d964a (accessed 7 February 2022). For one of the most resonant responses to the situation, see Sharif Abdel Kouddous, 'City Limits of the Dead', *Mada Masr*, 21 July 2020, www.madamasr.com/en/2020/07/21/opinion/u/city-limits-of-the-dead/ (accessed 7 February 2022).

50 See, e.g., Ayyad, 2021.

51 On the video (and for a link to it), see, e.g., Thaer Mansour, 'Egypt Mocked Over Song for Newly Opened Prison', *The New Arab*, 1 November 2021, www.english.alaraby.co.uk/news/egypt-mocked-over-song-newly-opened-prison (accessed 7 February 2022).

52 Another example of such pharaonic-style juridical architecture is the 'reluctantly Postmodern' court in the Cairo suburb of Maadi, for which see Elshahed, 2020, p.210.

53 Fekri A. Hassan, 'Memorabilia: Archaeological Materiality and National Identity in Egypt', in *Archaeology Under Fire: Nationalism, Politics and Heritage in the Eastern Mediterranean and Middle East*, ed. Lynn Meskell (London, 1998), p.212.

INDEX